Advanced Software Testing—Vol. 1
2nd Edition

T0203511

About the Author

Rex Black
With over 30 years of software and systems engineering experience, Rex Black is president of RBCS (www.rbcs-us.com), a leader in software, hardware, and systems testing. For over 20 years, RBCS has delivered consulting, outsourcing, and training services in the areas of software, hardware, and systems testing and quality. Employing the industry's most experienced and recognized consultants, RBCS conducts product testing, builds and improves testing groups, and provides testing staff for hundreds of clients worldwide. Ranging from Fortune 20 companies to start-ups, RBCS clients save time and money through higher quality, improved product development, decreased tech support calls, improved reputation, and more.

As the leader of RBCS, Rex is the most prolific author practicing in the field of software testing today. He has written over 50 articles and ten books that have sold over 100,000 copies around the world, including numerous translations and foreign releases such as Japanese, Chinese, Indian, Spanish, Hebrew, Hungarian, and Russian editions. He is a popular speaker at conferences and events around the world.

Rex is the past president of the International Software Testing Qualifications Board (ISTQB) and of the American Software Testing Qualifications Board (ASTQB).

Rex Black

Advanced Software Testing—Vol. 1

**Guide to the ISTQB Advanced Certification
as an Advanced Technical Test Analyst**

2nd Edition

Advanced Software Testing—Vol.1, 2nd Edition

Rex Black
www.rbcs-us.com / rex_black@rbcs-us.com

Project editor: Michael Barabas
Project manager: Matthias Rossmanith and Lisa Brazieal
Marketing: Jessica Tiernan
Copyeditor: Stephanie Pascal
Layout and type: Josef Hegele
Cover design: Helmut Kraus

ISBN: 978-1-937538-68-2
2nd Edition (1st printing, December 2015)
© 2016 Rex Black
All images © Rex Black unless otherwise noted

Rocky Nook Inc.
802 E. Cota Street, 3rd Floor
Santa Barbara, CA 93103
USA

www.rockynook.com

Distributed in the U.S. by Ingram Publisher Services
Distributed in the UK and Europe by Publishers Group UK

Library of Congress Control Number: 2015949667

Preface

I've worked as a software engineer for over 30 years. When I started as a programmer, I learned to unit test my code as I wrote it. When I became a professional tester about 25 years ago, I tested my own code and other people's code.

I received my degree in software engineering in the 1980s at the University of California, Los Angeles, which is a prestigious university. However, I learned very little about testing there. So, when I became a professional tester, I found that I had to teach myself the skills, both from books and from experience.

In the 1980s, software testing was just emerging as a separate discipline within software engineering. It's no surprise that universities, even prestigious universities, would not provide much education on the topic of software testing at that time.

Unfortunately, software testing education at universities and colleges has not advanced much in the intervening 30 years. Training on software testing from private firms, including my own company, RBCS, has helped fill that gap. However, practitioners often obtain education in a piecemeal fashion, without continuity between subjects. So, many practitioners of software testing remain self-taught or educated in disparate concepts without a unifying set of ideas to help them understand that whole field. This has created a situation where many practitioners do not understand the foundational and advanced concepts of software testing.

The International Software Testing Qualifications Board (ISTQB) is addressing this situation by defining a set of syllabi (or bodies of knowledge, if you prefer) that suggest what practitioners should know at various points in their careers as software testing professionals. I have served as president of the International Software Testing Qualifications Board and the American Software Testing Qualifications Board. I have also served on the ISTQB's Foundation Level Working Group, Advanced Level Working Group, and other working groups to help create these syllabi.

I previously wrote a book, with Dorothy Graham and Erik van Veenendaal, called *Foundations of Software Testing*. That book addressed the Foundation Level syllabus.

This book addresses the Advanced Test Analyst syllabus. Here, I will cover the concepts that practitioners should apply as they reach an advanced point in their careers as software testing professionals. It is my hope that, after reading this book, you will feel more comfortable in your understanding and application of these concepts. In the next 15 years, before I retire from this field, I intend to help us move beyond a piecemeal, disparate, inchoate understanding of software testing to a point where software testing becomes a true, respected, professionally practiced specialty. I hope that this book will help you be among its respected practitioners.

Acknowledgements

A complete list of people who deserve thanks for helping me along in my career as a test professional would probably make up its own small book. Here I'll confine myself to those who had an immediate impact on my ability to write this particular book.

First, I'd like to thank my colleagues on the American Software Testing Qualifications Board and the International Software Testing Qualifications Board, and especially the Advanced Syllabus Working Party, who made this book possible by creating the process and the material from which this book grew. Not only has it been a real pleasure sharing ideas with and learning from each of the participants, but I have had the distinct honor of being elected president of both the American Software Testing Qualifications Board and the International Software Testing Qualifications Board twice. In the time since I finished my statutory last term as president, I've remained involved in both boards, and I'm very proud of what we continue to accomplish for the software testing profession. I hope this book serves as a suitable expression of the gratitude and professional pride I feel toward what we have done for the field of software testing.

Next, I'd like to thank the people who helped me create the material that grew into this book. The materials in this book, our Advanced Level Test Analyst instructor-led training course, and our Advanced Level Test Analyst e-learning course were reviewed, re-reviewed, and polished with hours of dedicated assistance by José Mata, Judy McKay, Jamie Mitchell, Paul Jorgensen, Amr Ali Abdel-Naby, Pat Masters, Bernard Homés, Gary Rueda Sandoval, Jan Sabak, Joanna Kazun, Corné Kruger, Ed Weller, and Dawn Haynes.

Once the materials were created, the task of assembling the first rough draft of this book from scripts, slides, the syllabus, and a rough framework fell to Dena Pauletti, RBCS's extremely competent and meticulous senior systems engineer. This book would have taken literally months longer to prepare without her intrepid and timely assistance.

Of course, the Advanced Test Analyst syllabus could not exist without a foundation, specifically the ISTQB Foundation syllabus. I had the honor of working with that Working Party as well. I thank them for their excellent work over the years, creating the fertile soil from which the Advanced Test Analyst syllabus and thus this book sprang.

In the creation of the training courses and the materials that make up this book, I have drawn on all the experiences I have had as an author, practitioner, consultant, and trainer. So, I have benefited from individuals too numerous to list. I thank those of you who have bought one of my previous books, for you contributed to my skills as a writer. I thank those of you who have worked with me on a project, for you have contributed to my abilities as a test manager, test analyst, and technical test analyst. I thank those of you who have hired me to work with you as a consultant, for you have given me the opportunity to learn from your organizations. I thank those of you who have taken a training course from me, for you have collectively taught me much more than I taught each of you. I thank my readers, colleagues, clients, and students, and hope that my contributions to you have repaid the debt of gratitude that I owe you.

For over twenty years, I have run a testing services company, RBCS. From humble beginnings, RBCS has grown into an international consulting, training, and outsourcing firm with clients on six continents. While I have remained a hands-on contributor to the firm, over 100 employees, subcontractors, and business partners have been the driving force of our ongoing success. I thank all of you for your hard work for our clients. Without the success of RBCS, I could hardly avail myself of the luxury of writing technical books, which is a source of great pride but not a whole lot of money. Again, I hope that our mutual successes together have repaid the debt of gratitude that I owe each of you.

Finally, I thank my family, especially my wife, Laurel; my daughters, Emma and Charlotte; and the canine crew, Kibo and Eeland. Laurel, as my wife and business partner, is the one who does all the really hard work in the family and the business. I'm sure she has ended up doing a number of business tasks just because I rambled off into the office to work on some book or other, including this one. I published my first book before my first daughter, Emma, was born, and so she and her sister Charlotte have grown up thinking it's normal to have a father who writes books and travels the world talking about a very specialized subject with a small but important audience. They are off to college in a few short years, where they'll be reading other people's books on very specialized subjects.

Regarding the canines, Kibo is our Golden Retriever puppy, a smart and headstrong youngster with a bright future of jogging, ball chasing, swimming, and other fun activities ahead of him. If he had any idea what I was doing as I write this text, he'd probably be wondering why I would waste my time when there were plenty of chew toys I could be throwing for him. As for Eeland, he's not really our dog. He is a US military working dog, a Belgian Malinios, whom we got to foster as a puppy for six months. He reported for duty in March and is apparently tearing up the training. It was a joy and a privilege to do our small part to help raise one of these dogs, which are estimated to save hundreds of lives when deployed.

Table of Contents

Introduction

This is a book on advanced software testing for test analysts. This means that I address topics that a practitioner who has chosen software testing as a career should know. I focus on skills and techniques related to test analysis, test design, test execution, and test results evaluation. I assume that you know the basic concepts of test engineering, test design, test tools, testing in the software development lifecycle, and test management. You are ready to mature your level of understanding of these concepts and to apply these mature, advanced concepts to your daily work as a test professional.

This book follows the International Software Testing Qualifications Board's (ISTQB) Advanced Test Analyst syllabus. As such, this book can help you prepare for the Advanced Level Test Analyst exam. You can use this book to self-study for that exam or as part of an e-learning or instructor-led course on the topics covered in those exams. If you are taking an ISTQB-accredited Advanced Level Test Analyst training course, this book is an ideal companion text for that course.

However, even if you are not interested in the ISTQB certification, you will find this book useful to prepare yourself for advanced work in software testing. If you are a test manager, test director, test analyst, technical test analyst, automated test engineer, manual test engineer, or programmer, or in any other field where a sophisticated understanding of software testing is needed, then this book is for you.

This book focuses on test analysis. The book consists of eight chapters:

1. Testing Process
2. Test Management: Responsibilities for the Test Analyst
3. Test Techniques
4. Testing Software Quality Characteristics
5. Reviews
6. Defect Management

7. Test Tools
8. Preparing for the Exam

What should a test analyst be able to do? Or, to ask the question another way, what should you have learned to do—or learned to do better—by the time you finish this book?

- Perform the appropriate testing activities based on the software development lifecycle being used.
- Determine the proper prioritization of the testing activities based on the information provided by the risk analysis.
- Select and apply appropriate testing techniques to ensure that tests provide an adequate level of confidence, based on defined coverage criteria.
- Provide the appropriate level of documentation relevant to the testing activities.
- Determine the appropriate types of functional testing to be performed.
- Assume responsibility for the usability testing for a given project.
- Effectively participate in formal and informal reviews with stakeholders, applying knowledge of typical mistakes made in work products.

In this book, we focus on these main concepts. I suggest that you keep these high-level objectives in mind as we proceed through the material in each of the following chapters.

In writing this book and the companion volumes on technical test analysis and test management, I've kept foremost in my mind the question of how to make this material useful to you. If you are using this book to prepare for an Advanced Level Analyst exam, then I recommend that you read Chapter 8 first and then read the other seven chapters in order. If you are using this book to expand your overall understanding of testing to an advanced level, but do not intend to take the Advanced Level Test Analyst exam, then I recommend that you read Chapters 1 through 7 only. If you are using this book as a reference, then feel free to read only those chapters that are of specific interest to you.

Each of the first seven chapters are divided into sections. For the most part, I have followed the organization of the Advanced Test Analyst syllabus to the point of section divisions, but subsections and subsubsection divisions in the syllabus might not appear. You'll also notice that each section starts with a text box describing the learning objectives for that section. If you are curious about how to interpret those K2, K3, and K4 tags in front of each learning objective, and how learning objectives work within the ISTQB syllabi, read Chapter 8.

Software testing is in many ways similar to playing the piano, cooking a meal, or driving a car. How so? In each case, you can read books about these activities, but, until you have practiced, you know very little about how to do it. So, I've included practical, real-world exercises for the key concepts. I encourage you to practice these concepts with the exercises in the book. Then, make sure you take these concepts and apply them on your projects. You can only become an advanced software test professional by doing software testing.

1 Testing Process

Put the lime in the coconut and drink 'em both together,
Put the lime in the coconut, then you'll feel better...

From the lyrics of "Coconut," by Harry Nilsson

The first chapter of the Advanced Test Analyst syllabus is concerned with the overall test process, which serves as the context in which the rest of the activities in the syllabus occur. There are nine sections.

1. Introduction
2. Testing in the Software Development Lifecycle
3. Test Planning, Monitoring, and Control
4. Test Analysis
5. Test Design
6. Test Implementation
7. Test Execution
8. Evaluating Exit Criteria and Reporting
9. Test Closure Activities

Let's look at each section and how it relates to test analysis.

1.1 Introduction

Learning objectives
Recall of content only.

In the Foundation syllabus, the fundamental test process is defined as:

- Planning and control
- Analysis and design

- Implementation and execution
- Evaluating exit criteria and reporting
- Test closure activities

In the Advanced syllabi, we have refined that process to separate certain activities, thus providing finer-grained resolution of the process as a whole as well as its constituent activities. This fine-grained breakdown allows us to focus refinement and optimization efforts, to tailor the test process better within the software development lifecycle, and to help us gain better insight into project and product status for responsive, effective test monitoring and control. The refined activities are:

- Planning, monitoring, and control
- Analysis
- Design
- Implementation
- Execution
- Evaluating exit criteria and reporting
- Test closure activities

These activities may overlap or be concurrent, in spite of the appearance of sequencing in the syllabus—and in the images shown in Figure 1–1. In addition, it's usually necessary to tailor these activities, both in terms of the specific tasks performed as well as the order in which they occur in a project, based on the needs of the project and the type of system being tested. In fact, in my years as a test manager and test consultant, I can't remember ever seeing any testing done exactly according to the fundamental test process, but I have seen every activity and task described within the fundamental test process play an important part in at least one project. Therefore, in set theory terms, you can think of the fundamental test process as the union of all tasks that can be important in testing, organized into a hierarchy that corresponds roughly to the timeline of testing on a project following a sequential lifecycle.

> **ISTQB Glossary**
>
> **Exit criteria:** The set of generic and specific conditions, agreed upon with the stakeholders, for permitting a process to be officially completed. The purpose of exit criteria is to prevent a task from being considered completed when there are still outstanding parts of the task that have not been finished. Exit criteria are used to report against and to plan when to stop testing.

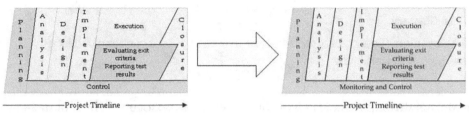

Figure 1–1   *Fundamental test process*

Since the fundamental test process was introduced at the Foundation level, I recommend that you review Chapter 1, Section 4 of the Foundation syllabus prior to or immediately after going through this chapter. Remember that, to the extent that the Foundation syllabus material forms an underpinning of the Advanced Test Analyst material, it may be examined. If the Advanced Test Analyst material refines or modifies the Foundation material in any way, then you should expect the exam to follow the Advanced Test Analyst material.

While the fundamental test process discusses tasks carried out by both managers and testers, in this book we will focus on the testers' perspective.

1.2   Testing in the Software Development Lifecycle

Learning objectives
(K2) Explain how and why the timing and level of involvement for the test analyst varies when working with different lifecycle models.

Software testing, by itself, does not have any value. Software testing only has value when it delivers value to some other part of the software development lifecycle. As discussed in the Foundation syllabus and in the Advanced Test Manager syllabus, the way testing fits into the software development lifecycle should be defined in the testing strategy. This is true regardless of which lifecycle you are following.

That said, each software development lifecycle model has a significant effect on how testing is done and how test analysts participate in the software development process. For example, in Agile lifecycles, the tester should be involved from the inception of the project, during release planning. Of course, that upfront test involvement is also theoretically true in V-model projects, though frequently that is not the case. Sometimes, the testers on V-model projects have

> **ISTQB Glossary**
>
> **Test execution:** The process of running a test on the component or system under test, producing actual result(s).

input during the requirements phase, but are expected to focus the bulk of their attention on test execution in another project. This leads to suboptimal contributions by the testers to the requirements, which, as was discussed at the Foundation level, is a significant missed opportunity.

In V-model projects—at least ones following a formal lifecycle model—you'll find extensive requirements documents created during a requirements phase, while in Agile projects the requirements evolve throughout the project and are documented as relatively terse user stories.

In order to be successful on any project, you need to make sure you understand what you will do, when you will do it, and whom you will do it for. The expectations of other project participants and stakeholders matter. Make sure you understand organizational relationships. Make sure you understand the deliverables you will receive, as well as those that you will create for others.

In addition, be aware that lifecycle models are heavily tailored by each organization. You might be thinking, "Oh, this is a Scrum project, and I've worked on Scrum projects in other organizations, so I know what is going to happen." What we have seen with our clients is that, whether following Rational Unified Process, Scrum, the V-model, or some other lifecycle, there's always a significant difference between how that lifecycle is described in the books and what it is actually doing.

Test Touchpoints

As just discussed, proper alignment between the testing process and other processes in the lifecycle is critical for success. This is especially true at key interfaces and handoffs between testing and other lifecycle activities. For example:

- Requirements engineering and management
- Project management
- Configuration and change management
- Software development and maintenance
- Technical support
- Technical documentation
- User documentation

Let's look at two examples of alignment.

In a sequential lifecycle model, a key assumption is that the project team will define the requirements early in the project and then manage the (hopefully limited) changes to those requirements during the rest of the project. In such a situation, if the team follows a formal requirements process, an independent test team in charge of the system test level can follow an analytical requirements-based test strategy.

Using such a strategy in a sequential model, the test team would start—early in the project—planning and designing tests following an analysis of the requirements specification to identify test conditions. This planning, analysis, and design work might identify defects in the requirements, making testing a preventive activity. Failure detection would start later in the lifecycle, once system test execution began.

However, suppose the project follows an Agile methodology like Scrum. Now, the testers won't receive a complete set of requirements early in the project. While user stories are defined in release planning, those user stories are subject to change. The test team will receive final user stories at the beginning of each sprint.

Rather than analyzing requirements during release planning, the best the testers can do is to identify and prioritize key quality risk areas; i.e., they can follow an analytical risk-based test strategy. During iteration planning, testers should be involved in user story grooming and estimation, which is another place where a more detailed quality risk analysis can and should occur, as this involvement and these activities enable the defect-preventing role of testing. Specific test design and implementation will occur immediately before test execution. Defect detection starts very early in the project, as test execution at all levels starts on the first sprint, and continues in repetitive, short cycles throughout the project. In such a case, testing activities in the fundamental testing process overlap and are concurrent with each other as well as with major activities in the software lifecycle.

No matter what the lifecycle—and indeed, especially with the more fast-paced Agile lifecycles—good change management and configuration management are critical for testing. A lack of proper change management results in an inability of the test team to keep up with what the system is and what it should do. A lack of proper configuration management, as was discussed in the Foundation, leads to loss of changes, an inability to say what was tested at what point in time, and severe lack of clarity around the meaning of the test results.

Learning objectives
Test design: (1) A document specifying the test conditions
(coverage items) for a test item, specifying the detailed test
approach, and identifying the associated high-level test cases.
(2) The process of transforming general testing objectives into
tangible test conditions and test cases.

Example: V-model Alignment

Let's take a closer look at this concept of alignment. We'll use the V-model as
shown in Figure 1–2 as an example. We'll further assume that we are talking
about the system test level.

In a properly run V-model, with a well-aligned test process, test planning
occurs concurrently with project planning. In other words, the moment of
involvement of testing is at the very start of the project.

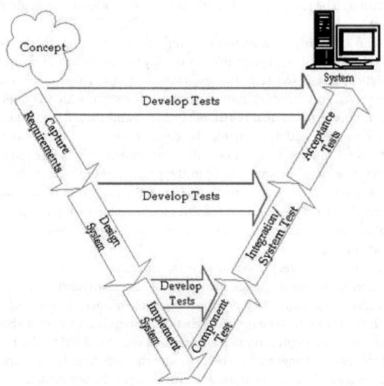

Figure 1–2   *V-model*

ISTQB Glossary

Test control: A test management task that deals with developing and applying a set of corrective actions to get a test project on track when monitoring shows a deviation from what was planned.

Test planning: The activity of establishing or updating a test plan.

Once the test plan is approved, test control begins. Test control continues through to test closure. Analysis, design, implementation, execution, evaluation of exit criteria, and test results reporting are carried out according to the plan. Deviations from the plan are managed.

Test analysis starts immediately after or even concurrently with test planning. Test analysis and test design happen concurrently with requirements, high-level design, and low-level design. Test implementation, including test environment implementation, starts during system design and completes just before test execution begins.

Test execution begins when the test entry criteria are met. More realistically, test execution starts when most entry criteria are met and any outstanding entry criteria are waived. In V-model theory, the entry criteria would include successful completion of both component test and integration test levels. Test execution continues until the test exit criteria are met, though again some of these criteria will often be waived.

Evaluation of test exit criteria and reporting of test results occurs throughout test execution.

Test closure activities occur after test execution is declared complete.

This kind of precise alignment of test activities with each other and with the rest of the system lifecycle absolutely **will not** just happen by accident. Additionally you cannot expect to be able to instill this alignment continuously throughout the process, without any forethought.

Rather, for each test level, no matter what the selected software lifecycle and test process, testers must ensure this alignment. Not only must this happen during the test and project planning, but test control includes acting to ensure ongoing alignment.

No matter what test process and software lifecycle are chosen, each project has its own quirks. This is especially true for complex projects such as the systems of systems projects common in the military and among RBCS's larger clients. In such a case, the testers must plan not only to align test processes, but also to modify them. Off-the-rack process models, whether for testing alone or for the entire software lifecycle, don't fit such complex projects well.

Example: Iterative Alignment

Traditional iterative and incremental models, such as Rapid Application Development (RAD) and Rational Unified Process (RUP), will have an effect on how testing is done. In these models, the development work is broken into iterations or increments. Test planning typically happens before the start of the first increment, and test closure only after the last increment, but otherwise all parts of the test process occur within each increment.

In each increment, some portion of the product's functionality is defined, designed, developed, and tested. Sometimes the increments themselves are sequential, as shown in Figure 1–3, but sometimes they overlap such that analysis, design, and development work for subsequent iterations is happening even while test execution of earlier iterations is still ongoing. In the case of sequential increments, sometimes these increments are organized as small V-model projects, each building upon the previous increment.

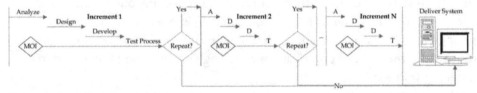

Figure 1–3   *Iterative model*

Another variation of the iterative/V-model hybrid approach is where the project follows a V-model at first, doing the standard requirements specification and design work. However, there is then a sequence of iterations. In each iteration, a subset of the features is selected, the design is refined, code is written, and some of the testing for those features occurs. The testing might well focus on the lower levels only, though, with system testing and acceptance testing saved for after the final increment. This can work acceptably if the testers are involved throughout the project, including helping with the lower levels of testing. However, if testers don't get any opportunity to participate until system testing is about to start, the usual dysfunctions associated with "throwing code over the wall to the testers" will occur.

No matter the flavor of iterative model used, testers are ideally involved from the very beginning of the first increment, as shown by the diamond marked MOI in the figure. In the case of overlapping increments, there can be challenges when testers become decoupled from the natural focus of the project, the ongoing development. Significant bug backlogs can develop and retard both the testing work and the development work. In one such situation, I saw an organization that routinely developed bug backlogs that approached 10,000 known, reported, yet-unfixed bugs, and these situations would persist for months during the project. I estimated that this situation cost them about twenty person-years of productivity annually, which is about $3 million in terms of labor costs. This was complicated by the fact that testers didn't get involved until after the first increment was fully coded and delivered for test execution, which meant that the testers were always behind.

Example: Agile Alignment

Agile methods are similar to traditional iterative methods, in that the software is built and tested in increments, also called *iterations* or *sprints*. However, the iterations are typically very short, two to four weeks, rather than months. In addition, the iterations are supposed to be sequential, in that all of the development and testing work associated with one iteration should be complete before the next iteration starts, as shown in Figure 1–4. That said, some organizations have certain test levels, especially system integration test and acceptance test, that happen after the iterations or that trail each iteration, and this can work if organized properly.

Testers who have worked on traditional lifecycles—whether V-model or iterative—often have a certain degree of culture shock when first assigned to an Agile project. Testing is supposed to be less siloed and self-contained, more integrated into the team. For example, as opposed to test entry and exit criteria, you often see cross-functional criteria for what's called the *Definition of Done*, or *DoD*, which defines all tasks and criteria—not just test and quality criteria—that must be achieved before something is considered done. Testers should work collaboratively to define these criteria.

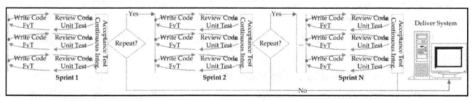

Figure 1–4   *Agile model*

Testers work closely with the whole team, including developers and business stakeholders. This collaboration is less by formal documentation and more through verbal communication. In a properly organized Agile project, testers are embedded within the project teams from the first day, and they play a key role in all levels of testing. Testers are also involved in informal review processes. These include user story grooming, which is the clarification of requirements (called *user stories*) by the testers, developers, and business stakeholders at the beginning of each sprint. Another example is pairing, where a tester might work with a developer to create unit tests, review code, or define high-level tests.

A challenge to testers used to traditional methods is that change is allowed throughout the process. Early creation of test cases, test environments, and test data, prior to the iteration in which they'll be needed, may result in those deliverables requiring significant changes—or complete rework—prior to their actual use, due to changes in the user stories. Close communication with the business stakeholders and developers is critical before such advanced work is undertaken

1.3   Test Planning, Monitoring, and Control

Learning objectives
(K2) Summarize the activities performed by the test analyst in support of planning and controlling the testing.

While test planning, monitoring, and control are primarily roles played by the test manager—at least in sequential and traditional iterative lifecycles such as RUP—the test analyst has a strong supporting role to play, helping the test manager carry out the relevant tasks. If you are working as a tester in an Agile lifecycle, many test management roles will devolve to you, due to the Agile principle of self-directing, self-organizing teams. In this case, not only do you need to understand how to support the test manager, but you should probably plan to obtain more education in test management and project management tasks.

One of these important tasks is participating in the creation of the test plan and estimate. Not all test managers have direct, hands-on, previous experience with the full range of test activities, so make sure that both functional and non-functional test types are adequately represented. Remember that non-functional test types are often overlooked, and you may be more business focused than technically focused. Therefore, involving a technical test analyst can be helpful for the non-functional tests.

You'll want to help the test manager make sure that the plan and estimate include adequate tasks and time for the parts of the test process that don't involve executing tests and reporting results, as these preparatory tasks are often forgotten or underestimated. The plan and estimate should also be well aligned with the chosen lifecycle, and you'll want to check that they are. The test environment must be configured, tested, and supported, including testing of the installation process for the software into the test environment. You'll need to plan to obtain and test the technical and user documentation, including any web-based support and online help. You'll need to think about whether enough time is in the schedule for a thorough quality risk analysis. In addition, if you are testing a complex system, with multiple test basis documents, a large set of test conditions to cover, and what is expected to be a large set of automated and manual test cases, make sure to plan for how all that will be managed, including traceability.

Test Analyst in Monitoring and Control

During test analysis, design, implementation, and execution, you'll need to measure your progress toward established goals. You need to capture coverage information as tests are designed and implemented. You need to ensure that test case status is correctly captured, so that progress toward completion of the tests is clear. During test execution, defect information will become critical, including determining the actual root cause of defects—at least, if your organization has the intent of learning from the defects, which of course it should.

Test execution also includes monitoring test case status, in terms of what has been run, what passes, what fails, and what is blocked. All too often, people stop with this and believe that test case status and defect status alone are sufficient to report test progress and product quality. They are not. The status of the test basis items, determined by using traceability, is essential to knowing what quality risks have been adequately mitigated, what requirements are known to be met (at least under tested conditions), what supported environments work properly, and the status of other test basis items. Therefore, proper coverage analysis and traceability are essential.

It's important to remember that the information that is sufficient for immediate task completion is not sufficient to provide adequate data for good project monitoring and control. All too often, I see test teams that operate acceptably in terms of fulfilling the immediate tactical needs of daily work, but don't capture information to support smart project decision making, much less smart process improvements. Work with the test manager to ensure that you are gathering all the data necessary, in a timely and objective fashion.

Example: Breakdown in Test Monitoring

Here's an example of why timely, objective, accurate data gathering at the tester level is so important. We did an assessment for one client, a Fortune 50 company with a billion-dollar annual IT budget. We found that somewhere between $100 million and $250 million of that money was being wasted, since most bugs were being discovered and removed in system integration testing, acceptance testing, and—worse yet—in production.

The obvious next question was, "Why is this happening?" Unfortunately, we could not answer that question. The defect data was full of inconsistencies, holes, and just plain random classification selections. We could not figure out what exactly was happening in the process.

The most dramatic example of these problems had to do with invalid bug reports. Invalid bug reports are situations where a false positive was not recognized as such, but rather was reported as a failure. Ideally, the rate of invalid bug reports should be 5% or less. In this organization, depending on which of four fields we looked at, 22%, 27%, 28%, or 34% of defect reports were invalid. Notice that the highest number is 50% greater than the lowest, which is a very high error rate. Would you want to make $100 million decisions based on data that was so unreliable? Unfortunately, many times important decisions are made based on flawed data, and, of course, those decisions are therefore flawed.

The moral of this story is that, without valid measurements, management can't make smart decisions. This is as true for decisions made based on test results as for anything else.

1.4   Test Analysis

Learning objectives
(K2) Summarize the activities performed by the test analyst in support of planning and controlling the testing.

Test analysis is the process of determining the test conditions, which is to say, determining what we need to test. Taking into account the defined mission and objectives of testing—which should specify what's in scope and what's out of scope—test analysts should analyze the test basis to identify the test conditions. Keep in mind that the test basis can and should be thought of broadly, including the following:

- External work products, such as requirements specifications, use cases, and user stories
- Internal work products created in collaboration with other stakeholders, such as quality risk catalogs
- Internal work products created and maintained by the test team, such as bug taxonomies, major functional areas, and important quality characteristics
- Conversations held with important stakeholders, such as discussions with a developer and a product owner

Since the analysis proceeds from the test basis documents—and I'm using the word *document* loosely here, in the sense of any readable repository of information, including your notes on a conversation—before you start analysis, you need access to at least one or more of these test basis documents.

Ideally, these documents should have been reviewed by other project participants and stakeholders before test work starts. In addition, the test basis should give the testers adequate insight to the test object so that they won't forget to cover anything important. Further, adequate time and money should be available for the entire test process. Of course, in the real world, some of these entry criteria are not entirely met before test analysis starts, and might not even be met when test execution ends. As testers, we have to be ready to play the hand we're dealt.

Test Analysis and Design Process

Figure 1–5 shows an example of the test analysis process. It assumes we're following a requirements-based and risk-based test strategy. Business stakeholders supply test basis documents such as requirements and user stories, while technical stakeholders supply test basis documents such as test design and architecture. Business and technical stakeholders participate in quality risk analysis. The test analysts combine all this information into a catalog of test conditions, making sure to retain traceability between each of these test conditions and its source. This catalog of test conditions is then reviewed by the stakeholders, updated if needed based on the review, and then used as the basis for the next step in the test process, test design, which we'll discuss in the next section.

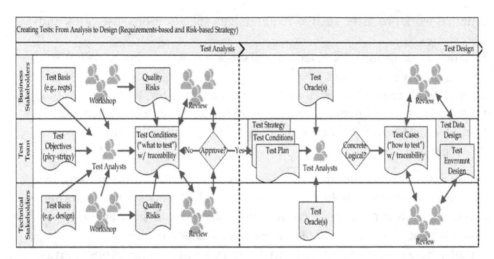

Figure 1–5   *Test analysis process*

Test Conditions

I've used the phrase "test condition" loosely to describe what should be tested. In reality, test conditions can take on many different forms. Some may be very high level, as in, "Test credit card purchases" for an e-commerce application. Others may be very detailed, as these for the same application:

- Test American Express successful purchase
- Test American Express declined purchase attempt
- Test MasterCard successful purchase
- Test MasterCard declined purchase attempt
- Test Visa successful purchase
- Test Visa declined purchase attempt
- Test JCB successful purchase
- Test JCB declined purchase attempt

Notice that you might start at a high level, use that level of detail for the stakeholder review, and then create the detailed conditions as a next step.

Previously, I mentioned that test conditions should trace back to their source. If you are using a blended risk-based and requirements-based test strategy, for example, some of the test conditions will derive entirely from the requirements, and should be linked only to one (or more) requirements. Some test conditions will derive entirely from the quality risks, and should be linked only to one (or more) quality risk items. Some test conditions will derive from both requirements and quality risks. You need to configure your test management or lifecycle management tool to accommodate traceability in all three cases.

At the end of the test analysis process, you should have a catalog of test conditions in your test management tool. Each test condition should have properly established traceability to its source. You should be confident that, if each test condition is covered by the proper number of tests, sufficient testing will occur to meet the objectives of testing. Typical objectives of testing include:

- Finding bugs, especially important bugs
- Reducing risk of failure in production to an acceptable level prior to release
- Building confidence in the adequacy of testing and, if the test results warrant, in the readiness of the product for release
- Providing information to the key project participants and stakeholders to enable smart project, process, and product decisions

This list of objectives is not exhaustive or prescriptive, but does tend to reflect the most common objectives I find with our clients.

Example: Agile Analysis and Design

The same process shown in Figure 1–5 applies, with some variation, regardless of lifecycle. For example, one of our clients follows an Agile lifecycle to develop software for investment banks, which in turn use that software to manage large, sophisticated, and high-value stock portfolios.

At the beginning of each iteration, they carry out the standard Agile process of user story grooming. During this process, they identify the test conditions relevant to each user story. Thanks to the business stakeholders' involvement, these test conditions are also prioritized.

Once each user story is finalized—and approved as part of the iteration backlog—test design and implementation start on the associated test conditions, at the same time that the programmer is creating the code. Test data is generated. Acceptance criteria are finalized—again with the help of the business and technical stakeholders—and then translated into acceptance test–driven development tests, typically using FitNesse or some similar test tool.

Test Analysis Exercise

Read the HELLOCARMS system requirements document, provided as Appendix B. This document is for a hypothetical project, though I derived it from a real project that RBCS helped to test.

Assume that HELLOCARMS is following an iterative lifecycle model and using a blended requirements-based and risk-based analytical test strategy. Identify the tasks testers would need to carry out during test analysis. Next, identify the tasks testers would need to carry out during test design.

Test Analysis Debrief

Test analysis would happen during project initiation and would then be refined at the beginning of each iteration. During test analysis, testers would:

- Review the HELLOCARMS system requirements document (focusing on new or changed content in subsequent iterations)
- Review the HELLOCARMS quality risk analysis (focusing on new or changed risks in subsequent iterations)
- Evaluate the testability of the requirements, the risks, and HELLOCARMS as a whole (again, focusing on new or changed items in subsequent iterations)
- Identify test conditions based on these reviews, prioritizing the conditions based on requirement priority or level of risk, as appropriate

Test design would happen at the start of each iteration. During test design, testers would:

- Design and prioritize high-level test cases based on test conditions (in subsequent iterations, this could include redesign and reprioritization of existing tests based on changes)
- Identify the test data needed for these test conditions and test cases (in subsequent iterations, this could include identifying changes needed to test data based on changes)
- Design the test environment (note: the amount of additional work on this task in each subsequent iteration would depend on the realism of the initial environment and whether additional configurations are supported in later iterations)
- Identify any required infrastructure and tools for the test cases and test environment
- Capture bidirectional traceability between test bases (in this case, the requirements and the risks) and the test cases that have been designed

You might have identified some additional tasks in either or both activities.

1.5   Test Design

Learning objectives

(K2) Explain why test conditions should be understood by the stakeholders.

(K4) Analyze a project scenario to determine the most appropriate use for low-level (concrete) and high-level (logical) test cases.

In test design, we translate test conditions into test cases. This is a simple statement, but it raises a number of questions.

First, at what level of detail do we document the test cases? Concrete or low-level test cases supply specific inputs and specific expected results, while logical or high-level test cases give rules for generating the inputs and for evaluating the expected results. We'll examine this topic in more detail later in this section, because it's important—and often overlooked.

Second, what test design technique or techniques should we use to create these test cases? Are tools available and perhaps even needed to support the techniques? As we go through the material on test design techniques in Chapters 3 and 4, we'll talk about the techniques available and how to select them, based on what you're trying to test.

Third, what is the order in which we should create the tests and run the tests? In Chapter 2, we'll look at how to identify and assess quality risk so that we can use the level of risk to determine the priority of our tests.

ISTQB Glossary

Logical test case: A test case without concrete (implementation level) values for input data and expected results. Logical operators are used; instances of the actual values are not yet defined and/or available.

Concrete test case: A test case with concrete (implementation level) values for input data and expected results. Logical operators from high-level test cases are replaced by actual values that correspond to the objectives of the logical operators.

High-level test case: A test case without concrete (implementation level) values for input data and expected results. Logical operators are used; instances of the actual values are not yet defined and/or available.

Low-level test case: A test case with concrete (implementation level) values for input data and expected results. Logical operators from high-level test cases are replaced by actual values that correspond to the objectives of the logical operators.

Test Design and Implementation Process

In Figure 1–6, we see what happens in the next step of the test process, test design. Test analysts use the test conditions as the primary input to create test cases. However, they also need to adhere to the parameters, constraints, and guidelines provided in the test strategy and the relevant test plans. They will need access to one or more test oracles, often provided by business stakeholders, technical stakeholders, or both.

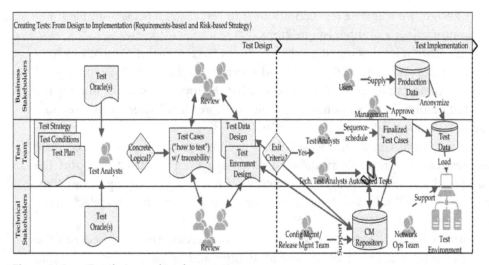

Figure 1–6   *Test design and implementation*

These inputs will be used to create the test cases, documented at the appropriate level of detail. Test analysts should capture traceability between the test cases and the test conditions as the test cases are created. As the tests are created, test analysts should be designing the test data and test environment that will be required.

Before the test cases are considered complete, some organizations like to have them reviewed by technical and business stakeholders. My experience is that, provided sufficiently detailed test conditions were already reviewed and approved, such further review might be unnecessary or even counterproductive. I have had business analysts and developers tell me that they have participated in test case reviews that didn't help them understand what was being tested, because it provided too much detail. However, we also have clients that successfully use acceptance test-driven development and behavior-driven development, both of which involve business and technical stakeholders in the review of concrete test cases. You, your fellow testers, and your test manager will need to decide what's right for your team.

However you come down on that question, it is a good idea to have the test data design reviewed by business stakeholders, especially if your plan is to use production data for testing. (More on that topic in the next section.) It's also a good idea to have the test environment design reviewed by the relevant technical stakeholders, especially those on whom you will rely to configure or reconfigure the test environment.

Only once you are confident that the test cases are complete, the test data will be adequate, and the test environment will allow you to cover realistic usage scenarios should you consider test design complete.

Tips for Test Design

Here are some tips to consider during test design.

First, not all test conditions need to be turned into test cases, if you plan to use reactive testing as part of your test strategy. Techniques such as exploratory testing, defect taxonomies, and software attacks are often associated with such reactive testing. Remember that, in reactive testing, rather than relying on pre-designed tests, we react to the system actually presented to us. In reactive testing, you can use the test conditions as part of the test charter.

Next, make sure that you have a reliable test oracle, so that you can determine whether a test has passed or failed. In most cases, there is very little point in running a test if you have no way of saying what the expected result is. Boris Beizer, in his usual inimitable style, described doing so as "playing kiddie pool," as in whacking the balls around the pool table and hoping that they end up in a pocket, any pocket.[1] We'll revisit this topic in a moment, since it's critical.

Now, when you're documenting the tests, keep in mind that you might not be documenting them just for yourself. What other testers will need to run them? Will the tests be reviewed by other project stakeholders? This is a common mistake, and it relates to the logical-versus-concrete topic we'll revisit in a moment.

Finally, when you're designing tests, look beyond just the user interface. Ask yourself if the application consists of components that talk to each other, such as a business logic layer and a data repository, and what should happen in those communications? Are there multiple systems in the test object, and what might

---

1. This comment, along with many other useful ideas for testers, is found in *Software Testing Techniques*.

be happening across those interfaces during the test? Are there batch processes that will run during this test, whether as part of it or independently, and what should the result of those batch processes be? What interrupts could occur during the test, and how can you force those to occur? How else, besides a graphical user interface, does the software interact with the world?

Logical or Concrete?

Now, let's address this question of whether to create logical or concrete test cases. A concrete test case is one that provides the specific information needed to run the test. This includes an exact description of the test data to use, the inputs to supply, the steps to carry out, and the expected results, down to the level of field inputs, screen shots, and so forth. These are useful when the requirements are well defined, because they provide worked-out examples of how the system behaves. For example, acceptance test–driven development uses concrete test cases this way.

Concrete test cases can be run by an automated tool in some cases, or by a person. Since the tests leave nothing to the imagination or discretion of the tester, any tester can run them, regardless of experience. Any tester can repeat the test exactly as was it was run before. In addition, anyone can verify exactly what was tested, which can be useful in regulatory situations.

However, concrete test cases require a lot of documentation. This documentation is expensive to produce and even more expensive to maintain over the long term. Further, the level of detail can limit creativity and lead to testers ignoring important possible variations in what to test.

A logical test, as I said before, provides guidelines for the specific inputs, data, steps, and expected results. The tester must use their judgment and experience to choose those items, and also has discretion to vary the test as opportunities present themselves. These are useful if the requirements are not well defined, especially if they are subject to change, since you aren't tied to specifics. If the testers have a lot of experience, and there are no external auditors to satisfy, perhaps you don't need to create concrete tests.

All things being equal, such logical tests will provide better coverage than an equivalent set of concrete tests, because testers will tend to vary the tests each time they are run, addressing nuances of system behavior. Since logical test cases may be anywhere from 10 to 100 times less verbose than concrete test cases, they are much cheaper to create and maintain. However, any time the test is run, it will be run differently, even if the same person runs it twice. So, reproducibility is low.

Now, one way to create concrete tests is to start with logical tests and then elaborate those. In Agile projects, you see an example of this when acceptance criteria are defined, and then automated tests are created using techniques like acceptance test–driven development and behavior-driven development to evaluate those acceptance criteria. Since the tool has no discretion, experience, or judgment, automated tests are always concrete tests.

This decision about the right level of detail and whether to document at multiple levels of detail must be a team decision, made prior to test design, and kept consistently by all test analysts throughout the project and across multiple projects. I've seen lots of test repositories that were full of inconsistently documented tests, some with excruciating and useless levels of detail and others so vague as to barely be test conditions. This is not an efficient or effective way to deal with test documentation. The test manager, with the advice of test analysts, should look at factors such as project risks, the need to reuse documentation over time, any relevant standards or regulations that might result in auditing, the lifecycle model and how documentation is treated within that model, and the level of detail required in the traceability of the tests.

Example: Use of Logical Test Cases

Here's an example of how we used logical test cases on one project. When we updated our RBCS website in 2015, we needed to test that update. We used an experienced test engineer, one who had worked with us for years, to do an acceptance test for us. He didn't need detailed test cases. Instead, we took the statement of work and created test conditions from it.

We sent those test conditions to the contractor building our website as a form of fair warning, saying, "This is our interpretation of the contract and we won't accept a website that doesn't meet those test conditions. Now is your chance to object before payment becomes an issue."

Once we had approval of the test conditions, we created very lightweight logical tests. The tester could then run the tests and report his results based on the test conditions themselves, as we had traceability. In situations where the statement of work was unclear, the tester was allowed to use his expertise to define the expected behavior.

Creating Good Test Cases

What can we say about the process of creating good test cases? First, the process is usually one of elaborating test conditions into test cases through a process of stepwise refinement. I say "usually" because some test strategies, such as reactive test strategies, don't always use written tests. For the moment, let's assume that we want to specify test cases that are repeatable, verifiable and traceable back to requirements, quality risks, or whatever else our tests are based on.

If we are going to create test cases, then, for a given test condition—or two or more related test conditions—we can apply various test design techniques to create test cases. These techniques are covered in Chapters 3 and 4. Keep in mind that you can and should blend techniques in a single test case.

I mentioned traceability to the requirements, quality risks, and other test bases. We can capture that traceability directly, by relating the test case to the test basis element or elements that gave rise to the test conditions from which we created the test case. Alternatively, we can relate the test case to the test conditions, which are in turn related to the test basis elements.

So, can we say anything else about the test design process? Well, the specific process of test design depends on the technique. However, it typically involves defining the following:

- Objective
- Preconditions
- Test environment requirements
- Test inputs and other test data requirements
- Expected results
- Postconditions

Defining the expected result of a test can be tricky, especially as expected results are not only screen outputs, but also data and environmental postconditions. Solving this problem requires that we have what's called a test oracle, which we'll look at in a moment.

Notice the mention of test environment requirements. It is vital to remember that testing involves more than just the test objects and the testware. There is a test environment, and this isn't just hardware. It includes rooms, equipment, personnel, software, tools, peripherals, communications equipment, user authorizations, and all other items required to run the tests.

Test Oracle

Let's address this issue of the test oracle in more detail and start by defining what a test oracle is.

A *test oracle* is some source to determine the expected results of a test. We can compare these expected results with the actual results from the test. Some test oracles are existing systems. Some are user manuals. Some are people's specialized knowledge. We should never use the code itself as an oracle, even for structural testing, because that's simply testing that the compiler, operating system, and hardware work. The expected results include what you see on the screen, but there's more to it than that. You have to consider postconditions in the test data and the test environment. You have to consider data that might flow across interfaces or through inter-process communications, as mentioned earlier.

So, what is the oracle problem? Well, if you haven't experienced this first-hand, ask yourself how, in general, we know what the correct results are for a test? The difficulty of doing so was termed the oracle problem, yet another phrase we as test professionals owe to Boris Beizer.

If you've just entered the workforce from the ivory towers of academia, you might have learned about perfect software engineering projects. You might have heard stories about detailed, clear, and consistent test bases like requirements and design specifications that define all expected results. These stories were myths, if you heard them.

In the real world, on real projects, test basis documents such as requirements are vague. Two documents, such as a marketing requirements document and a system requirements document, will often contradict each other. They have gaps, leaving out any discussion of important characteristics of the product—especially non-functional characteristics, and especially usability and user interface characteristics.

Sometimes they are missing entirely. Sometimes they exist, but are so superficial as to be useless. One of my clients showed me a handwritten scrawl on letter-size paper, complete with crude illustrations, which was all he received by way of requirements on a project that involved 100 or so person-months of effort.

When test basis documents are delivered, they are often delivered late, often too late to wait for them to be done before we begin test design (at least if we want to finish test design before we start test execution).

Even with the best intentions on the part of business analysts, sales and marketing staff, and users, test basis documents won't be perfect. Real-world applications are complex and not entirely amenable to complete, unambiguous specification.

So, we have to augment the written test basis documents we receive with tester expertise or access to expertise, along with judgment and professional pessimism. Using all available oracles—written and mental, provided and derived—the tester can define expected results before and during test execution.

Since I've been talking a lot about requirements in this section, you might assume that the oracle problem applies only to high-level tests like system test and acceptance test. Nope. The oracle problem and its solutions apply to all test levels. The test bases will vary from one level to another, though. Higher test levels like acceptance test and system test rely more on requirements specifications, use cases, and defined business processes. Lower test levels like component test and integration test rely more on low-level design specifications.

While this is a hassle, remember that the oracle problem must be solved in your testing. If you run tests with no way to evaluate the results, you are wasting your time. You will provide low, zero, or negative value to the team. Such testing generates false positives and false negatives. It distracts the team with spurious results of all kinds. It creates false confidence in the system.

By the way, as for my sarcastic aside about the ivory tower of academia a moment ago, let me mention that, in my studies at UCLA quite a few years ago, I remember my software engineering professors letting me in on this problem right from the start. I guess I couldn't say I wasn't warned about what I was up against!

Test Design Considerations

A missed opportunity for a number of organizations is not applying this process of test design at all levels. This process certainly can be applied at all levels, provided people keep in mind that the test basis inputs and the objectives of testing will vary. For example, business analysts creating user acceptance tests should use requirements specifications as their primary test basis, while developers creating unit tests will generally refer to the code. Developers creating unit tests focus on the functionality of the component they're testing, while test analysts creating system tests focus on end-to-end functionality.

The test target has a strong influence on the level of detail issue we addressed before. In addition, the tools used for test automation vary quite a bit. For example, we have clients that use frameworks like JUnit to implement unit tests for individual components, Cucumber for feature verification tests of individual user stories, and Selenium for system testing across all the features.

Another common mistake is to focus the test target too narrowly, leaving out important quality characteristics. This is especially true for non-functional quality characteristics. It's even worse when such characteristics are clearly within scope based on the test strategy or test plan, but are simply omitted during test design.

At this juncture, let me remind you of three important ideas from the Foundation syllabus. One is the value of static testing early in the lifecycle to catch defects when they are cheap and easy to fix. The next is the preventive role testing can play when involved early in the lifecycle. The last is that testing should be involved early in the project. These three ideas are related, because test analysis and design are forms of static testing. Test analysis and design are synergistic with other forms of static testing, but we can only exploit that synergy if we are involved at the right time.

Notice that, depending on when the test analysis and design work is done, you could possibly define test conditions and test cases in parallel with reviews and static analyses of the test basis. In fact, you could prepare for a requirements review meeting by doing test analysis and design on the requirements. Test analysis and design can serve as a structured, failure-focused static test of a requirements specification generating useful inputs to a requirements review meeting.

Of course, we should also take advantage of the ideas of static testing, and early involvement if we can, to have test and non-test stakeholders participate in reviews of various test work products, including risk analyses, test designs, test cases, and test plans. We should also use appropriate static analysis techniques on these work products.

As mentioned earlier, make sure that you don't forget the test environment and other important supporting infrastructure during test design. All too often, I see clients wasting huge amounts of test execution time resolving issues in their test environments and infrastructure that clearly could have been resolved earlier, before test execution started. Whatever lifecycle you're following, test execution time is always at a premium. Don't squander it through intellectual laziness by saying, "Well, these environment and infrastructure issues are hard to predict in advance, so we'll just see what happens when we start running tests."

On a related note, make sure that you know what else must be done before test execution starts. Having a written checklist for important test execution entry criteria is a good idea. Whether this is documented in a test plan, as it would be in a traditional lifecycle, or just part of the definition of done in an Agile lifecycle, such a checklist will help you avoid shooting yourself in the foot.

Example: Understanding Test Conditions

Let's look at an example of a test oracle, from the real world.

I was once working on a project to develop a banking application to replace a legacy system. There were two test oracles. One was the requirements specification, such as it was. The other was the legacy system. We faced two challenges.

For one thing, the requirements were vague. The original concept of the project, from the vendor's side, was, "Give the customer whatever the customer wants," which they then realized was a good way to go bankrupt given the indecisive and conflicting ideas about what the system should do among the customer's users. The requirements were the outcome of a belated effort to put more structure around the project.

For another thing, sometimes, the new system differed from the legacy system in minor ways. I remember one infamous situation, a bug report that we opened, then deferred, then reopened at least four or five times, regarding situations where the monthly payment varied by one cent.

The absence of any reliable, authoritative, consistent set of oracles led to a lot of bug report ping-pong. We also had bug report prioritization issues as people argued over whether some problems were problems at all. We had high rates of false positives and negatives. The entire team—including the test team—was frustrated.

So, you can see, the oracle problem is not some abstract concept; it has real-world consequences.

Test Design Exercise

Assume that HELLOCARMS is following an iterative lifecycle model and using a blended requirements-based and risk-based analytical test strategy. Assume also that some amount of reactive testing will occur. Identify where you would use concrete test cases and where you would use logical test cases, as well as additional factors that you would need to clarify to make the decision on which type to use.

Test Design Debrief

The requirements for this project are reasonably well defined, though some gaps remain that would need to be filled. While those gaps remain, logical test cases can be developed. If appropriate, those logical test cases can be elaborated into concrete test cases once the requirements specification is complete.

If the project is subject to regulations or company standards that require traceability of tests and their results back to the requirements, subject to audit, then concrete test cases are probably required. In addition, a lack of testing and banking experience among the testers who execute the test cases may require the use of concrete test cases.

If regulations or standards do not apply, and testers are experienced with testing and banking applications, then logical test cases might be useful to save effort on test development and maintenance. In fact, they could even allow for testers to do some creative additional tests that they might have forgotten if they were following detailed test scripts.

However, since the project is following an iterative lifecycle, there is a need to manage regression risk during the second and subsequent iterations. This can be addressed by automating tests during or after each iteration, in which case reproducibility of the tests is not a concern. If the regression testing must be manual, and if a high degree of confidence is needed that the same test conditions were covered in the same way each time the test is run, then concrete tests are required.

For the reactive testing, no test cases are required, as the test conditions serve as charters for unscripted testing sessions. During test design, it would be important to determine which test conditions were suitable for reactive testing, so that no effort was spent creating test cases for them.

1.6   Test Implementation

Learning objectives
(K2) Describe the typical exit criteria for test analysis and test design and explain how meeting those criteria affects the test implementation effort.

Implementation includes a disparate collection of activities. Part of implementation is finalizing the tests to whatever level of detail is required, based on the factors discussed in the previous section. This is the point where you would ensure that all organizational standards for tests are satisfied, and, where applicable, any regulations that affect the tests are also satisfied.

Test automation is also assigned to the implementation process. That can be a little deceiving, because certainly automation work must be happening at a very early stage in order for the automated tests to be ready when test execution starts. For example, in acceptance test-driven development and behavior-driven development in Agile projects, automation work is happening from the moment work starts on the user story.

Another part of implementation is simply making sure everything is ready for test execution. In traditional lifecycle projects, this would involve evaluating exit criteria for test analysis and design and entry criteria for test execution. These criteria would be documented in a test strategy (where universal across projects) and in a test plan (where specific to this project). In Agile projects, these criteria can and should be part of the DoD for various tasks and work products. We'll revisit this topic in a moment.

Part of being ready for test execution is to understand the order in which the tests will be run. In Agile projects, especially those Agile lifecycles using elements of Kanban, this can be less of an issue, since it is a whole-team responsibility to optimize the flow of work, including through the testing activities. Further, in any given iteration, there are fewer tests to run. However, in traditional lifecycles, especially sequential lifecycles, there can be a very large number of tests to run, and the sequence of those tests is not obvious.

Regardless of lifecycle, when considering the sequencing of tests, factors to consider include the following:

- Logical collections of tests that are similar in type, tested quality characteristics, or functional area, sometimes called test suites
- The level of risk associated with each test, as will be discussed in Chapter 2
- Dependencies and constraints, such as hardware availability, the order of feature delivery, and the like
- Where in the test schedule reactive test strategies will be used—e.g., how frequently periods will be set aside for error guessing, exploratory testing, bug hunting, or software attacks[2]

Once test sequencing decisions are made, this information should be captured and put into action. For example, in Agile projects, development work would start earlier for user stories that are associated with high-priority tests. In sequential projects, testers often work with system operations teams or test environment specialists to resolve potential test environment issues before they block test execution later. Regardless of lifecycle, there should be forethought put into how the test items, the test environments, the people, and any other

---

2. The first mention of reactive test strategies and experience-based test techniques is found in Glenford Myers's *The Art of Software Testing*, published in the 1970s. More recently, James Whittaker has written books discussing software attacks and exploratory testing over the last fifteen years, and Elisabeth Hendrickson has been promulgating her approach to bug hunting for over ten years.

resources needed will be in place when a particular test needs to run, and how those test environments will be supported during test execution.

Test implementation should also include verifying how test results will be gathered and reported. In Agile projects, these decisions would be made during release planning, often called *sprint zero* in Scrum projects, and would span the whole team. Reporting mechanisms such as task management tools, task boards, and daily stand-up meetings would all be agreed on and put into place. In traditional lifecycles, status reporting is often siloed for each group, such as business analysts, testers, and developers, so the test strategy or test plan will discuss how the results will be reported. During implementation, testers should check that all the tools necessary for results reporting are in place.

Another part of implementation is validating and loading any test data needed, unless loading that data is part of the test itself. If there is data that's needed as inputs or as data to be loaded during the test, that must be checked for readiness and correctness during implementation. This includes any data needed for automated tests.

In a similar vein, the test environments must be finalized, verified for correctness and completeness (ideally using a checklist so nothing is forgotten), and validated (ideally by running some kind of smoke test against an early version of the test object). If this is done after the test data is loaded, this process can cover both the test environment and the test data.

You'll also need to make sure that you have a defined process for delivering software into the test environment. In Agile projects, this is often embedded within the continuous integration process and automated. Care must be taken that such automated deployment of test objects into the test environment doesn't interfere with or invalidate the results of tests already underway. While these same continuous integration frameworks can be used in traditional lifecycles, it's more typical for me to see organizations with defined handover processes where release engineering staff deliver test releases to the test team for installation. Whether automated or manual, in order to avoid chaos, make sure the test release process is well defined and robust. The best practice is to test that process at least once prior to the start of test execution.

Test Analysis and Design Exit Criteria

Let's return to this topic of exit criteria for test analysis and test design, or, if you prefer, the definition of done for these activities. While organizational, product, and project realities can result in significant differences, you should consider the following:

- Have you designed the test environment and all other relevant and necessary test infrastructure?
- Have you designed all the test data that must be loaded prior to test execution, and the test data that will be used during test execution, including input data?
- Has the entire test basis been covered, to the appropriate depth, and are the tests traceable back to the test basis elements they cover?
- Are the tests documented to whatever level of detail was previously decided?
- Has the oracle problem been solved for every test, so that expected results are either defined in the test itself or available through a reference given in the test?
- Are the tests prioritized according to the considerations discussed before?

Some implementation tasks will take longer or be blocked if these criteria are not satisfied before those tasks are started.

Test Implementation and Execution Process

In Figure 1–7, you can see the test implementation process. Test analysts work on finalizing, sequencing, and scheduling the manual test cases, which are checked into some type of repository, such as a task management tool, a test management tool, or a configuration management tool. Technical test analysts work on the same tasks for the automated tests.

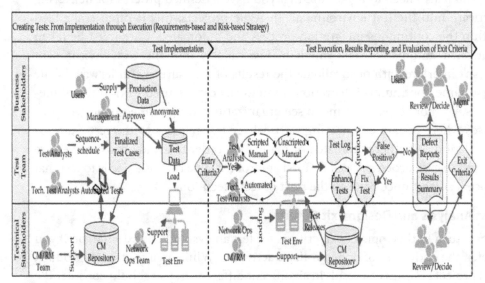

Figure 1–7   *Test implementation process*

The test repository is often supported by an external team, which is a release management team in the example below. We also see, in this figure, the test environment being configured and supported by a network operations team.

As mentioned in the previous section, it's possible that production data will be used for testing. If so, that data is supplied by users. Management usually must approve the use of such data for testing, and it will often insist that such data be anonymized before it is loaded into the test data repository and then into the test environment itself.

Finally, you see the test team checking entry criteria before declaring test implementation done and test execution ready to begin.

Example: DO-178C Design Exit Criteria

The United States Federal Aviation Administration provides a standard called DO-178C for avionics systems. In Europe, it's called ED-12C. A summary of the standard is shown in Table 1–1.

Table 1–1   *DO-178C*

Criticality	Potential Failure Impact	Required Coverage
Level A: Catastrophic	Software failure can result in a catastrophic failure of the system.	Modified Condition/ Decision, Decision, and Statement
Level B: Hazardous/ Severe	Software failure can result in a hazardous or severe/major failure of the system.	Decision and Statement
Level C: Major	Software failure can result in a major failure of the system.	Statement
Level D: Minor	Software failure can result in a minor failure of the system.	None
Level E: No effect	Software failure cannot have an effect on the system.	None

The standard assigns a criticality level, based on the potential impact of a failure. Based on the criticality level, a certain level of white-box test coverage is required.

Criticality level A, or Catastrophic, applies when a software failure can result in a catastrophic failure of the system. This is defined as, "Failure conditions which would result in multiple fatalities, usually with the loss of the airplane." For software with such criticality, the standard requires Modified Condition/ Decision, Decision, and Statement coverage.

Criticality level B, or Hazardous and Severe, applies when a software failure can result in a hazardous, severe, or major failure of the system. This is defined as, "Failure conditions which would reduce the capability of the airplane or the ability of the flight crew to cope with adverse operating conditions to the extent that there would be: (1) A large reduction in safety margins or functional capabilities, (2) Physical distress or excessive workload such that the flight crew cannot be relied upon to perform their tasks accurately or completely, or (3) Serious or fatal injuries to a relatively small number of the occupants other than the flight crew." For software with such criticality, the standard requires Decision and Statement coverage.

Criticality level C, or Major, applies when a software failure can result in a major failure of the system. This is defined as, "Failure conditions which would reduce the capability of the airplane or the ability of the crew to cope with adverse operating conditions to the extent that there would be, for example, a significant reduction in safety margins or functional capabilities, a significant increase in crew workload or in conditions impairing crew efficiency, or discomfort to flight crew, or physical distress to passengers or cabin crew, possibly including injuries." For software with such criticality, the standard requires only Statement coverage.

Criticality level D, or Minor, applies when a software failure can only result in a minor failure of the system. This is defined as, "Failure conditions which would not significantly reduce airplane safety, and which would involve crew actions that are well within their capabilities. Minor failure conditions may include, for example, a slight reduction in safety margins or functional capabilities, a slight increase in crew workload, such as routine flight plan changes, or some physical discomfort to passengers or cabin crew." For software with such criticality, the standard does not require any level of coverage.

Finally, criticality level E, or No effect, applies when a software failure cannot have an effect on the system. This is defined as, "Failure conditions that would have no effect on safety; for example, failure conditions that would not affect the operational capability of the airplane or increase crew workload." For software with such criticality, the standard does not require any level of coverage.

This makes a certain amount of sense. You should be more concerned about software that affects flight safety, such as rudder and aileron control modules, than you are about software that doesn't, such as video entertainment systems. However, there is a risk of using a one-dimensional white-box measuring stick to determine how much confidence we should have in a system. Coverage metrics are a measure of confidence, it's true, but we should use multiple coverage metrics, both white box and black box. Fortunately, the DO-178C standard does require additional coverage metrics, in terms of requirements.

By the way, if you found this example a bit confusing due to the references to code coverage, note that most of the white-box coverage metrics I mentioned were discussed in the Foundation syllabus, in Chapter 4. If you don't remember what they mean, you should go back and review that material in that chapter on white-box coverage metrics.

1.7 Test Execution

Learning objectives
(K3) For a given scenario, determine the steps and considerations that should be taken when executing tests.

We've now come to the point where we're ready to start test execution. To do so, we need the delivery of the test object or objects and the satisfaction (or waiver) of entry criteria.

Of course, this presumes that the entry criteria alone are enough to ensure that the various necessary implementation tasks discussed earlier in this chapter are complete. If not, then we have to go back and check those issues of test data, test environments, test dependencies, and so forth.

Now, during test execution, people will run the manual tests. To execute a test to completion, we'd expect that at least two things had happened. First, all of the test conditions or quality risk items traceable to the test were covered. Second, all of the steps of the test were carried out.

You might ask, "How could I carry out the test without covering all the risks or conditions?" In some cases, the test is written at a high level. In such situations, you would need to understand what the test was about, and augment the written test with on-the-fly details that ensure you cover the right areas.

You might also ask, "How could I cover all the risks and conditions without carrying out the entire test?" Some steps of a test are there more to enable testing than to cover conditions or risk. For example, some steps set up data or other preconditions, some steps capture logging information, and some steps restore the system to a known good state at the end.

A third kind of activity can apply during manual test execution. This is that some degree of exploratory testing can be incorporated into the tests themselves. One way to accomplish this is by leaving them somewhat vague and telling the tester to select their favorite way of carrying out a certain task. Another way is to tell the testers, as I often do, that a test is a road map to interesting places, and, when they get somewhere interesting, they should stop and look around. This has the effect of giving them permission to transcend, to go beyond, the tests. I've found it very effective.

Finally, during execution, tools will run automated tests. These tools follow the defined scripts without deviation. That can seem like an unalloyed good thing at first. However, if the scripts are not designed properly, that can mean that they get out of sync with the system under test and generate a bunch of false positives. If you move on to the technical test analyst book, Jamie Mitchell and I will talk more about that problem—and how to solve it.

At the heart of any test, of course, is a comparison of actual results to expected results. A discrepancy between them—known in ISTQB terms as an anomaly—should be investigated to determine whether the discrepancy results from a bug in the software under test. If so, then the anomaly is a failure. If the anomaly is due to some other reason—e.g., a problem with the test, a problem with the test environment, a problem with test data, etc.—then we have a false positive. In such an event, the underlying problem should be resolved and the test rerun.

In addition to false positives, we can also have false negatives, which is where we miss a failure that the test could have caught. For example, if two fields are supposed to be multiplied, but instead are added, testing with both fields having the value of two will not reveal the defect. Inattentiveness is another reason for false negatives, so pay attention.

In some cases, users or customers are involved in test execution. For example, in Agile projects, it's common for a business stakeholder or product owner to participate in acceptance testing or feature demos once a feature has been verified by the developer (via unit tests) and the tester (via feature verification tests and system tests).

Test Result Logging

Most testers like to run tests—at least the first few times they run them—but sometimes they don't like to log results. "Paperwork!" they snort. "Bureaucracy and red tape!" they protest.

If you are one of those testers, get over it. All the planning, analysis, design, and implementation were about getting to the point of running a test and comparing actual and expected results. Everything after that point is about using the value the comparison delivered. Well, you can't use the value if you don't capture it, and the test logs are about capturing the value.

So, remember that, as testers run tests, testers log results. Failure to log results means either doing the test over again (most likely) or losing the value of running the tests. When you do the test over, that is pure waste, a loss of your time running the test. Since test execution is usually on the critical path for project completion, that waste puts the planned project end date at risk. People don't like that.

A side note here, before we move on. I mentioned reactive test strategies and the problems they have with coverage earlier. Note that, with adequate logging, while you can't ascertain reactive test coverage in advance, at least you can capture it afterward. So, again, log your results, both for scripted and unscripted tests.

During test execution, there are many moving parts. The tests might be changing. The test object and each constituent test item are often changing. The test environment might be changing. The test basis might be changing. So, logging should identify the versions tested.

The military strategist Carl von Clausewitz referred famously to the "fog of war." What he meant was not a literal fog—though black-powder cannons and firearms of his day created plenty of that—but rather a metaphorical fog whereby no one observing a battle, be they an infantryman or a general, could truly grasp the whole picture.

Clausewitz would recognize his famous fog if he were to come back to life and work as a tester. Test execution periods tend to have a lot of fog. Good test logs are the fog cutter. Test logs should provide a detailed, rich chronology of test execution.

To do so, test logs need to be test by test and event by event. Each test, uniquely identified, should have status information logged against it as the test goes through the test execution period. This information should support not only understanding the overall test status, but also the overall test coverage.

Events that occur during test execution and affect the test execution process—directly or indirectly—should be logged as well. We should document anything that delays, interrupts, or blocks testing.

Test analysts are not always also test managers, but they should work closely with the test managers. Test managers need logging information for test control, test progress reporting, and test process improvement. Test analysts need it, too, along with the test managers, for measurement of exit criteria, which we'll cover in the next section.

Finally, let me point out that the extent, type, and details of test logs will vary based on the test level, the test strategy, the test tools, and various standards and regulations. Automated component testing results in automated gathering of test logging information. Manual acceptance testing usually involves the test manager compiling the test logs or at least collating the information coming from the testers. If we're testing regulated, safety-critical systems like pharmaceutical systems, we might have to log certain information for audit purposes.

Special Considerations for Execution

During test execution, here are some tips to keep in mind:

- Explore the seemingly irrelevant. Sometimes that minor, odd behavior is the loose thread on the sweater which, when pulled, unravels the whole thing.
- Check that the system does what it is supposed to do and doesn't do what it's not supposed to do. Negative testing is important. Look for the inability to handle typical mistakes, and typical security hacks. Look for the presence of features that are not required and perhaps not even specified—i.e., the so-called Easter eggs.
- Enhance tests over time, especially to fill discovered coverage gaps. Expect to grow and maintain your tests.
- Use the defect tracking tool as a source of test enhancement inspiration, especially defects from unscripted tests. Defect-based testing isn't just for exploratory testing, bug hunting, and attacks. It can also be used to augment your written tests.
- Take notes for knowledge transfer on the next test effort. These notes will be useful during the test retrospective in test closure.
- Never let an anomaly slide based on the assumption that you can catch it in the next test cycle. Many a known bug has escaped to the customers based on this assumption.
- Use regression tests for confidence building, not defect finding. It's a common misunderstanding that regression tests will find bugs, but remember the pesticide paradox. Finding bugs is not why you're running regression tests.

Test execution periods can be hectic, rushed, and confusing, but try to remain calm.

Test Execution and Results Reporting

In Figure 1–8, you can see the processes of test execution, test results reporting, and the evaluation of exit criteria. We'll talk about results reporting and evalua- tion of exit criteria in the next section. We've changed a bit from previous fig- ures, because in this figure, the test strategy includes reactive testing.

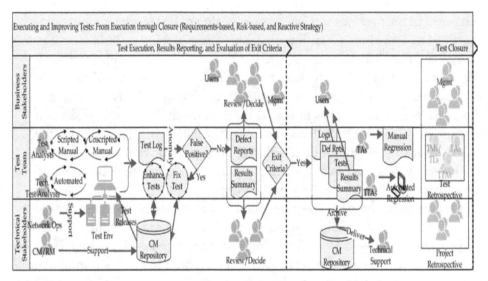

Figure 1–8   *Test execution, test results reporting, and evaluation of exit criteria*

As you can see, the test analysts are running both scripted and unscripted man- ual tests, while the technical test analysts are running automated tests. That's not always the way it works, since properly designed automated tests can be run by test analysts. We also see network operations supporting the test environment, as well as the release management team supporting test releases and the test repository.

As test execution continues, the testers log the test results. If they observe anomalies, testers first check for a false positive. If so, they fix the test and run it again. Testers may also rerun tests after enhancing the tests to improve coverage, efficiency, or some other attribute.

1.8   Evaluating Exit Criteria and Reporting

Learning objectives
(K2) Explain why accurate test case execution status information is important.

As discussed in the previous section, proper logging of test results is an important part of test execution. Common mistakes in test logging include failing to properly assign test status, such as whether the test has been run, whether it passes, whether it fails, or whether it is blocked. Improper classification of defects, especially in terms of severity or affected subsystem, is also common.

Bad results logging, or gaps in results logging, mean that people make bad project, process, and product decisions. A lack of alignment between, on the one hand, the exit criteria or the definition of done, and, on the other hand, the results logging will also mean that we can't evaluate test progress. Poorly defined or subjective exit criteria have the same problem.

When results are properly logged, the test manager can use test information to give other project stakeholders accurate, reliable, regular test reports. When major problems occur—whether defects or blockages to tests—the test manager can submit exception reports to get problems resolved. At the end of testing, the test manager can summarize the findings.

Test Execution and Results Reporting

Referring back to Figure 1–8, let's finish the discussion about results reporting and evaluation of exit criteria. As you can see, anomalies that are not false positives become defect reports. Those are reviewed by business and technical stakeholders to decide what should happen. Should the bug be fixed, deferred, rejected as not a real bug, or accepted as a permanent limitation?

The test logs and the bug reports are the raw material for the test results summary. This is also reviewed by technical and business stakeholders. These stakeholders use the test results to make important project, process, and product decisions, including deciding whether test execution can be declared done. In traditional projects, that is decided based on exit criteria, while Agile projects use a DoD (definition of done).

Example: System Test Exit Review

Let's look at a case study. Figure 1–9 shows an excerpt of the exit criteria for an Internet appliance we tested. You'll see that we have graded the criteria as part of a system test exit review.

System Test Exit Review

Per the Test Plan, System Test was planned to end when following criteria were met:

1. All design, implementation, and feature completion, code completion, and unit test completion commitments made in the System Test Entry meeting were either met or slipped to no later than four (4), three (3), and three (3) weeks, respectively, prior to the proposed System Test Exit date.
   STATUS: RED. Audio and demo functionality have entered System Test in the last three weeks. The modems entered System Test in the last three weeks. On the margins of a violation, off-hook detection was changed significantly.

2. No panic, crash, halt, wedge, unexpected process termination, or other stoppage of processing has occurred on any server software or hardware for the previous three (3) weeks.
   STATUS: YELLOW. The servers have not crashed, but we did not complete all the tip-over and fail-over testing we planned, and so we are not satisfied that the servers are stable under peak load or other inclement conditions.

3. Production Devices have been used for all System Test execution for at least three (3) weeks.
   STATUS: GREEN. Except for the modem situation discussed above, the hardware has been stable.

Figure 1–9   *System test exit review*

Each of the three criteria here is graded on a three-point scale:

> Green: Totally fulfilled, with little remaining risk.
> Yellow: Not totally fulfilled, but perhaps an acceptable risk.
> Red: Not in any sense fulfilled, and even poses a substantial risk.

Of course, you'd want to provide additional information and data for the yellows and the reds.

Evaluating Exit Criteria Exercise

Consider the complete set of actual exit criteria from the Internet appliance project, which is shown at the end of the exercise setup. Toward the end of the project the test team rated each criterion on the three-point scale given above.

You can see the ratings we gave each criterion in the status block below the criterion itself.

We used this evaluation of the criteria as an agenda for a system test exit review meeting. I led the meeting and walked through each criterion. As you can imagine, the red ones required more explanation than the yellow and green ones.

While narrative explanation is provided for each evaluation, perhaps more information and data are needed. So, for each criterion, determine what kind of data and other information you'd want to collect to support the conclusions shown in the status evaluations for each. Subhed calls this an exercise, implicating that it would be, well, an exercise, but it's a list/example of something that someone already did.No, because it's asking for the supporting information and data.

Per the test plan, system test was planned to end when following criteria were met: This just repeats the above image, so I'm puzzled again. Check the section subheds and see whether these are meant to go under those subheds or maybe be combined into one, or subbed down into one more level.No, there are most items on this list, most of which aren't shown above. Did she read the entire text?

1. All design, implementation, and feature completion, code completion, and unit test completion commitments made in the system test entry meeting were either met or slipped to no later than four, three, and three weeks, respectively, prior to the proposed system test exit date.
   STATUS: RED. Audio and demo functionality have entered system test in the last three weeks. The modems entered system test in the last three weeks. On the margins of a violation, off-hook detection was changed significantly.

2. No panic, crash, halt, wedge, unexpected process termination, or other stoppage of processing has occurred on any server software or hardware for the previous three weeks.
   STATUS: YELLOW. The servers have not crashed, but we did not complete all the tip-over and fail-over testing we planned, and so we are not satisfied that the servers are stable under peak load or other inclement conditions.

3. Production devices have been used for all system test execution for at least three weeks.
   STATUS: GREEN. Except for the modem situation discussed above, the hardware has been stable.

4. No client systems have become inoperable due to a failed update for at least three weeks.
    STATUS: YELLOW. No system has become permanently inoperable during update, but we have seen systems crash during update and these systems required a reboot to clear the error.
5. Server processes have been running without installation of bug fixes, manual intervention, or tuning of configuration files for two weeks.
    STATUS: RED. Server configurations have been altered by change committee-approved changes multiple times over the last two weeks.
6. The test team has executed all the planned tests against the release candidate hardware and software releases of the device, server, and client.
    STATUS: RED. We had planned to test procurement and fulfillment, but disengaged from this effort because the systems were not ready. Also, we have just received the release candidate build; complete testing would take two weeks. In addition, the servers are undergoing change committee-approved changes every few days, and a new load balancer has been added to the server farm. These server changes have prevented volume, tip-over, and fail-over testing for the last week and a half. Finally, we have never had a chance to test the server installation and boot processes because we never received documentation on how to perform these tasks.
7. The test team has retested all priority one and two bug reports over the life of the project against the release candidate hardware and software releases of the device, server, and client.
    STATUS: RED. Testing of the release candidate software and hardware has been schedule limited to one week, which does not allow for retesting of all bugs.
8. The development teams have resolved all "must-fix" bugs. "Must-fix" will be defined by the project management team.
    STATUS: RED. Referring to the attached open/closed charts and the "Bugs Found Since November 9" report, we continue to find new bugs in the product, though there is good news in that the find rate for priority one bugs has leveled off. Per the closure period charts, it takes on average about two weeks—three weeks for severity one bugs—to close a problem report. In addition, both open/close charts show a significant quality gap between cumulative open and cumulative closed, and it's hard to believe that taken all together, a quantity of bugs that significant doesn't indicate a pervasive fit-and-finish issue with the product. Finally, note that Web and e-commerce problems are design issues—the selected browser is basically incompatible

with much of the Internet—which makes these problems much more worrisome.

9. The test team has checked that all issues in the bug tracking system are either closed or deferred, and, where appropriate, verified by regression and confirmation testing.
STATUS: RED. A large quality gap exists, and has existed for months. Because of the limited test time against the release candidate build, the risk of regression is significant.

10. The open/close curve indicates that we have achieved product stability and reliability.
STATUS: RED. The priority-one curve has stabilized, but not the overall bug-find curve. In addition, the run chart of errors requiring a reboot shows that we are still showing about one crash per eight hours of system operation, which is less stable than a typical Windows laptop. (One of the ad claims is improved stability over a PC.)

11. The project management team agrees that the product, as defined during the final cycle of system test, will satisfy the customer's reasonable expectations of quality.
STATUS: YELLOW. We have not really run enough of the test suite at this time to give a good assessment of overall product quality.

12. The project management team holds a system test exit meeting and agrees that we have completed system test.
STATUS: In progress.

Evaluating Exit Criteria Debrief

For each of the criteria, discussed below, I have added a section called "ADDITIONAL DATA AND INFORMATION." In that section, you'll find my own solution to this exercise, based both on what kind of additional data and information I actually had during this meeting and what I would have brought if I knew then what I know now.

1. All design, implementation, and feature completion, code completion, and unit test completion commitments made in the system test entry meeting were either met or slipped to no later than four, three, and three weeks, respectively, prior to the proposed system test exit date.
STATUS: RED. Audio and demo functionality have entered system test in the last three weeks. The modems entered system test in the last three weeks. On the margins of a violation, off-hook detection was changed significantly.

ADDITIONAL DATA AND INFORMATION: The specific commitments made in the system test entry meeting. The delivery dates for the audio functionality, the demo functionality, the modem, and the off-hook detection functionality.

2. No panic, crash, halt, wedge, unexpected process termination, or other stoppage of processing has occurred on any server software or hardware for the previous three weeks.

    STATUS: YELLOW. The servers have not crashed, but we did not complete all the tip-over and fail-over testing we planned, and so we are not satisfied that the servers are stable under peak load or other inclement conditions.

    ADDITIONAL DATA AND INFORMATION: Metrics indicate the percentage completion of tip-over and fail-over tests. Details on which specific quality risks remain uncovered due to the tip-over and fail-over tests not yet run.

3. Production devices have been used for all system test execution for at least three weeks.

    STATUS: GREEN. Except for the modem situation discussed above, the hardware has been stable.

    ADDITIONAL DATA AND INFORMATION: None. Good news requires no explanation.

4. No client systems have become inoperable due to a failed update for at least three weeks.

    STATUS: YELLOW. No system has become permanently inoperable during update, but we have seen systems crash during update, and these systems required a reboot to clear the error.

    ADDITIONAL DATA AND INFORMATION: Details, from bug reports, on the system crashes described.

5. Server processes have been running without installation of bug fixes, manual intervention, or tuning of configuration files for two weeks.

    STATUS: RED. Server configurations have been altered by change committee–approved changes multiple times over the last two weeks.

    ADDITIONAL DATA AND INFORMATION: List of tests that have run prior to the last change, along with an assessment of the risk posed to each test by the change. (Note: Generating this list and the assessment could be a lot of work unless you have good traceability information.)

6. The test team has executed all the planned tests against the release-candidate hardware and software releases of the device, server, and client.

    STATUS: RED. We had planned to test procurement and fulfillment, but disengaged from this effort because the systems were not ready. Also, we have just received the release-candidate build; complete testing would take two weeks. In addition, the servers are undergoing change committee-approved changes every few days, and a new load balancer has been added to the server farm. These server changes have prevented volume, tip-over, and fail-over testing for the last week and a half. Finally, we have never had a chance to test the server installation and boot processes because we never received documentation on how to perform these tasks.

ADDITIONAL DATA AND INFORMATION: List of procurement and fulfillment tests skipped, along with the risks associated with those tests. List of tests that will be skipped due to time compression of the last pass of testing against the release candidate, along with the risks associated with those tests. List of changes to the server since the last volume, tip-over, and fail-over tests along with an assessment of reliability risks posed by the change. (Again, this could be a big job.) List of server install and boot process tests skipped, along with the risks associated with those tests.

7. The test team has retested all priority one and two bug reports over the life of the project against the release-candidate hardware and software releases of the device, server, and client.

STATUS: RED. Testing of the release-candidate software and hardware has been schedule limited to one week, which does not allow for retesting of all bugs.

ADDITIONAL DATA AND INFORMATION: The list of all the priority one and two bug reports filed during the project, along with an assessment of the risk that those bugs might have reentered the system in a change-related regression not otherwise caught by testing. (Again, potentially a huge job.)

8. The development teams have resolved all "must-fix" bugs. "Must-fix" will be defined by the project management team.

STATUS: RED. Referring to the attached open/closed charts and the "Bugs Found Since November 9" report, we continue to find new bugs in the product, though there is good news in that the find rate for priority one bugs has leveled off. Per the closure period charts, it takes on average about two weeks—three weeks for priority one bugs—to close a problem report. In addition, both open/close charts show a significant quality gap between cumulative open and cumulative closed, and it's hard to believe that taken all together, a quantity of bugs that significant doesn't indicate a pervasive fit-and-finish issue with the product. Finally, note that Web and e-commerce problems are design issues—the selected browser is basically incompatible with much of the Internet—which makes these problems much more worrisome.

ADDITIONAL DATA AND INFORMATION: Open/closed charts, list of bugs since November 9, closure period charts, and a list of selected important sites that won't work with the browser. (Note: The two charts mentioned are covered in the Advanced Test Manager course, if you're curious.)

9. The test team has checked that all issues in the bug tracking system are either closed or deferred, and, where appropriate, verified by regression and confirmation testing.

   STATUS: RED. A large quality gap exists and has existed for months. Because of the limited test time against the release-candidate build, the risk of regression is significant.

   ADDITIONAL DATA AND INFORMATION: List of bug reports that are neither closed nor deferred, sorted by priority. Risk of tests that will not be run against the release-candidate software, along with the associated risks for each test.

10. The open/close curve indicates that we have achieved product stability and reliability.

    STATUS: RED. The priority-one curve has stabilized, but not the overall bug-find curve. In addition, the run chart of errors requiring a reboot shows that we are still showing about one crash per eight hours of system operation, which is no more stable than a typical Windows laptop. (One of the ad claims is improved stability over a PC.)

    ADDITIONAL DATA AND INFORMATION: Open/closed chart (run for priority-one defects only and for all defects). Run chart of errors requiring a reboot—i.e., a trend chart that shows how many reboot-requiring crashes occurred each day.

11. The project management team agrees that the product, as defined during the final cycle of system test, will satisfy the customer's reasonable expectations of quality.

    STATUS: YELLOW. We have not really run enough of the test suite at this time to give a good assessment of overall product quality.

    ADDITIONAL DATA AND INFORMATION: List of all the tests not yet run against the release-candidate build, along with their associated risks.

12. The project management team holds a system test exit meeting and agrees that we have completed system test.

    STATUS: In progress.

    ADDITIONAL DATA AND INFORMATION: None.

1.9 Test Closure Activities

Learning objectives
(K2) Provide examples of work products that should be delivered
by the test analyst during test closure activities.

Test closure includes both prospective and retrospective tasks. Prospective tasks are those we carry out to transfer the value of testing into the future. We want to make sure that important work products such as defect reports, tests, test environments, and, especially if they exist, automated regression test sets are available for use on future projects, or given to people who could use them right now. Information about the tests that were run and the results of those tests is also useful.

As a test analyst, you should work collaboratively with the test manager. Advise her or him on what you think would be useful on future projects. The test manager should then write the test plan or test strategy to ensure that the right information is delivered and archived.

Retrospectives

Retrospective tasks are about learning from the project, to make future projects go better. These can and should happen at both a project level and a test level. We should identify what went well, and look for ways to ensure that happens consistently on future projects. We should also identify what didn't go well, and look for ways to eliminate the root causes of those problems.

As a test analyst, you have a good perspective to contribute to these meetings. You often have a more realistic grasp of what project metrics mean than others on the project, who might be more optimistic. You should either attend yourself or make sure you've passed on your input to the test manager.

Test Closure

In Figure 1–10, you see the process of test closure. As you can see, the various test work products are delivered to business and technical stakeholders, as well as being archived. The test analysts create and archive manual regression tests. The technical test analysts create and archive automated regression tests. The right side of the figure shows the test manager, test leads, test analysts, and technical test analysts holding a test retrospective, as well as one or more test representatives attending the project retrospective.

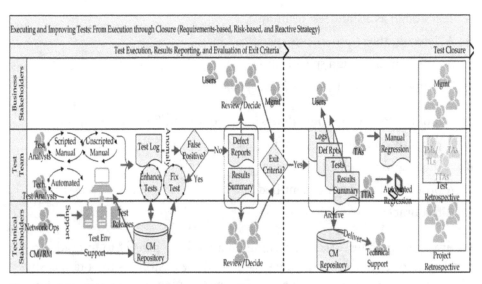

Figure 1–10   *Test closure process*

1.10 Sample Exam Questions

To end each chapter, you can try one or more sample exam questions to reinforce your knowledge and understanding of the material and to prepare for the ISTQB Advanced Level Test Analyst exam.

1. Which of the following can be useful as a test oracle the first time a test is run?

   A. Bug reports from previous test execution

   B. Requirements specification

   C. Tester's annual performance evaluation

   D. The source code

   E. Legacy system

2 Assume you are a test analyst working on a banking project to upgrade an existing automated teller machine system to allow customers to obtain cash advances from supported credit cards. During test design, you identify a discrepancy between the list of supported credit cards in the requirements specification and the design specification. This is an example of what?

A. Test design as a static test technique

B. A defect in the requirements specification

C. A defect in the design specification

D. Starting test design too early in the project

3. Which of the following is *not always* a pre-condition for test execution?

A. A properly configured test environment

B. A thoroughly specified test procedure

C. A process for managing identified defects

D. A test oracle

4. Assume you are a test analyst working on a banking project to upgrade an existing automated teller machine system to allow customers to obtain cash advances from supported credit cards. During test planning, an exit criterion was approved that requires successful cash advances during testing of at least 500 euros for all supported credit cards. The correct list of supported credit cards is American Express, Visa, Japan Credit Bank, Eurocard, and Master-Card.

After test execution, a complete list of cash advance test results shows the following:

   American Express allowed advances of up to 1,000 euros.

   Visa allowed advances of up to 500 euros.

   Eurocard allowed advances of up to 1,000 euros.

   MasterCard allowed advances of up to 500 euros.

Which of the following statements is true?

A. The exit criterion fails due to excessive advances for American Express and Eurocard.

B. The exit criterion fails due to a discrepancy between American Express and Eurocard on the one hand and Visa and MasterCard on the other hand.

C. The exit criterion passes because all supported cards allow cash advances of at least the minimum required amount.

D. The exit criterion fails because we cannot document Japan Credit Bank results.

2 Test Management: Responsibilities for the Test Analyst

"If a tree falls in the forest, and we've already sold it, does it have quality?" —The pointy-haired boss of the Dilbert cartoon strip, mutilating the famous Zen kōan to respond to Ratbert the tester's protestations that the test results do not support product release.

The second chapter of the Advanced Test Analyst syllabus is concerned with test management as seen from the test analyst's perspective. There are four sections:

1. Introduction
2. Test Progress Monitoring and Control
3. Distributed, Outsourced, and Insourced Testing
4. The Test Analyst's Tasks in Risk-Based Testing

Let's look at each section and how it relates to test analysis.

2.1 Introduction

Learning objectives
Recall of content only.

As part of your daily work, you'll often interact with a test manager. This can involve supplying information to the test manager, for planning, control, and results reporting purposes, as described in Chapter 1. Even in organizations using Agile methods, the emerging best practice is to have a test manager—sometimes referred to as a test coach—who supervises a matrixed team of testers, with one or more testers assigned to each Agile team. In fact, in Agile teams, testers take on even more management roles.

In this chapter, we'll look at how you will work with, support, and, in some cases, act as a test manager.

2.2   Test Progress Monitoring and Control

Learning objectives
(K2) Explain the types of information that must be tracked during testing to enable adequate monitoring and controlling of the project.

There are five main dimensions of test progress monitoring:

- Quality risks, also called product risks. When you're doing risk-based testing (more on that later in this chapter), one main test basis is the quality risk catalog. Using traceability, you can track progress in terms of addressing these risks. During test design and implementation, you'll need to monitor which risks are covered with tests and which are not. During test execution, you'll need to monitor which risks are fully mitigated (e.g., all tests associated with those risks have been run and have passed) and which risks are not fully mitigated (e.g., some or all of the tests are not yet run, or some of the tests have failed).
- Defects. Common metrics here are the defect discovery rate on a daily or weekly basis, the total number of defects found, and the total number remaining to be found.
- Tests. Here we are usually looking at the total number of tests planned, implemented, run, passed, failed, and blocked. Be careful not to aggregate test counts with dissimilar-sized tests, such as unit tests and system tests.
- Coverage. In addition to risk coverage as described above, we can similarly track coverage of all the other test bases, including requirements, supported configurations, user personas, and the like. Again, traceability is key.
- Confidence. This is sometimes reported subjectively, but that can be a mistake, unless your opinion of confidence is informed by metrics in the four other dimensions. Confidence should be based especially on risk, coverage, and defects, and less influenced by test progress, as test counts are notoriously misleading in terms of product quality.

ISTQB Glossary

User story testing: A black-box test design technique in which test cases are designed based on user stories to verify their correct implementation.

During the entire test process, you'll need to make sure that you gather the data necessary to support test progress monitoring. This data must be accurate. Otherwise, as discussed in Chapter 1, the overall test results reports will be inaccurate. People will then misunderstand the actual situation and make bad decisions. I have seen such bad decisions arising from bad test progress data—resulting in multimillion-dollar mistakes—so beware. I have also seen test teams get caught by stakeholders while reporting inaccurate or incomplete results, leading to significant damage to the test team's credibility.

Risk and Defect Monitoring

As I mentioned, when monitoring risks, use traceability to determine which risks are mitigated and which are not. Track defects in terms of discovery, total found, and the backlog. With a properly configured test management tool, properly captured traceability information for risks and classification information for defects, and the ability to manage defects through their lifecycle from discovery to resolution, these tasks are much easier. Without proper tools and traceability, these tasks are basically impossible.

Test Case Monitoring

When monitoring test execution, as mentioned, you'll need to track which tests are planned, implemented, executed, passed, failed, and blocked. For the tests failed or blocked, you'll need to be able to track additional information, such as the associated defects that cause the test to fail or be unable to run. In some cases, especially in regulated situations, you might need to capture screenshots and other evidence for all tests run, passed or failed.

Test counts are notoriously misleading in terms of product quality. Just because 90% of the tests have been run and have passed is no reason to have a high level of confidence in the product. What if the other 10% of the tests have failed, revealing showstopping bugs? Of course, the converse does work: If 90% of the tests are failing, you do know you have a quality problem. But of course, if that 90% figure is calculated by aggregate tests of vastly dissimilar size, such as unit tests, feature verification tests, system tests, and user acceptance tests, that figure is just as meaningless as an average temperature calculated using a mix of unconverted Celsius, Kelvin, and Fahrenheit measurements.

It's also important to keep in mind that the software development lifecycle will influence how you track tests, since the tools used are often different. Many of our clients report using tools like Rally and JIRA for test tracking in Agile projects. Whatever the merits of those tools for Agile task management, our clients report that they clearly were not designed by or for testers.

Example: Core 4

The following material describes an example of a test results reporting dashboard built for another client's senior management and executives. It is called the Core 4.

The executive summary in Figure 2–11 shows the current status of each test basis element (requirement, risk, configuration, non-functional quality characteristic, etc.): okay (green), not okay (red), or unknown (black). The test basis element status is determined by using traceability to classify each element based on test run/pass/fail status and any associated defect reports. This figure tells us to what extent the product works across all the important dimensions of coverage, to what extent problems are known, and to what extent we remain in the dark about some areas.

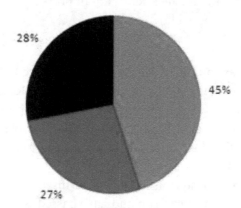

Figure 2–11   *Executive summary*

The coverage breakdown in Figure 2–12 shows test coverage in a finer-grained fashion, which conveys the degree of testing and level of bugginess of each functional area. The green/red bar is the breakdown of test execution (pass and fail) for each major functional area, and the yellow/blue bar is the breakdown of the defect reports across all functional areas. This graph tells us the level of confidence that we should have in each functional area and which functional areas need extra attention in terms of bug fixing and testing.

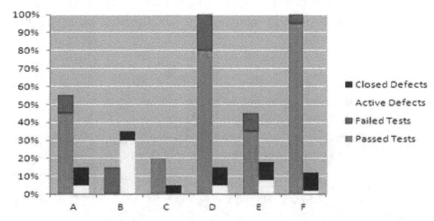

Figure 2–12   *Coverage breakdown*

The defect trend chart in Figure 2–13 is a version of the opened/closed/backlog chart commonly used by test teams. It gives us the trend of defects reported, closed, and active, in context of project targets. It tells us the remaining level of risk in the application (which is directly proportional to the rate of defect reporting and number of defects active) and whether we are on track to end testing on time.

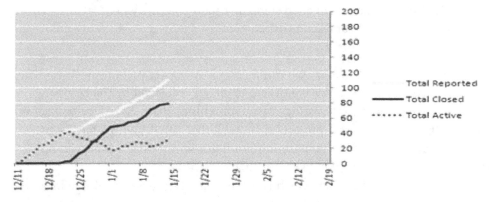

Figure 2–13   *Defect trend*

Finally, the test execution progress chart in Figure 2–14 shows the trend of actual, passed, and failed tests, against the plan, in context of project targets. It tells us whether the test team is on track to complete test execution on time, whether the development team is on track to complete defect repair on time, and what the remaining level of risk is in the application (being directly proportional to the number of failed tests).

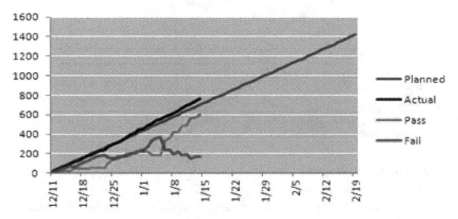

Figure 2–14   *Test execution progress*

2.3   Distributed, Outsourced, and Insourced Testing

Learning objectives
(K2) Provide examples of good communication practices when working in a 24-hour testing environment.

Back in the early days of software development, most development projects took place in a single location, with a collocated team, all employed by the company developing the software, interacting often, sometimes daily, in a face-to-face fashion. While there are still projects that work that way—and, in fact, some people will say all Agile projects must only work that way—what we see with our clients is that there are many ways that teams work now.

There is distributed testing, which is where testing occurs in multiple locations, such as using a testing service provider to perform some of the testing work. Since this example involves using testers who are not employees of the developing company, this is often referred to as outsourced testing. Centralized testing happens when all the testing occurs at a single location. If some of the testers are employees of the developing company, then that's referred to as insourced.

In any of these situations, communication and information transfer require careful attention. When people who are all employed by the same company work side by side, many informal communication channels exist. In fact, this is why many Agile advocates push for this form of team organization. However, in some cases, cost considerations, organizational realities, systems-of-systems projects, vendor-client development, and other management factors require distributed, outsourced, or insourced testing. When the testing will happen in such a way that some testing will be happening at all hours of the day—"follow the sun" or 24-hour testing—then the handoff of information, the clear definition of responsibilities and assignments, and the proper use of tools become even more critical.

Communication

In distributed, outsourced, or insourced testing situations, it's usually not possible to have daily, direct interaction between all members of the team. So, managers often define ways to replace that interaction, using email, status reports, test management tools, and defect tracking tools. Test management tools are useful to hand out work assignments, such as tests to be run by testers in various locations, and to track the results of testing. Similarly, defect management tools manage the routing of defects across organizational and geographical boundaries.

Example: Acceptance Test Status Email

Figure 2–15 shows an example of test communication. This is an excerpt of an email to a vendor about the results of acceptance testing of our company website. You might want to pause the audio to spend a minute reading this.

The first paragraph is to communicate that this is a careful, thought-out analysis, not just one of the dozens of fired-off emails someone is likely to get. The message is, "Pay attention to this email, please, because I did." This paragraph also refers the reader to further details in the attached document.

The second paragraph—including the bullet list and closing sentence— summarizes what needs to be done to complete the acceptance testing and move into deployment.

The third paragraph clarifies the meaning of the deferral of certain bugs. I wanted to make sure that I was not waiving any legal rights RBCS had to insist on these problems being fixed later.

I have spent a couple hours reviewing the current status of the site and
the acceptance test. Please see attached [documents] with deferred bug reports
and [test status]...for pass 2.

The following issues are must-fix to move forward with deployment:

o   Consistency of messages and UI (for examples, see bug 85, 91, 92, 95, 97)

o   Newsletter link...not in place as agreed (see bug 98)

o   Identification and resolution of internal dead links (see bug 103)

While some of these issues might strike the casual reader as picayune, please
understand that our target customers...are sensitive to any errors...

In the interests of moving forward and having this critical marketing collateral in
place...I have agreed to defer a number of bugs from pass 1 that either failed
verification testing or which related to advertised product features that [the
vendor] retroactively and unilaterally withdrew... Please note that deferral of
these bugs does not indicate acceptance by RBCS of the disposition of those bugs
for all time.

Finally, please note that there were eighteen (18) new bug reports filed
during the second pass.

Figure 2–15   *Acceptance test status email*

The final paragraph is a subtle—I hope—hint that we were disappointed to be
still finding problems.

This type of email is appropriate for me to send as a customer to a vendor,
explaining test results. Would you send it to your development colleagues?
Probably not. The important point here is that every word and every sentence
of that email had a communication objective.

2.4 The Test Analyst's Tasks in Risk-Based Testing

Learning objectives
(K3) For a given project situation, participate in risk identification,
perform risk assessment, and propose appropriate risk mitigation.

As a test analyst, you will put into action whatever test strategies are selected by
the test manager. If the test manager has selected risk-based testing, you'll need
to be ready to participate in risk identification, risk assessment, and risk mitigation. We'll discuss these three tasks on the next few pages. As a test analyst, you'll
be expected to provide special insight in terms of business domain risks.

While I will cover them in that order—identification, assessment, and mitigation—you should remember that these tasks tend to occur iteratively in the

> **ISTQB Glossary**
>
> **Risk mitigation:** The process through which decisions are reached and protective measures are implemented for reducing risks to, or maintaining risks within, specified levels.
>
> **Test strategy:** A high-level description of the test levels to be performed and the testing within those levels for an organization or program (one or more projects).

project, even on sequential lifecycle projects. Regardless of the development lifecycle, you should expect to learn about new quality risks as the project proceeds. You'll also gain information that changes the level of risk associated with each quality risk. So, you'll need to evaluate your test findings and other project information to be ready to adapt to these changes, as well as to communicate your test findings in terms of risk.

Risk Identification

For proper risk-based testing, we need to identify quality risks. Quality risks, also called product risks, are potential problems in the system that would affect the level of quality, which is the degree to which the system is fit for purpose. We can identify quality risks using techniques such as:

- Interviews with domain experts, users, and others with insight into the risks
- Independent assessments
- Use of risk templates
- Including quality risk identification as part of project retrospectives
- Risk workshops and brainstorming with users, product owners, and other business and technical stakeholders
- Checklists of important risk areas
- Calling on past experience with similar systems or projects
- Holding workshops to try to anticipate the effects risks would have if they became actual problems

As a test analyst, you bring a business-oriented tester focus to this process. (Technical test analysts can provide a more technically oriented tester perspective.) You should especially consider quality attributes that are particularly important from a business perspective, such as accuracy, usability, and learnability.

> **ISTQB Glossary**
>
> **Risk analysis:** The process of assessing identified risks to estimate their impact and probability of occurrence (likelihood).
>
> **Risk identification:** The process of identifying risks using techniques such as brainstorming, checklists, and failure history.

Remember that the goal is to identify as many quality risks as possible, since these quality risks will make up an important part of your test basis. If you miss some risks, that could result in gaps in your test coverage.

Project risks—and not just for testing, but also for the project as a whole—are often identified as by-products of quality risk analysis. In addition, if you use a requirements specification, design specification, use cases, user stories, and the like as inputs into your quality risk analysis process, you should expect to find defects in those documents as another set of by-products. These are valuable by-products, which you should plan to capture and escalate to the proper person.

The most important thing to remember about risk identification is that you'll need to involve representatives of all possible stakeholder groups. For the risk identification activities, the broadest range of stakeholders will yield the most complete, accurate, and precise risk identification. The more stakeholder group representatives you omit from the process, the more missing risk items and even whole risk categories.

Risk Assessment

The next step in the risk management process is risk assessment. Risk assessment involves the study of the identified risks. We typically want to categorize each risk item appropriately and assign each risk item an appropriate level of risk.

In categorization of risk items, we can use any good checklist of quality categories or attributes to organize the risk items. It doesn't matter so much what category a risk item goes into, usually, so long as we don't forget it. However, in complex projects and for large organizations, the category of risk can determine who has to deal with the risk. A practical implication of categorization such as this will make the categorization important.

The other part of risk assessment is determining the level of risk. This often involves likelihood and impact as the two key factors. Likelihood arises from technical considerations, typically, while impact arises from business considerations.

What factors should we consider when determining likelihood? Here's a list to get you started:

- Complexity of technology and teams
- Personnel and training issues
- Intra-team and inter-team conflict
- Supplier and vendor contractual problems
- Geographical distribution of the development organization, as with outsourcing
- Legacy or established designs and technologies versus new technologies and designs
- The quality—or lack of quality—in the tools and technology used
- Bad managerial or technical leadership
- Time, resource, and management pressure, especially when financial penalties apply
- Lack of earlier testing and quality assurance tasks in the lifecycle
- High rates of requirements, design, and code changes in the project
- High defect rates
- Complex interfacing and integration issues.

What factors should we consider when determining impact? Here's a list to get you started:

- The frequency of use of the affected feature
- Potential damage to image
- Loss of customers and business
- Potential financial, ecological, or social losses or liability
- Civil or criminal legal sanctions
- Loss of licenses, permits, and the like
- The lack of reasonable workarounds
- The visibility of the failure and the associated negative publicity

When determining the level of risk, we can try to work quantitatively or qualitatively. In quantitative risk analysis, we have numerical ratings for both likelihood and impact. Likelihood is a percentage, and impact is often a monetary quantity. If we multiply the two values together, we can calculate the cost of exposure, which is called—in the insurance business—the expected payout or expected loss.

While it will be nice someday in the future of software engineering to be able to routinely calculate risk quantitatively, typically the level of risk is determined qualitatively. Why? Because we don't have statistically valid data on which to perform quantitative quality risk analysis. So, we can speak of likelihood being very high, high, medium, low, or very low, but we can't say—at least, not in any meaningful way—whether the likelihood is 90%, 75%, 50%, 25%, or 10%.

This is not to say—by any means—that a qualitative approach should be seen as inferior or useless. In fact, given the data most of us have to work with, use of a quantitative approach is almost certainly inappropriate on most projects. The illusory precision produced by quantitative methods will mislead the stakeholders about the extent to which you actually understand and can manage risk. What I've found is that if I accept the limits of my data and apply appropriate lightweight quality risk management approaches, the results are not only perfectly useful, but also indeed essential to a well-managed test process.

Unless your risk analysis is based on extensive and statistically valid risk data, your risk analysis will reflect perceived likelihood and impact. In other words, personal perceptions and opinions held by the stakeholders will determine the level of risk. Again, there's absolutely nothing wrong with this, and I don't bring this up to condemn the technique at all. The key point is that project managers, programmers, users, business analysts, architects, and testers typically have different perceptions and thus possibly different opinions on the level of risk for each risk item. By including all these perceptions, we distill the collective wisdom of the team.

However, we do have a strong possibility of disagreements between stakeholders. So, the risk analysis process should include some way of reaching consensus. In the worst case, if we cannot obtain consensus, we should be able to

---

ISTQB Glossary

Risk level: The importance of a risk as defined by its characteristic impact and likelihood. The level of risk can be used to determine the intensity of testing to be performed. A risk level can be expressed either qualitatively (e.g., high, medium, low) or quantitatively.

Risk management: Systematic application of procedures and practices to the tasks of identifying, analyzing, prioritizing, and controlling risk.

escalate the disagreement to some level of management to resolve it. Otherwise, risk levels will be ambiguous and conflicted, and thus not useful as a guide for risk mitigation activities—including testing.

Risk Mitigation

We have four main options for risk control:

- Mitigation, where we take preventive measures to reduce the likelihood and/or the impact of a risk.
- Contingency, where we have a plan or perhaps multiple plans to reduce the impact if the risk becomes an actuality.
- Transference, where we get another party to accept the consequences of a risk.
- Finally, we can ignore or accept the risk and its consequences.

For any given risk item, selecting one or more of these options creates its own set of benefits and opportunities as well as costs and, potentially, additional risks associated with each option.

Analytical risk-based testing is focused on creating risk mitigation opportunities for the test team, including for test analysts, especially for quality risks. Risk-based testing mitigates quality risks through testing throughout the entire lifecycle.

Let me mention that, in some cases, there are standards that can apply. We've already looked at one such standard, the FAA's DO-178C.

It's important too that project risks be controlled. As test analysts, we're particularly concerned with test-affecting project risks like:

- Test environment and tools readiness
- Test staff availability and qualification
- Low quality of inputs to testing
- Too frequent changes in the test basis
- Lack of standards, rules, and techniques for the testing effort

While it's usually the test manager's job to make sure these risks are controlled, the lack of adequate controls in these areas will affect the test analyst.

One idea discussed in the Foundation syllabus, a basic principle of testing, is the principle of early testing and QA. This principle stresses the preventive potential of testing. Preventive testing is part of analytical risk-based testing. We should try to mitigate risk before test execution starts. This can entail early preparation of testware, pretesting test environments, pretesting early versions of the product well before a test level starts, ensuring requirements for and designing for testability, participating in reviews including retrospectives for earlier project activities, participating in problem and change management, and monitoring of the project progress and quality.

In preventive testing, we take quality risk control actions throughout the lifecycle. Test analysts should look for opportunities to control risk using various techniques, such as:

- Choosing an appropriate test design technique
- Reviews and inspection
- Reviews of test design
- An appropriate level of independence for the various levels of testing
- The use of the most experienced person on test tasks
- The strategies chosen for confirmation testing (retesting) and regression testing

Preventive test strategies acknowledge that quality risks can and should be mitigated by a broad range of activities, many of them not what we traditionally think of as "testing." For example, if the requirements are not well written, perhaps we should institute reviews to improve their quality, rather than relying on tests that will be run once the badly written requirements become a bad design and ultimately bad, buggy code. Testing is not effective against all kinds of quality risks. In some cases, it's possible to estimate the risk reduction effectiveness of testing in general and specific test techniques for given risk items. There's not much point in using testing to reduce risk where there is a low level of test effectiveness.

Once we get to test execution, we use test execution to mitigate quality risks. Where testing finds defects, testers reduce risk by providing the awareness of defects and opportunities to deal with them before release. Where testing does not find defects, testing reduces risk by ensuring that under certain conditions the system operates correctly.

Test Prioritization

In risk-based testing, we use the level of risk to make a number of decisions. First, the amount of test effort to expend in mitigating any given quality risk is determined by the level of risk. Second, we select more rigorous and thorough test design techniques, and often a greater number of test design techniques, for quality risks with a high level of risk, and we would also use a more extensive set of test data and try to mitigate the risk before test execution even starts. Third, we sequence the tests we do execute based on the level of risk.

Risk-based test sequencing can work in a variety of ways, with two extremes, referred to as depth first and breadth first. In a depth-first approach, all of the highest-risk tests are run before any lower risk tests, and tests are run in strict risk order. In a breadth-first approach, we select a sample of tests across all the identified risks using the level of risk to weight the selection while at the same time ensuring coverage of every risk at least once.

As we run tests, we should measure and report our results in terms of residual risk. The higher the test coverage in an area, the lower the residual risk. The fewer bugs we've found in an area, the lower the residual risk. Of course, in doing risk-based testing, if we test only based on our risk analysis, this can leave blind spots, so we need to use testing outside the predefined tests to see if we have missed anything.

If, during test execution, we need to reduce the time or effort spent on testing, we can use risk as a guide. If the residual risk is acceptable, we can curtail our tests. Notice that, in general, whatever tests were not run are less important than those that were. If we do curtail further testing, that serves to transfer the remaining risk onto the users, customers, help desk and technical support personnel, or operational staff.

Adjusting Risk

Risk identification and assessment are ongoing, continuous processes in risk-based testing. Periodically, you adjust your risk analysis—and thus your testing—for further test cycles based on what you've learned from your current testing. First, you revise your risk analysis. Then, you reprioritize existing tests and possibly add new tests. What should you look for to decide whether to adjust your risk analysis? Main factors include these:

- Totally new or very much changed product risks
- Unstable or defect-prone areas discovered during the testing
- Risks, especially regression risk, associated with fixed defects
- Discovery of unexpected bug clusters
- Discovery of business-critical areas that were missed

Each time you start a new test cycle, consider revising your quality risk analysis first. You should also update the quality risk analysis at each project milestone.

Example: Quality Risk Analysis

In Figure 2–16 you see an example of a quality risk analysis document. It is a case study of an actual project. This document—and the approach we used—followed the Pragmatic Risk Analysis and Management approach.

Quality Risks Analysis Form

System Name: SYSVIEW	Release: v12
Product Manager: Bob Carpenter	Target Release Date: [TBD]
Project Managers: [Jim: Please complete]	Prepared By: Rex Black, Peter Nash
Test Manager: Jim Kaste	Analysis Date: April 29, 2008
Stakeholders in Risk-Based Analysis Session: Jim Kaste, Jim Cray, Jim Gubala, David Jones Phyllis Casella, Bob Carpenter, Jim Williams	Revision Date[s]: [TBD]

Risk ID Number	Quality Risk Category	Specific Quality Risk	Likelihood	Impact	RPN	Extent of Testing	Other Action Needed	PRS/DDS Tracing	Total Items	Total Rated	Percent Rated
1.000	Functionality	Failures that cause specific features not to work							24	19	79%
1.001		Unix System services compatibility issue	4	3	12						
1.002		MQ Agent not properly removed from product	3	5	15						
1.003		Data collection changes incorrect	3	2	6						
1.004		Incompatibility with previous Sysview	5	2	10						
1.005		New commands do not function.	TBD	TBD	##		[Jim: Might need to break this out for each new command?]				
1.006		Changed commands do not function	TBD	TBD	##		[Jim: Might need to break this out for each new command?]				
1.007		Data lib commands don't work	3	2	6		[Jim: Might need to break this out for each command?]				
1.008		Problems with exploitation of z/OS 1.10 functionality	3	TBD	##		[Jim: Need to get list of 1.10 functions to determine impact.]				
1.009		Audit logs too vague	TBD	TBD	##						
1.010		System overview changes incorrect	4	5	20						
1.011		Parallel Sysplex compatibility issues	5	2	10						

Project Risks / Miscellaneous / Risk Levels and Test Extent / Initial QRA

Figure 2–16 *Quality risk analysis document*

In this project, at the end of the quality risk analysis session, we had identified 92 non-duplicate quality risk items. Of those, the team had successfully rated the impact and likelihood for about 40%. We then asked one team member to assign tentative risk levels to the remaining risk items, subject to the approval of the team. You can see some of the risk items and their risk ratings in Figure 2–16. As you can see, some of the risk ratings were TBD (to be determined) at the end of the session.

The next day, the team members worked collaboratively but individually to successfully rate the remaining unrated items. In some cases, this required splitting a given risk item into two or more items in order to assign an appropriate impact to each aspect of the risk. At the end of this process, we had 104 fully rated quality risk items.

Functional Quality Risks Analysis Exercise

Using the HELLOCARMS system requirements document, perform quality risk analysis for this project. Since this is a book focused mainly on domain testing, identify and assess risks for *functional* quality characteristics only. Use the template shown in Figure 2–17.

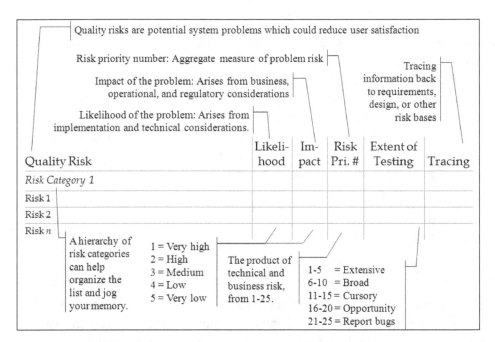

Figure 2–17   *Quality risk analysis template*

In Figure 2–17 you see a template that you can use to capture the information you identify in quality risk analysis.

The quality risk analysis process consists of the following activities. First, you will identify the quality risks, and then you will assess their level of risk. Based on the level of risk, you will determine the overall priority of testing and the extent of testing. Finally, if the risks arise from specific requirements or design specification elements, establish traceability back to these elements. Let's look at these activities and how they generate information to populate this template.

First, remember that quality risks are potential system problems that could reduce user or stakeholder satisfaction. We can use a hierarchy of risk categories to organize the list and to jog your memory. Working with the stakeholders, we identify one or more quality risks in each category and populate the template.

Having identified the risks, we can now go back and assess the level of risk, because we see the risk items in relation to each other. Usually, I use two main factors for assessing risk.

The first is the likelihood of the problem, which is influenced mostly by technical considerations. So, I sometimes call this *technical risk* to remind me of that fact.

The second is the impact of the problem, which is influenced mostly by business or operational considerations. So, I sometimes call this business risk to remind me of that fact.

Both likelihood and impact can be rated on an ordinal scale such as high, medium, or low. I prefer to use a five-point scale, from very high to very low.

Given likelihood and impact, I need a single, aggregate measure of risk for the quality risk item. I use the phrase *risk priority number* for this. To create the risk priority number, I combine likelihood and impact. One way is to translate the ordinal scale into a numerical scale, for example:

1 = Very high
2 = High
3 = Medium
4 = Low
5 = Very low

I can then calculate the risk priority number as the product of the two numbers—e.g., very high likelihood and medium impact means the risk priority number is 1 times 3, or 3. It's rather kludgy, but it works. Feel free to devise your own formulas for calculating this number if simple multiplication doesn't work for you.

Now, you can use the risk priority number to sequence the tests. However, I still need to determine the extent of testing. One way to do this is to split the risk priority number into five groups and use those to determine test effort:

1–5   = Extensive testing
6–10   = Broad testing
11–15 = Cursory testing
16–20 = Opportunity testing
21–25 = Report bugs only

Again, feel free to fine-tune these groups to match your needs.

While you go through the quality risk analysis process, remember to capture the by-products I mentioned earlier, such as implementation assumptions, project risks, and problems with the requirements, design, or other input documents.

Functional Quality Risk Analysis Debrief

You can see my solution to the exercise in Table 2–1. Immediately after Table 2–1 are two lists of by-products. One is the list of project risks discovered during the analysis. The other is the list of requirements document defects discovered during the analysis.

As a first pass for this quality risk analysis, I went through each functional requirement and identified one or more risk items for it. I assumed that the priority of the requirement was a good surrogate for the impact of the risk, so I used that. Even using all of these shortcuts, it took me about an hour to get through this.

Table 2–1 *Functional quality risk analysis for HELLOCARMS*

No.	Quality Risk	Likeli-hood	Impact	Risk Pri. #	Extent of Testing	Tracing
1.1.000	Functionality: Suitability					
1.1.001	Reject all applications for home equity loans.	5	1	5	Extensive	010-010-010
1.1.002	Reject all applications for home equity lines of credit.	5	1	5	Extensive	010-010-010
1.1.003	Reject all applications for reverse mortgages.	5	1	5	Extensive	010-010-010
1.1.004	Fail to properly process some home equity applications.	3	1	3	Extensive	010-010-190
1.1.005	Fail to properly process some home equity line of credit applications.	3	2	6	Broad	010-010-200
1.1.006	Fail to properly process some home equity reverse mortgage applications.	3	3	9	Broad	010-010-210
1.1.007	Fail to properly process some combined products (e.g., home equity and credit cards).	3	4	12	Cursory	010-010-220
1.1.008	Fail to properly process some original mortgage applications	3	5	15	Cursory	010-010-230
1.1.009	Fail to properly process some preapproved applications.	3	4	12	Cursory	010-010-240
1.1.010	Scripts not available for all fields and screens.	4	2	8	Broad	010-010-020
1.1.011	Customer source data not collected.	3	2	6	Broad	010-010-030
1.1.012	Customer source data categories not well defined.	2	2	4	Extensive	010-010-030
1.1.013	Accepts invalid data at input fields.	1	1	1	Extensive	010-010-040

No.	Quality Risk	Likeli-hood	Impact	Risk Pri. #	Extent of Testing	Tracing
1.1.014	Existing trade lines not displayed and/or processed properly.	3	1	3	Extensive	010-010-050 010-010-100
1.1.015	Trade line payoff details not passed to LoDoPS.	2	1	2	Extensive	010-010-050 010-010-100
1.1.016	Loan to be paid off included in debt-to-income calculations.	4	3	12	Cursory	010-010-110
1.1.017	Cannot resume incomplete/ interrupted applications.	3	2	6	Broad	010-010-060
1.1.018	Applicant not asked about existing relationship.	5	2	10	Broad	010-010-070
1.1.019	Applicant existing relationship not passed to GLADS.	3	2	6	Board	010-010-070
1.1.020	Loan status information lost after initiation.	3	2	6	Broad	010-010-080
1.1.021	Cannot abort or abandon an application cleanly (e.g., must close browser).	4	3	12	Cursory	010-010-090
1.1.022	Cannot retrieve existing application by customer ID.	4	4	16	Opportunity	010-010-120
1.1.023	Loans over $500,000 not transferred for approval.	4	1	4	Extensive	010-010-130
1.1.024	Loans over $500,000 automatically denied.	3	1	3	Extensive	010-010-130
1.1.025	Property valuation over $1,000,000 not transferred for approval.	4	2	8	Broad	010-010-140
1.1.026	Property valuation over $1,000,000 automatically denied.	3	2	6	Extensive	010-010-140
1.1.027	Inbound telemarketing operations fail in supported region.	1	2	2	Extensive	010-010-150
1.1.028	Outbound telemarketing operations fail in supported region.	1	2	2	Extensive	010-010-150
1.1.029	Branding for brokers and other business partners not supported.	4	2	8	Broad	010-010-160
1.1.030	Untrained users (e.g., end customers) cannot enter applications via Internet.	4	3	12	Cursory	010-010-170
1.1.031	Product operations for retail bank branches not supported.	4	4	16	Opportunity	010-010-180

No.	Quality Risk	Likeli-hood	Impact	Risk Pri. #	Extent of Testing	Tracing
1.1.032	Flexible pricing schemes not supported.	4	5	20	Opportunity	010-010-250
1.2.000	Functionality: Accuracy					
1.2.001	Customer presented with products for which they are ineligible.	3	1	3	Extensive	010-020-010
1.2.002	Customer not presented with products for which they are eligible.	4	1	4	Extensive	010-020-010
1.2.003	Application decisioning inconsistent with Globobank credit policies.	3	1	3	Extensive	010-020-010
1.2.004	Risk-based pricing miscalculated based on credit score, loan to value, and debt to income.	4	1	4	Extensive	010-020-020
1.2.005	New loan payment not included in credit scoring.	3	2	6	Broad	010-020-030
1.2.006	Pricing add-ons not calculated correctly.	3	3	9	Broad	010-020-040
1.2.007	Government retirement income not handled properly.	3	1	3	Extensive	010-020-050
1.2.008	Duration of additional income not captured.	4	3	12	Cursory	010-020-060
1.3.000	Functionality: Interoperability					
1.3.001	Can't pull information from GloboRainBQW into HELLOCARMS.	2	2	4	Extensive	010-030-010
1.3.002	HELLOCARMS and Scoring Mainframe reject joint applications.	3	1	3	Extensive	010-030-020
1.3.003	HELLOCARMS and Scoring Mainframe cannot handle/resolve duplication of information on joint applications.	1	2	2	Extensive	010-030-030
1.3.004	HELLOCARMS trade line communication to LoDoPS fails.	3	1	3	Extensive	010-030-040 010-030-070
1.3.005	Loan status information from LoDoPS to HELLOCARMS lost or corrupted.	5	2	10	Broad	010-030-050 010-030-140

No.	Quality Risk	Likeli-hood	Impact	Risk Pri. #	Extent of Testing	Tracing
1.3.006	HELLOCARMS can't continue if the Scoring Mainframe indicates an undischarged bankruptcy or foreclosure.	4	3	12	Cursory	010-030-060
1.3.007	HELLOCARMS communication of government retirement income to LoDoPS fails.	5	1	5	Extensive	010-030-080
1.3.008	HELLOCARMS application information not passed to Scoring Mainframe properly.	3	1	3	Extensive	010-030-090
1.3.009	HELLOCARMS does not receive information from Scoring Mainframe properly.	3	1	3	Extensive	010-030-100
1.3.010	Decisioning requests not queued for Scoring Mainframe as needed.	4	2	8	Broad	010-030-110
1.3.011	Tentatively approved, customer-accepted loans not passed to LoDoPS.	5	2	10	Broad	010-030-120
1.3.012	Declined applications not passed to LoDoPS.	5	2	10	Broad	010-030-130
1.3.013	Changes made in loan information in LoDoPS not propagated back to HELLOCARMS.	5	2	10	Broad	010-030-140
1.3.014	Computer-telephony integration not supported.	3	5	15	Cursory	010-030-150
1.3.015	Applicant existing relationship not passed to GLADS.	4	3	12	Broad	010-010-070
1.4.000	Functionality: Security					
1.4.001	Agreed-upon security requirements not supported.	1	2	2	Extensive	010-040-010
1.4.002	"Created By" and "Last Changed By" audit trail information lost.	3	1	3	Extensive	010-040-020
1.4.003	Outsourced telemarkets see actual credit scores and other privileged information.	3	2	6	Broad	010-040-030
1.4.004	Internet applications insecure against intentional attacks.	1	2	2	Extensive	010-040-040
1.4.005	Internet applications insecure against unintentional attacks.	3	2	6	Broad	010-040-040

No.	Quality Risk	Likeli-hood	Impact	Risk Pri. #	Extent of Testing	Tracing
1.4.006	Anonymous browsing on Internet not permitted.	2	4	8	Broad	010-040-050
1.4.007	Fraud detection too lenient.	3	1	3	Extensive	010-040-060
1.4.008	Fraud detection too strict.	3	1	3	Extensive	010-040-060
1.5.000	Functionality: Compliance					
1.5.001	[Functional risks related to functional compliance go in this section.]					

Project Risk By-Products

In the course of preparing the quality risk analysis document, I observed the following project risk inherent in the requirements. Given the lack of clarity around security requirements (see 010-040-010), there's a strong chance that the necessary infrastructure won't be in place as needed to support this project's schedule.

Requirements Defect By-Products

In the course of preparing the quality risk analysis document, I observed the following defects in the requirements.

1. For 010-010-150, what are the supported States, Provinces, and Countries?
2. For 010-010-150, the phrase "all support States" should be "all supported States."
3. For 010-020-020, the phrase "dept-to-income" should be "debt-to-income."
4. For some requirements, the ID number is duplicated—e.g., 010-030-140.
5. Not all requirements are prioritized—e.g., 010-030-150.
6. For 010-040-010, what are the agreed-upon security approaches discussed here?
7. There don't appear to be any direct mentions of regulatory compliance requirements, though certainly many would apply for a bank.

2.5   Sample Exam Questions

1. Assume you are a test analyst working on a banking project to upgrade an existing automated teller machine system to allow customers to obtain cash advances from supported credit cards. The system should allow cash advances of at least 500 euros for all supported credit cards. The correct list of supported credit cards is American Express, Visa, Japan Credit Bank, Eurocard, and MasterCard.

   Among the various quality risk items you identify during risk analysis, you have the following, listed in order of perceived level of risk from most risky to least risky:

   - Visa and MasterCard unable to obtain any cash advances
   - American Express or Eurocard unable to obtain any cash advances
   - Japan Credit Bank unable to obtain any cash advances
   - Visa or MasterCard cash advances improperly limited
   - American Express or Eurocard cash advances improperly limited
   - Japan Credit Bank cash advances improperly limited

   Assume that, in the following list, each test case requires exactly one hour of test analyst effort to run. Which of the following is a semicolon-separated, sequenced list of tests that covers these risks in a way that is appropriate to the level of risk and that minimizes test effort?

   A. Test minimum American Express and Eurocard advances; test minimum Visa and MasterCard advances; test minimum Japan Credit Bank advances.

   B. Test minimum and maximum Visa and MasterCard advances; test minimum and maximum American Express and Eurocard advances; test minimum and maximum Japan Credit Bank advances.

   C. Test minimum Visa and MasterCard advances; test minimum American Express and Eurocard advances; test minimum Japan Credit Bank advances; test maximum Visa and MasterCard advances; test maximum American Express and Eurocard advances; test maximum Japan Credit Bank advances.

   D. Test maximum American Express and Eurocard advances; test maximum Visa and MasterCard advances; test maximum Japan Credit Bank advances.

2. Assume you have the following three documents or reports available to you at the appropriate point during a project:

   I. Checklist of important quality characteristics for your product

   II. Historical information from similar past projects on where defects were found and how serious those defects were

   III. A Pareto analysis of the subsystems where defects have been discovered so far during test execution on this project

   Which of the following statements matches each of these items with the risk management activity the item will most benefit?

   A. I: risk identification; II: risk assessment; III: risk control

   B. I: risk control; II: risk assessment; III: risk identification

   C. I: risk identification; II: risk control; III: risk assessment

   D. I: risk assessment; II: risk control; III: risk identification

3   Test Techniques

"You've got to understand the basics of aerodynamics in a thing like this."

—The Gyro Captain

"Shut up, shut up!" — "Mad" Max Rockatansky

Max politely declines a just-in-time lesson in aeronautical engineering principles from the gyrocopter pilot, as scripted by

Terry Hayes and George Miller in *The Road Warrior*

The third chapter of the Advanced syllabus is concerned with test techniques. To make the material manageable, it uses a taxonomy—a hierarchical classification scheme—to divide the material into sections and subsections. Conveniently, it uses a similar taxonomy of test techniques as that given in the Foundation syllabus. Where the Foundation provides for specification-based, structure-based, and experience-based techniques, at the Advanced level we add a fourth category of technique, defect-based. We also add additional techniques and further explanation in each category. We also cover both static and dynamic analysis. There are four sections.

1. Introduction
2. Specification-Based Techniques
3. Defect-Based Techniques
4. Experience-Based Techniques

Let's look at each section and how it relates to test analysis.

3.1   Introduction

Learning objectives
Recall of content only.

This chapter, as the name indicates, is focused on the test design techniques used by test analysts. Using Figure 3–1, let's review the breakdown of test design techniques at the Advanced level, which differs slightly from the breakdown at the Foundation level.

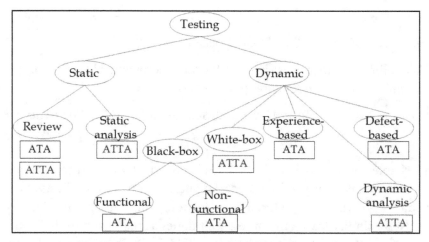

Figure 3–1   *Advanced Test Analyst and Advanced Technical Test Analyst test techniques*

As at the Foundation level, testing is defined to include any technique to evaluate the quality of a work product. This includes both static techniques, which do not involve executing the work product being evaluated, and dynamic techniques, which do involve executing the work product being evaluated. Static techniques can be divided into reviews and static analysis. Static analysis typically involves a single individual using a tool to find defects in a work product such as a piece of code. Reviews are group activities where people find the defects. Static analysis is covered in the Advanced Technical Test Analyst book, while reviews are covered in this book and the Advanced Technical Test Analyst book.

Dynamic test techniques are divided into black-box (or behavioral) techniques, white-box (or structural) techniques, experience-based techniques, defect-based techniques, and dynamic analysis. White-box techniques and

> **ISTQB Glossary**
>
> **Defect-based technique:** A procedure to derive and/or select test cases targeted at one or more defect categories, with tests being developed from what is known about the specific defect category.

dynamic analysis are covered in the Advanced Technical Test Analyst book. In this book, we cover black-box techniques for both functional and non-functional testing. We will also cover experience-based and defect-based techniques. Note that, in the Foundation, defect-based techniques are included in the experience-based category.

3.2 Specification-Based Techniques

Learning objectives

(K2) Explain the use of cause-effects graphs.

(K3) Write test cases from a given specification item by applying the equivalence partitioning test design technique to achieve a defined level of coverage.

(K3) Write test cases from a given specification item by applying the boundary value analysis test design technique to achieve a defined level of coverage.

(K3) Write test cases from a given specification item by applying the decision table test design technique to achieve a defined level of coverage.

(K3) Write test cases from a given specification item by applying the state transition test design technique to achieve a defined level of coverage.

(K3) Write test cases from a given specification item by applying the pairwise test design technique to achieve a defined level of coverage.

(K3) Write test cases from a given specification item by applying the classification tree test design technique to achieve a defined level of coverage.

K3) Write test cases from a given specification item by applying the use case test design technique to achieve a defined level of coverage.

Learning objectives

(K2) Explain how user stories are used to guide testing in an Agile project.

(K3) Write test cases from a given specification item by applying the domain analysis test design technique to achieve a defined level of coverage.

(K4) Analyze a system, or its requirement specification, in order to determine likely types of defects to be found and select the appropriate specification-based technique(s).

Let's start with a broad overview of specification-based tests, before we dive into the details of each technique.

In specification-based testing—which is also called black-box testing and, perhaps most accurately, behavioral testing—we derive and select tests by analyzing the test basis. Remember that the test bases are the documents that tell us, directly or indirectly, how the component or system under test should and shouldn't behave and what it is required to do and how it is required to do it. These are the documents we can base the tests on—hence the name *test basis*.

It's probably worth a quick compare and contrast with the term *test oracle*, which is similar and related, but not the same as the test basis. The test oracle is anything we can use to determine expected results that we can compare with the actual results of the component or system under test. Anything that can serve as a test basis can also be a test oracle, of course. However, an oracle can also be an existing system, either a legacy system being replaced or a competitor's system. An oracle can also be someone's specialized knowledge. An oracle should not be the code, because otherwise we are only testing whether the compiler works.

For structural or white-box tests—which were covered in the Foundation—the internal structure of the system is the test basis but not the test oracle. However, for specification-based tests, we do not consider the internal structure at all—at least theoretically.

Beyond being focused on behavior rather than structure, what's common in specification-based test techniques? Well, for one thing, there is some model, whether formal or informal. The model can be a graph or a table. There is some systematic way to derive or create tests using the model. And, typically, each technique has a set of coverage criteria that tell you, in effect, when the model has run out of interesting and useful test ideas. It's important to remember that fulfilling coverage criteria for a particular test design technique does not mean

> **ISTQB Glossary**
>
> **Requirements-based testing:** An approach to testing in which test cases are designed based on test objectives and test conditions derived from requirements—e.g., tests that exercise specific functions or probe non-functional attributes such as reliability or usability.
>
> **Specification-based technique:** Procedure to derive and/or select test cases based on an analysis of the specification, either functional or non-functional, of a component or system without reference to its internal structure.

that your tests are in any way complete or exhaustive. Instead, it means that the model has run out of useful tests to suggest, based on that technique.

These models are focused on different aspects of the software's behavior and are particularly apt for certain scenarios. They can also be particularly inapt. We'll discuss enablers and disablers for each technique in this chapter and then again in Chapter 4. The models can also be combined where appropriate, which we'll demonstrate here in this chapter.

There is also typically some family of defects that the technique is particularly good at finding. Boris Beizer, in his books on test design, referred to this as the bug hypothesis.[1] He meant that, if you hypothesize that a particular kind of bug is likely to exist, you could then select the technique based on that hypothesis. This provides an interesting linkage with the concept of defect-based testing, which we'll cover in a later section of this chapter.

Often, specification-based tests are requirements based. Requirements specifications often describe behavior, especially functional behavior. (The tendency for non-functional requirements to be under-specified is a whole separate quality-influencing problem that we'll not address at this point, but simply accept as a given.) So, we can use the description of the system behavior in the requirements to create the models. We can then derive tests from the models.

Combining Techniques

As I mentioned, you can combine these techniques when creating tests, which will make for an even more powerful set of tests. When you do so, you create the models for all the techniques first. You then derive tests following the procedure associated with whatever technique you expect to generate the most tests. As you

---

1. Specifically, Beizer's main books on test design include *Software Testing Techniques, Software System Testing and Quality Assurance*, and *Black-Box Testing*.

do so, you check the coverage criteria for all applicable models. Once you have finished generating tests with the first technique, check to see if all coverage criteria for all techniques have been satisfied. If not, repeat the process of selecting the next technique and generating tests with it, tracking coverage as you go. Repeat this process until all criteria are satisfied.

Whether selecting one technique or multiple techniques, you'll need to consider whether it is applicable to your testing problem. You should also consider any limitations and difficulties associated with the technique. Ask yourself whether the types of defects detected by this technique are the kind you'd expect to find in this testing situation. Also, consider your coverage goals, especially based on risk as discussed in the previous chapter.

As we work through the coming subsections, we'll look at how to combine techniques when creating tests.

3.2.1   Equivalence Partitioning

We start with the most basic of specification-based test design techniques, equivalence partitioning.

Conceptually, equivalence partitioning is about testing various groups that are expected to be handled the same way by the system and exhibit similar behavior. Those groups can be inputs, outputs, internal values, calculations, or time values, and should include valid and invalid groups. We select a single value from each equivalence partition, and this allows us to reduce the number of tests. We can calculate coverage by dividing the number of equivalence partitions tested by the number identified, though generally the goal is to achieve 100% coverage by selecting at least one value from each partition.

This technique is universally applicable at any test level, in any situation where we can identify the equivalence partitions. Ideally, those partitions are independent, though some amount of interaction between input values does not preclude the use of the technique. This technique is also very useful in constructing smoke tests, though testing of some of the less-risky partitions frequently is omitted in smoke tests. This technique will find primarily functional defects where data is processed improperly in one or more partitions. The key to this technique is to take care that the values in each equivalence partition are indeed handled the same way; otherwise, you will miss potentially important test values.

In equivalence partitioning, the underlying model is a graphical or mathematical one that identifies equivalent classes—which are also called *equivalent*

ISTQB Glossary

Equivalence partitioning: A black-box test design technique in which test cases are designed to execute representatives from equivalence partitions. In principle, test cases are designed to cover each partition at least once.

partitions—of inputs, outputs, internal values, time relationships, calculations, or just about anything else of interest. These classes or partitions are called *equivalent* because they should be handled the same way by the system. Some of the classes can be called *valid equivalence classes* because they describe valid situations that the system should handle normally. Other classes can be called *invalid equivalence classes* because they describe invalid situations that the system should reject or at least escalate to the user for correction or exception handling.

Once we've identified the equivalent classes, we can derive tests from them. Usually, we are working with more than one set of equivalence classes at one time; for example, each input field on a screen has its own set of valid and invalid equivalence classes. So, we can create one set of valid tests by selecting one valid member from each equivalence partition. We continue this process until each valid class for each equivalence partition is represented in at least one valid test.

Next, we can create invalid tests. For each equivalence partition, we select one invalid member for one equivalence partition and a valid member for every other equivalence partition. This rule—don't combine multiple invalid members in a single test—prevents us from running into a situation where the presence of one invalid value might mask the incorrect handling of another invalid value. We continue this process until each invalid class for each equivalence partition is represented in at least one invalid test.

Notice the coverage criteria implicit in the discussion above. Every class, both valid and invalid, is represented in at least one test.

What is our bug hypothesis with this technique? For the most part, we are looking for a situation where some equivalence class is handled improperly. That could mean the value is accepted when it should have been rejected or vice versa, or that a value is properly accepted or rejected, but handled in a way appropriate to another equivalence class, not the class to which it actually belongs.

Visualizing Equivalence Partitioning

How can we visualize equivalence partitioning? Let's look.

As you can see in the top half of Figure 3–2, we start with some set of interest. This set of interest can be an input field, an output field, a test precondition or postcondition, a configuration, or just about anything we're interested in testing. The key is that we can apply the operation of equivalence partitioning to split the set into two or more disjoint subsets, where all the members of each subset share some trait in common that is not shared with the members of the other subset.

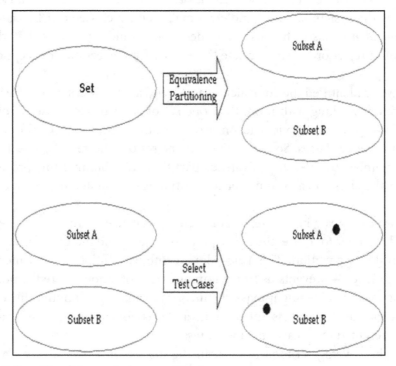

Figure 3–2   *Visualizing equivalence partitioning*

For example, if you have a simple drawing program that can fill figures in with red, green, or blue, you can split the set of fill colors into three disjoint sets: red, green, and blue.

In the bottom half of Figure 3–2, we see the selection of test values from the subsets. The dots in the subsets represent the value chosen from each subset to be represented in the test. This involves selecting at least one member from each subset. In pure equivalence partitioning, the logic behind this selection is outside the scope of the technique. In other words, you can select any member of the subset you please. If you're thinking, "Some members are better than others," that's fine; hold that thought for a few minutes, and we'll come back to it.

Now, at this point we'll generate the rest of the test. If the set that we partitioned was an input field, we might refer to the requirements specification to understand how each subset is supposed to be handled. If the set that we partitioned was an output field, we might refer to the requirements to derive inputs that should cause that output to occur. We might use other test techniques to design the rest of the tests.

Figure 3–3 shows that equivalence partitioning can be applied iteratively. In this figure, we apply a second round of equivalence partitioning to one of the subsets to generate three smaller subsets. Only at that point do we select four members—one from subset B and one each from subsets A1, A2, and A3—for tests. Note that we don't have to select a member from subset A, since each of the members from subsets A1, A2, and A3 are also members of subset A.

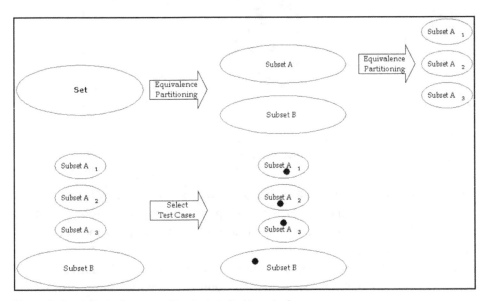

Figure 3–3   *Equivalence partitioning applied iteratively*

Avoiding Equivalence Partitioning Errors

Let me emphasize three key points.

One, as shown in the top half of Figure 3–4, the subsets must be disjoint. That is, no two of the subsets can have one or more members in common. The whole point of equivalence partitioning is to test whether a system handles different situations differently (and properly, of course). If it's ambiguous as to which handling is proper, then how do we define a test around this? "Try it out and see what happens"? Not much of a test!

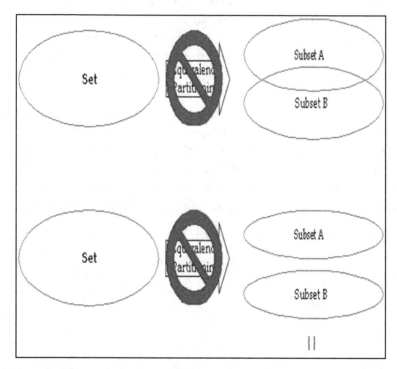

Figure 3–4   *Avoiding equivalence partitioning errors*

Two, as shown in the bottom half of Figure 3–4, none of the subsets may be empty. That is, if the equivalence partitioning operation produces a subset with no members, that's hardly very useful for testing. We can't select a member of that subset, because it has no members.

Third, while not shown graphically—in part because I couldn't figure out a clear way to draw the picture—note that the equivalence partitioning process does not subtract; it divides. What I mean by this is that, in terms of mathematical set theory, the union of the subsets produced by equivalence partitioning must be the same as the original set that was equivalence partitioned. In other words, equivalence partitioning does not generate "spare" subsets that are somehow disposed of in the process—at least, not if we do it properly. Notice that this is important, because, if this is not true, then we stand the chance of failing to test some important subset of inputs, outputs, configurations, or some other factor of interest that somehow was dropped in the test design process.

Composing Tests

When we compose test cases in situations where we've performed equivalence partitioning on more than one set, we select from each subset as shown in Figure 3–5.

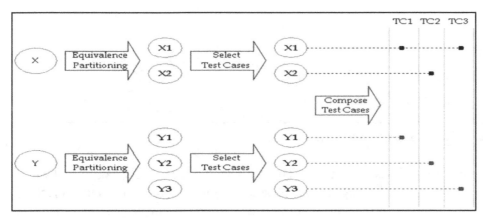

Figure 3–5 *Composing tests*

Here, we start with set X and set Y. We partition set X into two subsets, X1 and X2. We partition set Y into three subsets, Y1, Y2, and Y3. We select test values from each of the five subsets, X1, X2, Y1, Y2, and Y3. We then compose three tests, since we can combine the values from the X subsets with values from the Y subsets (assuming the values are independent and all valid).

For example, imagine you are testing a browser-based application. You are interested in two browsers, Chrome and Firefox. You are interested in three connection types, Wi-Fi, DSL, and cable modem. Since the browser and the connection types are independent, we can create three tests. In each of the tests, one of the connection types and one of the browser types will be represented. One of the browser types will be represented twice.

Earlier, I made a brief comment that we can combine values across the equivalence partitions when the values are independent and all valid. Of course, that's not always the case, as shown in Figure 3–6.

In some cases, values are not independent, in that the selection of one value from one subset constrains the choice in another subset. For example, imagine that you're trying to test combinations of applications and operating systems.

You can't test an application running on an operating system if there is not, version of that application available for that operating system.

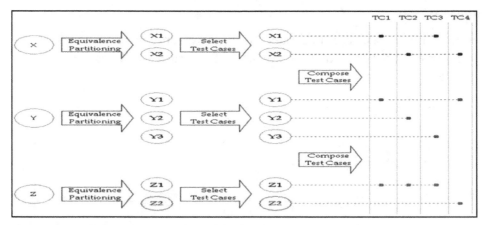

Figure 3–6   *Composing tests with invalid values*

In some cases, values are not valid. For example, in Figure 3–6, imagine that we are testing a project management application, something like Microsoft Project. Suppose that set X is the type of event we're dealing with, which can be either a task (X1) or a milestone (X2). Suppose that set Y is the start date of the event, which can be in the past (Y1), today (Y2), or in the future (Y3). Suppose that set Z is the end date of the event, which can be either on or after the start date (Z1) or before the start date (Z2). Of course, Z2 is invalid, since no event can have a negative duration.

So, we test combinations of tasks and milestones with past, present, and future start dates and valid end dates in test cases TC1, TC2, and TC3. In T4, we check that illegal end dates are correctly rejected. We try to enter a task with a start date in the past and an end date prior to the start date. If we wanted to subpartition the invalid situation, we could also test with a start date in the present and one in the future, together with an end date before the start date, which would add two more tests.

In this particular example, we had a single subset for just one of the sets that was invalid. The more general case is that many—perhaps all—of the sets will have invalid subsets. Imagine testing an e-commerce application. On the checkout screens of the typical e-commerce application, there are multiple required fields, and usually there is at least one way for such a field to be invalid.

ISTQB Glossary

Combinatorial testing: A means to identify a suitable subset of test combinations to achieve a predetermined level of coverage when testing an object with multiple parameters and where those parameters themselves each have several values, which gives rise to more combinations than are feasible to test in the time allowed.

When there are multiple invalid values, we have to select one invalid value per test—at least to start with. That way, we can check that any given invalid value is correctly rejected or in some way handled by the system.

Now, I said one invalid value per test to start with. If, after doing that, you want to test combinations of invalids, by all means, do so—if the risk is sufficient to justify it. Any time you start down the trail of combinatorial testing, you are taking a chance that you'll spend a lot of time testing things that aren't terribly important.

Example: Equivalence Partitioning

Here's a simple example of equivalence partitioning on a single value, in this case system configuration. On the Internet appliance project I've mentioned before, there were four possible configurations for the appliances. They could be configured for kids, teens, adults, or seniors. This configuration value was stored in a database on the Internet service provider server, so that, when an Internet appliance connected to the Internet, this configuration value became a property of its connection.

Based on this configuration value, there were two key areas of difference in the expected behavior. For one thing, for kids' and teens' systems, there was a filtering function enabled. This determined the allowed and disallowed websites the system could visit. The setting was most strict for kids and was somewhat less strict for teens. Adults and seniors, of course, were to have no filtering at all, and should be able to surf anywhere.

For another thing, each of the four configurations had a default set of e-commerce sites they could visit called the mall. These sites were selected by the marketing team and were meant to be age appropriate.

Of course, these were the expected differences. We were also aware of the fact that there could be weird unexpected differences that could arise, because that's the nature of some types of bugs. For example, performance was supposed to be the same, but it's possible that performance problems with the filtering software could introduce perceptible response-time issues with the kids and teens systems. We had to watch for those kinds of misbehaviors.

So, to test for the unexpected differences, we simply had at least one of each configuration in the test lab at all times, and spread the non-configuration-specific tests more or less randomly across the different configurations. (More on testing combinations of configurations in a subsequent part of this section.) To test expected differences related to filtering and e-commerce, we made sure these configuration-specific tests were run on the correct configuration. The challenge here was that, while the expected results were concrete for the mall—the marketing people gave us four sets of specific sites, one for each configuration—the expected results for the filtering were not concrete but rather logical. This led to an enormous number of very disturbing defect reports during test execution, as we found creative ways to sneak around the filters and access age-inappropriate materials on kids and teens configurations.

Equivalence Partitioning Exercise

A screen prototype for one screen of the HELLOCARMS system is shown in Figure 3–7.

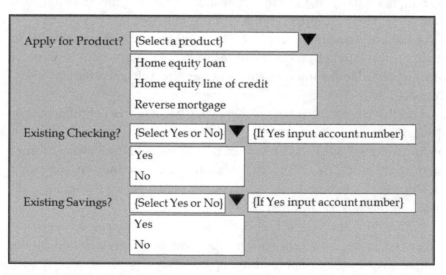

Figure 3–7   *Product screen prototype*

This screen asks for three pieces of information:

1. The product being applied for, which is one of the following:
   a. Home equity loan
   b. Home equity line of credit
   c. Reverse mortgage
2. Whether someone has an existing Globobank checking account, which is either Yes or No.
3. Whether someone has an existing Globobank savings account, which is either Yes or No.

If the user indicates an existing Globobank account, then the user must enter the corresponding account number. This number is validated against the bank's central database upon entry. If the user indicates no such account, the user must leave the corresponding account number field blank.

If the fields are valid, including the account number fields, then the screen will be accepted. If one or more fields are invalid, an error message is displayed.

The exercise consists of two parts:

1. Show the equivalence partitions for each of the three pieces of information, indicating valid and invalid members
2. Create test cases to cover these partitions, keeping in mind the rules about combinations of valid and invalid members

The answers to the two parts are shown in the debrief section that follows. You should review the answer to the first part (and, if necessary, revise your answer to the second part) before reviewing the answer to the second part.

Equivalence Partitioning Debrief

First, let's take a look at the equivalence partitions.

For the application-product field, the equivalence partitions are:

#	Partition
1	Home equity loan
2	Home equity line of credit
3	Reverse mortgage

Note that the screen prototype shows this information as selected from a pull-down list, so there is no possibility of entering an invalid product here.

For each of two existing-account entries, the situation is best modeled as a single input field, which consists of two subfields. The first subfield is the Yes/No field. This subfield determines the rule for checking the second subfield, which is the account number. If the first subfield is Yes, the second subfield must be a valid account number. If the first subfield is No, the second subfield must be blank.

So, the existing checking account information partitions are:

#	Partition
1	Yes-Valid
2	Yes-Invalid
3	No-Blank
4	No-Nonblank

And, the existing savings account information partitions are:

#	Partition
1	Yes-Valid
2	Yes-Invalid
3	No-Blank
4	No-Nonblank

Note that, for both of these, partitions 2 and 4 are invalid partitions, while partitions 1 and 3 are valid partitions.

Table 3–1   *Test cases for equivalence partitions*

Inputs	1	2	3	4	5	6	7
Product	HEL	LOC	RM	HEL	LOC	RM	HEL
Existing Checking?	Yes	No	No	Yes	No	No	No
Checking Account	Valid	Blank	Blank	Invalid	Nonblank	Blank	Blank
Existing Savings?	No	Yes	No	No	No	Yes	No
Savings Account	Blank	Valid	Blank	Blank	Blank	Invalid	Nonblank
Outputs							
Accept?	Yes	Yes	Yes	No	No	No	No
Error?	No	No	No	Yes	Yes	Yes	Yes

Now, let's create tests from these equivalence partitions. As we do so, I'm going to capture traceability information from the test case number back to the partitions. Once I have a trace from each partition to a test case, I'm done—provided that I'm careful to follow the rules about combining valid and invalid partitions! These tests and their traceability are shown in Table 3–1, Table 3–2, Table 3–3, and Table 3–4.

Product:

#	Partition	Test Case
1	Home equity loan (HEL)	1
2	Home equity line of credit (LOC)	2
3	Reverse mortgage (RM)	3

Table 3–2   *Product*

Checking:

#	Partition	Test Case
1	Yes-Valid	1
2	Yes-Invalid	4
3	No-Blank	2
4	No-Nonblank	5

Table 3–3   *Checking*

Savings:

#	Partition	Test Case
1	Yes-Valid	2
2	Yes-Invalid	6
3	No-Blank	1
4	No-Nonblank	7

Table 3–4   *Savings*

You should notice that these test cases do not cover all interesting possible combinations of factors here. For example, we don't test to make sure that for a person with both a valid savings and a valid checking account, both accounts work properly. That could be an interesting test because the accounts might have been established at different times and might have information that now conflicts in some way (e.g., in some countries it is still relatively common for a woman to take her husband's last name upon marriage). We also don't test the combination of invalid accounts or the combination of account numbers that are valid alone but not valid together (e.g., the two accounts belong to entirely different people).

We'll discuss techniques for testing combinations of conditions in subsequent portions of this section.

3.2.2 Boundary Value Analysis

Let's refine our equivalence partitioning test design technique with the next technique, boundary value analysis.

In boundary value analysis, we first use equivalence partitioning. Then, for those partitions that are ordered values, we select the minimum and maximum values—the boundary values—as test values. This technique can be applied at any level of testing. It can even be used during white-box testing when looking at loops, when looking at data structures such as lists and arrays, and during non-functional testing for boundaries in memory usage and performance.

Coverage is calculated as with equivalence partitioning, but counting the tested and identified boundary values. You must be careful only to apply this technique with ordered sets, and you must understand the precision of representation of the values. When used properly, this technique will find situations where boundaries are in the wrong place, boundaries are just plain missing, or undesired boundaries exist. In non-functional testing, performance and reliability problems under high levels of load are found with this technique.

Conceptually, boundary value analysis is about testing the edges of equivalence classes. In other words, instead of selecting one member of the class, we select the largest and smallest members of the class and test them.

The underlying model is again either a graphical or mathematical one that identifies two boundary values at the boundary between one equivalence class and another. (In some techniques, the model identifies three boundary values, which I'll address later.) Now, whether such a boundary exists for subsets where we've performed equivalence partitioning is another question that I'll get to in just a moment. Right now, notice that, assuming the boundary does exist, the boundary values are just special members of the equivalence classes that happen to be right next to each other and right next to the point where the expected behavior of the system changes. If the boundary values are members of a valid equivalence class, they are valid, of course, and if members of an invalid equivalence class, they are invalid.

ISTQB Glossary

Boundary value analysis (BVA): A black-box test design technique in which test cases are designed based on boundary values.

Deriving tests with boundary values as the equivalence class members is much the same as for plain equivalence classes. We test valid boundary values together and then combine one invalid boundary value with other valid values for the other classes.

We have to represent each boundary value in a test, analogous to the equivalence partitioning situation. In other words, the coverage criterion is that every boundary value, both valid and invalid, must be represented in at least one test.

The main difference is that there are at least two boundary values in each equivalence class. So, we'll have more tests, about twice as many.

Hmm, okay, more tests? That's not something we like unless there's a good reason for them. What is the point of these extra tests? That is revealed by the bug hypothesis for boundary value analysis. Since we are testing equivalence class members—every boundary value is an equivalence class member—we are testing for situations where some equivalence class is handled improperly. Again, that could mean acceptance of values that should be rejected or vice versa, or proper acceptance or rejection, but improper handling subsequently, as if it were in another equivalence class, not the class to which it actually belongs. However, by testing boundary values, we also test whether the boundary between equivalence classes is defined in the right place.

So, do all equivalence classes have boundary values? No, definitely not. Boundary value analysis is an extension of equivalence partitioning that applies only when the members of an equivalence class are ordered.

So, what does that mean? Well, an ordered set is one where we can say that one member is greater than or less than some other member if those two members are not the same. We have to be able to say this meaningfully, too. Just because some item is right above or below some other item on a pull-down menu does not mean that, within the program, the two items have a greater-than/less-than relationship.

Let's look at examples of where a test analyst can (and can't) use boundary value analysis on equivalence classes.

Pull-Down Menus

In Figure 3–8 you can see the Insert menu that you can pull down from the PowerPoint menu bar at the top of the screen. This is a typical pull-down menu.

Figure 3–8   *Pull-down menu*

For a situation like this, each selection is its own equivalence class. Yes, there is a first item and a last item on the menu, but the ordering of the set is arbitrary and has no meaning below the user interface. Inside the software, it's very unlikely that there is any greater-than/less-than relationship between the items on this menu. So, we can use equivalence partitioning (and we must test each selection on the menu) but not boundary values.

Notice that there is apparently no invalid selection possible here, as the only selections we can't choose are grayed out. Does that always work? Well, no. It's up to you to test that those things that should be grayed out are, those that shouldn't be grayed out aren't, and those that are grayed out are indeed inaccessible.

Example: Pull-Down Menu

So, for the menu in Figure 3–9, we will partition each menu selection into its own subset. Note that some are invalid selections.

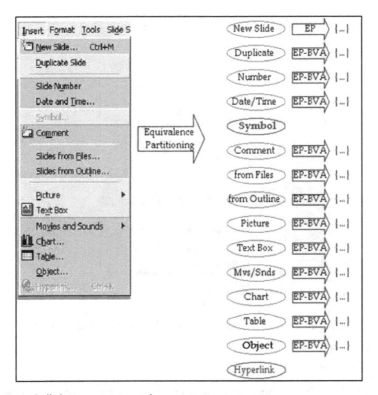

Figure 3–9   *Pull-down menu example*

For each valid menu selection, we'll need further equivalence partitioning and, in most cases, boundary value analysis. For example, we might want to try to insert slides from a file that contains only one slide, as well as a file that contains the maximum number of slides (whatever that is). We will also want to try inserting a file that contains zero slides (if that's possible) and a file that contains one more than the maximum number of slides.

Integer Fields

Not all pull-down menus are unordered sets. Some are menus that are sitting on top of an integer field. Integers are ordered sets.

For example, consider Microsoft Word font sizes. In this situation, the menu is one way to enter data, and direct, manual entry is another, as shown in Figure 3–10.

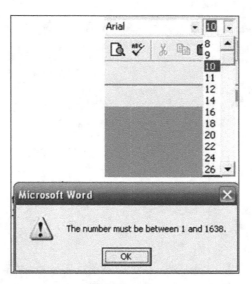

Figure 3–10   *Pull-down menu and manual entry*

So, we can use equivalence partitioning on ways to enter the font size:

Select from menu
Enter the value in the field

You might be saying, "Hey, these aren't disjoint sets, though, since I can select and then enter, and enter then select." You'd be right in that, but at any moment in time you're doing one or the other (if you're setting font sizes). Later, when we look at state transition testing, we'll examine a technique that allows us to deal with this situation.

Now, we can use boundary value analysis on each of the two ways to enter font sizes. Font size is an integer value in Word, and integer values are ordered sets. We can select the largest and smallest menu font. We can also test the largest and smallest entered font.

What are these largest and smallest font values? Well, ideally we'd have a requirements specification that would tell us. Barring that, though, we can try some experimentation, as I did here. You can see the smallest font size is 1 point and the largest 1638. Is that okay? Well, who knows? And all I know now are that these are the largest and smallest font sizes for the Arial font. It's possible that the font selection could influence the largest and smallest allowed font size. Must I try to figure out the limits for each font? What a testing nightmare that would be! So, it would be good to get clarification on these values before we start testing.

> **ISTQB Glossary**
>
> **State transition testing:** A black-box test design technique in which test cases are designed to execute valid and invalid state transitions.

Finally, notice that invalid values are not possible on the menu, but they are possible when entered. Also, the question of what the largest and smallest values are doesn't arise with the menu, either. From a testability point of view, requiring the user to select from a menu rather than allowing them to directly enter or directly edit fields is much better.

Example: Integer

In Figure 3–11 you can see the application of equivalence partitioning and boundary value analysis on the font size field, all the way down to the generation of test inputs.

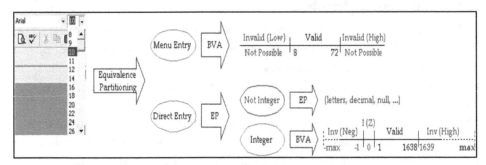

Figure 3–11   *Integer example*

Using these techniques, we can generate the following test input values.

From the menu, we would want to test 8 and 72. Any value lower or higher is impossible, at least from the menu.

From direct entry into the field, we can start with the invalid equivalence partition of non-integers. We could enter "a," 6.5, a null value (i.e., no entry at all), a slash character, a minus sign, and a plus sign. We could continue the generation of invalid values here to almost infinite length, but at some point, it gets silly.

For the equivalence partition of integers, we can enter -1, 0, 1, 1638 (the largest legal font size according to the message shown here), 1639 (the smallest illegal-too-large font size), some big positive number, and some big negative number. What is big in this situation? Well, one natural thing to try is to use the Notepad feature or some other simple text editor to generate a string of ten 9s, then copy-and-paste that into the field. If that works, copy and paste to generate twenty 9s. Then 40. Then 100. Again, at some point this gets silly.

The question of how deep you should go with these invalid inputs is, of course, a matter of risk. Overflowing buffers with invalid inputs is a well-known security attack. If your application has to deal with secure, private data—customer account data, for example—then running a whole array of carefully designed buffer overflow tests against every input field in your system makes sense. However, spending hours pumping invalid strings of various types into the font size input field in Word does not make sense. Be smart. Be risk based in your testing-depth decisions.

Tests consist of both an input and an expected result. So, for the invalid inputs, we expect the system to reject the input with a helpful error message. For the valid inputs, we expect the system to change the font size on the selected text.

Floating-Point (Decimal) Numbers

Integers are about the simplest ordered sets we deal with as testers. We also sometimes have to test floating-point numbers. Floating-point numbers are also called real numbers or decimal numbers. Floating-point numbers, like integers, are also ordered sets. However, while integers do not have decimal points, floating-point numbers do.

This immediately brings up the important testing question, "How many decimal points?" That is a question of the particular field's precision. This is sometimes referred to as epsilon or the smallest recognizable difference.

There are two reasons that this question of precision is an important testing question. First, we can't determine the boundary values without knowing the answer to this question. Second, problems with precision, and particularly ambiguity about it, are fertile ground for bugs.

Most software, by virtue of the programming language used, has a basic floating-point data type built in. One problem is that the precision of this data type can vary from one machine to another. Another potential testing challenge is that the range of the floating-point data type—i.e., its maximum and minimum values—can vary, too.

Without getting too technical about the issue, another problem arises from the way that floating-point data types are stored. The precision is not given in terms of digits before and after the decimal point, as you might expect. The precision is given in terms of total number of significant digits. There can be a very large number of zeros between the significant digits and the decimal point. For example, 999,999 trillion trillion is a very large number, but perhaps only the first six digits—the 999,999 part—will be stored as significant digits. This means that, with very large positive and negative numbers and very small positive and negative numbers—i.e., numbers very close to zero—we can have some interesting rounding errors that arise, especially in calculations.

When getting my computer science degree at UCLA, I spent an entire quarter studying numerical analysis. Lots of time is spent on issues like this in the field of computing, and the careless programmer can easily make many mistakes.

In Figure 3–12 you can see the Microsoft Calculator applet. The main input field is, by default, a floating-point field. Rather than rely on the internal representation of floating points, Microsoft provides a feature called Extended Precision. As shown here, this provides us with at least thirty-two decimal digits of precision. Furthermore, rational numbers—those numbers that can be written as fractions like ½ or ⅜—are stored as fractions to further promote accuracy of calculations. Of course, irrational numbers like pi and other such constants with unlimited digits after the decimal point will be inaccurate in any system like this with a fixed number of digits of accuracy.

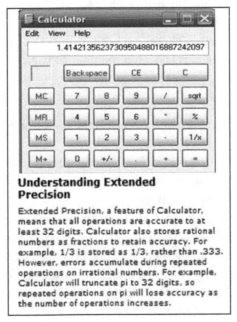

Figure 3–12   *Floating-point (decimal) numbers*

Example: Floating-Point Numbers

In Figure 3–13 you can see the application of equivalence partitioning and boundary value analysis on the calculator input field for the square root function, all the way down to the generation of test inputs.

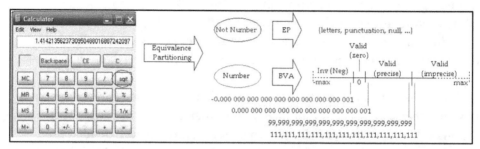

Figure 3–13   *Floating-point example*

The square root function accepts any floating-point number greater than or equal to zero as an input and returns a number that, if multiplied by itself, yields the original number.

Using the boundary value analysis and equivalence partitioning techniques, we can come up with the following test values.

As with integers, we can test non-numeric inputs like "a," ampersand, null (if that's possible), and so forth. There's no limit to the effort you could expend subpartitioning this equivalence class, so remember to use risk as your guide.

We can apply four equivalence classes to the numeric, floating-point inputs. There are three valid classes:

1. Zero, which is both the upper and lower boundary value of its own equivalence class.
2. Valid with thirty-two or fewer digits, and thus represented precisely. We have a small number close to zero, but not quite zero and a number with thirty-two 9s as the boundary values.
3. Valid with thirty-three or more digits, and thus represented imprecisely. It takes some effort to create these values, as you have to enter the largest possible values and then multiply them together to create even larger values. I spent a few minutes doing this, and could not find the point at which the calculator overflowed. I did find that the calculator would eventually take so long to complete a calculation that it would come back to me and ask per-

mission to continue! It would be best, again, to have this in a requirements specification somewhere.

There is one invalid class, the negative numbers. That starts with the negative number closest to zero. It continues up to the maximum negative number, which again might take some time to find without a requirements specification.

Financial Operations

Figure 3–14 shows an investment account screen from Quicken, the financial application. Testing of financial operations involves floating-point numbers, so all of the issues just discussed apply. However, notice that the question of precision has serious real-world implications. People tend to be very sensitive to rounding errors that involve things like money, investment account balances, and the like. Furthermore, there are regulations and contracts that often apply, along with any specified requirements, and even small breaches can be quite serious. So, testing financial applications involves a great deal of care when these kinds of issues are involved.

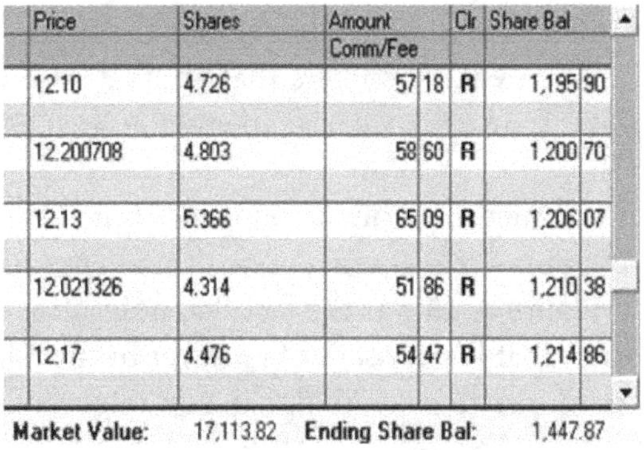

Price	Shares	Amount	Clr	Share Bal	
		Comm/Fee			
12.10	4.726	57 18	R	1,195 90	
12.200708	4.803	58 60	R	1,200 70	
12.13	5.366	65 09	R	1,206 07	
12.021326	4.314	51 86	R	1,210 38	
12.17	4.476	54 47	R	1,214 86	

Market Value: 17,113.82 Ending Share Bal: 1,447.87

Figure 3–14 *Investment account Quicken screen*

In Figure 3–15 you can see the application of equivalence partitioning and boundary value analysis to the input of a stock purchase transaction in Quicken. In Quicken, when you enter a stock purchase transaction, after entering the stock, you input the number of shares, the price per share, and the commission, if any. Quicken calculates the amount of the transaction.

First, for each of the three fields, number of shares, price per share, and commission, we can say that any non-numeric input is invalid. So, that's common across all three.

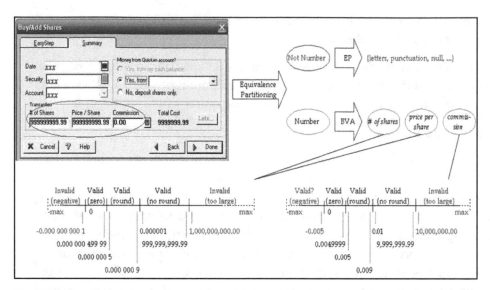

Figure 3–15 *Financial example*

For the numeric inputs, the price per share and the number of shares are handled the same. The number must be zero or greater. Notice the interesting rounding that happens, because we can enter numbers that aren't zero but are rounded down to zero. To be greater than zero, we have to enter at least .0000005, which is rounded up to .000001.

For the commission, something similar happens, but the rounding is to cents, which—pardon the pun—makes sense. One thing that didn't make much sense to me as I created Figure 3–15 was the fact that a negative commission is allowed. I guess sometimes that happens, but I've never been so lucky!

As Figure 3–15 is an information-dense figure, you might take a moment to study the various values identified for testing here.

Notice that you could apply the same approach to the Total Cost field. However, this is an output field, so you'd have to create inputs that would cause the output to be populated appropriately.

Presumably, you would use these various test values to populate some set of tests that involved entering stock purchase transactions. We'll look more at where those tests would come from when we talk about use cases.

Dates and Times

Dates and times are ordered sets, so both equivalence partitioning and boundary value analysis apply. They are more complex than integers and floating-point numbers, though, since dates and times are fields that consist of two or more subfields. In the case of dates, one or two subfields determine the valid range of another subfield. In the case of times, the format of the field determines validity of one of the subfields.

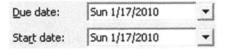

Figure 3–16   *Dates and times*

Now, there's mixed news for test analysts here. Most applications use standard libraries to validate date and time inputs, and we won't need to test those libraries so much. However, applications often accept as inputs two or more dates or times that have a relationship between them, like arrival and departure dates on airline flights. So, most test analysts will focus on testing relationships between dates, and this can be quite complicated.

In Figure 3–17 you can see the application of boundary value analysis and then equivalence partitioning to the relationship between the Start Date and Due Date fields of the task dialog box in Outlook. We can generate the test values, as well as decide on the means of entering them.

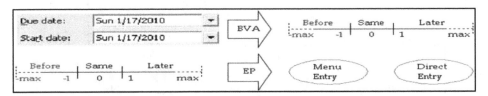

Figure 3–17   *Date and time example*

First, boundary value analysis allows us to generate the test values for the relationship between the due date and the start date. These include having the due date be the same day as the start date, which is valid. We can also have the due date be later than the start date, which is also valid. This can range from one day later up to some maximum number of days. Again, a requirements specification would help to determine what that maximum is.

For invalid inputs, note that we could try to enter a due day that is before the start date. That is definitely invalid. It could be one day before, up to some maximum number of days.

Now, we can use equivalence partitioning on the ways in which the dates are entered. This does matter in terms of when the validation happens, so we'd want to test it multiple ways. Pulling down a menu and selecting a date from it triggers immediate validation, while manually entering the date means the validation doesn't happen until you try to save the task.

Character Strings

Many inputs occur in free-form, editable fields, submitting character strings of various lengths and contents, as shown in Figure 3–18. The rules for validating these fields depend on what the field is. The boundary values and equivalence partitions that can exist arise not from the nature of the data itself—as was the case with integers, floating-point numbers, and so forth—but rather from rules imposed on the data by the application. So, in some cases there are boundary values for strings—especially in terms of length—while in other cases there aren't.

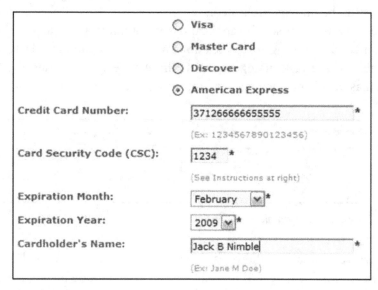

Figure 3–18   *Character strings*

As with dates, it's also quite possible for related fields to be individually valid but not valid together. You can see the payment processing screen from the RBCS website in Figure 3–19. Each of the six fields can be correct, yet the entire set of information not correspond to a real credit card.

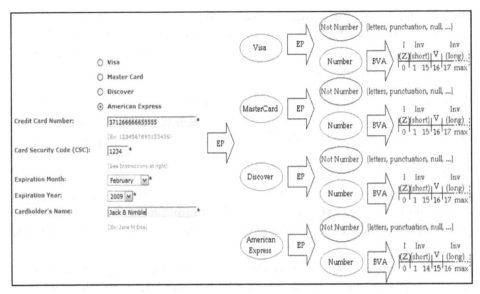

Figure 3–19   *Strings example*

In Figure 3–19 you can see the application of equivalence partitioning and boundary value analysis to the credit card type and the card number.

Using these techniques, we see that each card type is its own equivalence class. That's necessary because the specific leading digits and the number of digits will vary depending on the card type.

For each card type, we want to try the usual non-numeric inputs we've discussed for other fields.

For numeric inputs, we can use boundary value analysis on the length to determine validity. There are four equivalence classes:

1. The number has zero length; it is null, which is invalid. Okay, we already caught that one with the non-numeric tests, but that's not a problem. Better that our techniques generate the same interesting test values twice than not at all. Just remember, when this happens, that you don't actually have to test it twice!

2. The number is too short, which is invalid. We want to test with one digit to fifteen for most cards, though we want to test with fourteen for American Express because they have a fifteen-digit card number.

3. The number is the proper length, which makes it valid—at least from an input-field perspective. We'll address the question of whether the card number is actually valid in relationship to the other fields in a minute.

4. The number is too long, which is invalid. We want to test with seventeen digits for most cards, though we want to test with sixteen for American Express because they have a fifteen-digit card number. We also need to try some sort of maximum entry.

All of this hacking away at the credit card input field might strike you as absurd and overdone. However, from a security point of view, this screen is one you'll want to test heavily, right? Risk justifies extensive testing of these types of fields on such a screen.

I didn't have space to show the application of this approach to the card security code, expiration month and year, or to cardholder name. The card security code would look much like the equivalence partitioning for the card number, including the different number of digits for the American Express card compared to all the others.

The month and year are easy, because the RBCS website designers had the brains to restrict these two fields to pull-down menu selection only. That aids testability, because it's not possible to enter "Februly" as the month or 20ZB as the expiry year.

The cardholder name is a bit tricky, because here we'd need to know what the maximum and minimum lengths are for this field. Also, are there any rules about the characters allowed in this field? Again, a requirements specification would be useful.

Of course, what we've discussed so far covers only validation of the individual fields. Once the fields are individually validated, the payment method information has to be sent to the credit card processing company for validation. We could handle that with equivalence partitioning, but there is actually a whole set of conditions that determine this processing:

- Does the named person hold the credit card entered, and is the other information correct?
- Is the account still active or has it been canceled?
- Is the person within or over their limit?
- Is the transaction coming from a normal or a suspicious location?

We'll look at a technique that helps us test situations where conditions combine to determine outcomes when we cover decision tables in just a few moments.

Two Boundary Values or Three?

Let's wind down our discussion of boundary value analysis by mentioning a somewhat obscure point that can nevertheless arise if you do some reading about testing. This is the question of how many boundary values exist at a boundary.

In the material so far, I've shown just two boundary values per boundary. The boundary lies between the largest member of one equivalence class and the smallest member of the equivalence class above it. In other words, the boundary itself doesn't correspond to any member of any class.

However, some authors say there are three boundary values. Boris Beizer is probably the most notable. Why would there be three?

The difference arises from the use of a mathematical analysis rather than the graphical one that I've used. You can see that the two mathematical inequalities shown in Figure 3–20 describe the same situation as the graphical model. Applying Beizer's rule, you select the value itself as the middle boundary value, then you add the smallest possible amount to that value and subtract the smallest possible amount to that value to generate the two other boundary values. Remember, with integers as in this example, the smallest possible amount is one, while for floating points we have to consider that pesky issue of precision.

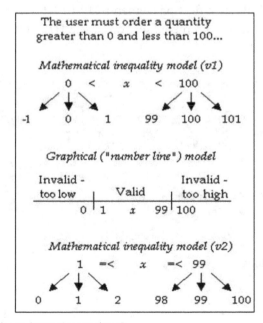

Figure 3–20   *Two boundary values or three?*

As you can see from this example, the mathematical boundary values will always include the graphical boundary values. To me, the three-value approach is wasteful of effort. We have enough to do already without creating more test values to cover, especially when those don't address any risks that haven't already been covered by other test values.

Boundary Value Analysis Exercise

A screen prototype for one screen of the HELLOCARMS system is shown in Figure 3–21. This screen asks for two pieces of information:

- Loan amount
- Property value

For both fields, the system allows entry of whole dollar amounts only (no cents), and it rounds to the nearest $100.

Assume the following rules apply to loans:

- The minimum loan amount is $5,000
- The maximum loan amount is $1,000,000
- The minimum property value is $25,000
- The maximum property value is $5,000,000

Refer also to requirements specification elements 010-010-130 and 010-010-140 in the Functional System Requirements section of the HELLOCARMS system requirements document.

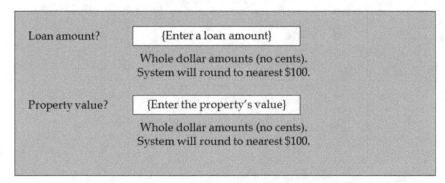

Figure 3–21   *Screen prototype*

If the fields are valid, then the screen will be accepted. Either the telephone banker will continue with the application, or the application will be transferred to a senior telephone banker for further handling. If one or both fields are invalid, an error message is displayed.

The exercise consists of two parts:

1. Show the equivalence partitions and boundary values for each of the two fields, indicating valid and invalid members and the boundaries for those partitions.
2. Create test cases to cover these partitions and boundary values, keeping in mind the rules about combinations of valid and invalid members.

The answers to the two parts are shown on the next pages. You should review the answer to the first part (and, if necessary, revise your answer to the second part) before reviewing the answer to the second part.

Boundary Value Analysis Debrief

First, let's take a look at the equivalence partitions and boundary values, which are shown in Figure 3–22.

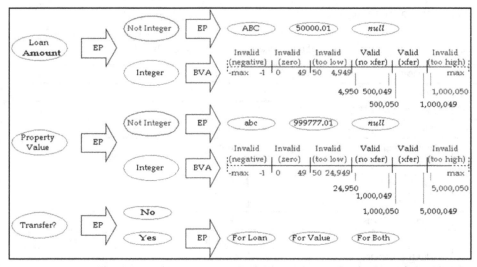

Figure 3–22 *Equivalence partitions and boundary values for amount, value, and transfer*

So, for the loan amount we can show the boundary values and equivalence partitions as shown in Table 3–5.

Table 3–5   *Boundary values and equivalence partitions for loan amount*

#	Partition	Boundary Value
1	Letter: ABC	-
2	Decimal: 50,000.01	-
3	Null	-
4	Invalid (negative)	-max
5	Invalid (negative)	-1
6	Invalid (zero)	0
7	Invalid (zero)	49
8	Invalid (too low)	50
9	Invalid (too low)	4,949
10	Valid (no transfer)	4,950
11	Valid (no transfer)	500,049
12	Valid (transfer)	500,050
13	Valid (transfer)	1,000,049
14	Invalid (too high)	1,000,050
15	Invalid (too high)	max

For the property value, we can show the boundary values and equivalence partitions as shown in Table 3–6.

Table 3–6   *Boundary values and equivalence partitions for property value*

#	Partition	Boundary Value
1	Letter: abc	-
2	Decimal: 999,777.01	-
3	Null	-
4	Invalid (negative)	-max
5	Invalid (negative)	-1
6	Invalid (zero)	0
7	Invalid (zero)	49
8	Invalid (too low)	50
9	Invalid (too low)	24,949
10	Valid (no transfer)	24,950
11	Valid (no transfer)	1,000,049
12	Valid (transfer)	1,000,050
13	Valid (transfer)	5,000,049
14	Invalid (too high)	5,000,050
15	Invalid (too high)	max

For the transfer decision, we can show the equivalence partitions for the loan amount as shown in Table 3–7.

Table 3–7   Equivalence partitions for loan amount

#	Partition
1	No
2	Yes, for the loan amount
3	Yes, for the property value
4	Yes, for both

Now, let's create tests from these equivalence partitions and boundary values, which you'll find in Table 3–8. I captured the traceability information from the test case number back to the partitions or boundary values, shown in Table 3–9, Table 3–10, and Table 3–11. As in the previous exercise, once I have a trace from each partition to a test case, I'm done—as long as I didn't combine invalids!

Table 3–8   Test cases for equivalence partitions and boundary values

Inputs	1	2	3	4	5	6
Loan amount	4,950	500,050	500,049	1,000,049	ABC	50,000.01
Property value	24,950	1,000,049	1,000,050	5,000,049	100,000	200,000
Outputs						
Accept?	Y	Y	Y	Y	N	N
Transfer?	N	Y (loan)	Y (prop)	Y (both)	-	-

Inputs	7	8	9	10	11	12
Loan amount	null	100,000	200,000	300,000	-max	-1
Property value	300,000	abc	999,777.01	null	400,000	500,000
Outputs						
Accept?	N	N	N	N	N	N
Transfer?	-	-	-	-	-	-

Inputs	13	14	15	16	17	18
Loan amount	0	49	50	4,949	1,000,050	max
Property value	600,000	700,000	800,000	900,000	1,000,000	1,100,000
Outputs						
Accept?	N	N	N	N	N	N
Transfer?	-	-	-	-	-	-

Inputs	19	20	21	22	23	24
Loan amount	400,000	500,000	600,000	700,000	800,000	900,000
Property value	-max	-1	0	49	50	24,949
Outputs						
Accept?	N	N	N	N	N	N
Transfer?	-	-	-	-	-	-

Inputs	25	26	27	28	29	30
Loan amount	1,000,000	555,555				
Property value	5,000,050	max				
Outputs						
Accept?	N	N				
Transfer?	-	-				

Table 3–9   *Loan amount*

#	Partition	Boundary Value	Test Case
1	Letter: ABC	-	5
2	Decimal: 50,000.01	-	6
3	Null	-	7
4	Invalid (negative)	-max	11
5	Invalid (negative)	-1	12
6	Invalid (zero)	0	13
7	Invalid (zero)	49	14
8	Invalid (too low)	50	15
9	Invalid (too low)	4,949	16
10	Valid (no transfer)	4,950	1
11	Valid (no transfer)	500,049	3
12	Valid (transfer)	500,050	2
13	Valid (transfer)	1,000,049	4
14	Invalid (too high)	1,000,050	17
15	Invalid (too high)	max	18

Table 3–10   *Property value*

#	Partition	Boundary Value	Test Case
1	Letter: abc	-	8
2	Decimal: 999,777.01	-	9
3	Null	-	10
4	Invalid (negative)	-max	19
5	Invalid (negative)	-1	20
6	Invalid (zero)	0	21
7	Invalid (zero)	49	22
8	Invalid (too low)	50	23
9	Invalid (too low)	24,949	24
10	Valid (no transfer)	24,950	1
11	Valid (no transfer)	1,000,049	2
12	Valid (transfer)	1,000,050	3
13	Valid (transfer)	5,000,049	4
14	Invalid (too high)	5,000,050	25
15	Invalid (too high)	max	26

Transfer decision:

#	Partition	Test Case
1	No	1
2	Yes, for the loan amount	2
3	Yes, for the property value	3
4	Yes, for both	4

Table 3–11   *Transfer decision*

Notice that's there's another interesting combination related to the transfer decision that we covered in our tests. This was when the values were rejected as inputs, in which case we should not even be able to leave the screen, not to mention transfer the application. We did test with both loan amounts and property values that would have triggered a transfer, had the other value been valid. I could have shown that as a third set of equivalence classes for the transfer decision.

3.2.3   Decision Tables

Equivalence partitioning and boundary value analysis are very useful techniques. They are especially useful, as we saw in the earlier parts of this section, when testing input field validation at the user interface. However, lots of testing that we do as test analysts involves testing the business logic that sits underneath the user interface. We can use boundary values and equivalence partitioning on business logic, too, but three additional techniques, decision tables, use cases, and state-based testing, will often prove handier and more powerful techniques. Let's start with decision tables.

Decision tables allow us to test the way that various combinations of conditions interact to produce certain results happening and not happening. The table arranges the combinations of conditions in columns, with the conditions on top and the associated actions taken and not taken shown at the bottom. When creating tests, we should make sure we have at least one test for each column, though in some cases boundary value analysis or equivalence partitioning on one or more conditions can create multiple tests for some or all columns. These tests can reveal situations where the wrong actions happen, or the right actions don't happen, or conditions interact in an undesirable way.[2]

Individual units usually don't have complex combinations of conditions—at least not if they are being written following the best programming practice of high cohesion—so decision tables are not typically useful for unit testing. However, at all levels of testing, wherever we can draw a flow chart or formulate business rules for interacting conditions, we can create a decision table, provided that we have enough information about the requirements and the expected results.

Conceptually, decision tables express the rules that govern handling of transactional situations. By their simple, concise structure, they make it easy for us to design tests for those rules, usually at least one test per rule.

When I said transactional situations, what I meant were those situations where the conditions—inputs, preconditions, etc.—that exist at a given moment in time for a single transaction are sufficient by themselves to determine the actions the system should take. If the conditions are not sufficient, but we must also refer to what conditions have existed in the past, then we'll want to use state-based testing, which we'll cover in a moment.

---

2. You can find a different description of decision tables in Lee Copeland's book, *A Practitioner's Guide to Software Test Design,* and in the book I cowrote with Dorothy Graham and Erik van Veenendaal, *Foundations of Software Testing.*

The underlying model is either a table—most typically—or a Boolean graph— less typically. Either way, the model connects combinations of conditions with the action or actions that should occur when each particular combination of conditions arises.

If the graph is used, this technique is also referred to as a cause-effect graph, because that is the formal name of the graph. However, it's important to keep in mind that any given decision table can be converted into a cause-effect graph, and any given cause-effect graph can be converted into a decision table. So, which one you choose to use is up to you. I prefer decision tables, and they are more commonly used, so I'll focus on them here. However, I'll show you how the conversion can be done.

To create tests from a decision table or a cause-effect graph, we are going to design test inputs that fulfill the conditions given. The test outputs will correspond to the action or actions given for that combination of conditions. During test execution, we check that the actual actions taken correspond to the expected actions.

We create enough tests that every combination of conditions is covered by at least one test. Often, that coverage criterion is relaxed to say the tests must cover those combinations of conditions that can determine the action or actions. If that's a little confusing—which it might be, depending on how you prepared for the Foundation exam, as this isn't always explained properly in books and classes. The distinction I'm drawing will become clear to you when we talk about collapsed decision tables.

With a decision table, the coverage criterion boils down to an easy-to-remember rule of at least one test per column in the table. For cause-effect graphs, you have to generate a truth table that contains all possible combinations of conditions and ensure you have one test per row in the truth table.

So, what is our bug hypothesis with decision tables? What kind of bugs are we looking for? There are two. First, under some combination of conditions, the wrong action might occur. In other words, there is some action that the system is not to take under this combination of conditions, yet it does. Second, under some combination of conditions, the system might not take the right action. In other words, there is some action that the system is to take under this combination of conditions, yet it does not.

Example: Decision Table (Full)

Earlier, we looked at the e-commerce section of the RBCS website, www.rbcs-us.com. Specifically, we worked through a complicated example of validating payment information, specifically credit card type, card number, card security code, expiration month, expiration year, and cardholder name. The objective was to apply boundary value analysis and equivalence partitioning to test the ability of the application to verify the payment information, as much as possible, before sending it to the server.

So, once that information goes to the credit card processing company for validation, how can we test that? Again, we could handle that with equivalence partitioning, but there are actually a whole set of conditions that determine this processing:

- Does the named person hold the credit card entered, and is the other information correct?
- Is the account still active or has it been canceled?
- Is the person within or over their limit?
- Is the transaction coming from a normal or a suspicious location?

Table 3–12   Decision table (full)

Conditions	1	2	3	4	5	6	7	8	9	10	11	12	13	14	15	16
Real account?	Y	Y	Y	Y	Y	Y	Y	Y	N	N	N	N	N	N	N	N
Active account?	Y	Y	Y	Y	N	N	N	N	Y	Y	Y	Y	N	N	N	N
Within limit?	Y	Y	N	N	Y	Y	N	N	Y	Y	N	N	Y	Y	N	N
Location okay?	Y	N	Y	N	Y	N	Y	N	Y	N	Y	N	Y	N	Y	N
Actions																
Approve?	Y	N	N	N	N	N	N	N	N	N	N	N	N	N	N	N
Call cardholder?	N	Y	Y	Y	N	Y	Y	Y	N	N	N	N	N	N	N	N
Call vendor?	N	N	N	N	Y	Y	Y	Y	Y	Y	Y	Y	Y	Y	Y	Y

The decision table shown in Table 3–12 shows how these four conditions interact to determine which of the following three actions will occur:

- Should we approve the transaction?
- Should we call the cardholder (e.g., to warn them about a purchase from a strange place)?
- Should we call the vendor (e.g., to ask them to seize the canceled card)?

Take a minute to study the table to see how this works. The conditions are listed at the top left of the table, and the actions are at the bottom left. Each column to the right of this leftmost column contains a business rule. Each rule says, in essence, "Under this particular combination of conditions (shown at the top of the rule), carry out this particular combination of actions (shown at the bottom of the rule)."

Notice that the number of columns—i.e., the number of business rules—is equal to 2 raised to the power of the number of conditions. In other words, $2 \times 2 \times 2 \times 2$, which is 16. When the conditions are strictly Boolean—true or false—and we're dealing with a full decision table (not a collapsed one) that will always be the case. Sometimes, conditions are not Boolean, but can take on three or more different values, in which case a larger number of combinations will be possible. For example, suppose that a card can be active, canceled, or suspended, i.e., one of three possible values. The number of columns in the full decision table would be 24.

Notice how I populated the conditions? The topmost condition changes most slowly. Half of the columns are Yes, then half No. The condition under the topmost changes more quickly but more slowly than all the others. The pattern is quarter Yes, then quarter No, then quarter Yes, then quarter No. Finally, for the bottommost condition, the alternation is Yes, No, Yes, No, Yes, etc. This pattern makes it easy to ensure you don't miss anything. If you start with the topmost condition, set the left half of the rule columns to Yes and the right half of the rule columns to No, then following the pattern I showed, if you get to the bottom and the Yes, No, Yes, No, Yes, etc., pattern doesn't hold, you did something wrong.

Example: Deriving Tests

Deriving tests from this example is easy: each column of the table is a test. When time comes to run the tests, we'll create the conditions that are each test's inputs. We'll replace the yes/no conditions with actual input values for credit card number, security code, expiration date, and cardholder name, either during test

> **ISTQB Glossary**
>
> **Decision table testing:** A black-box test design technique in which test cases are designed to execute the combinations of inputs and/or stimuli (causes) shown in a decision table.

design or perhaps even at test execution time. We'll verify the actions that are the test's expected results.

In some cases, we might generate more than one test per column. I'll cover this possibility more later, as we enlist our previous test techniques, equivalence partitioning and boundary value analysis, to extend decision table testing.

Notice that, in this case, some of the tests don't make much sense. For example, how can the account not be real but yet active? How can the account not be real but within limit?

This kind of situation is a hint that maybe we don't need all the columns in our decision table.

Collapsing a Decision Table

We can sometimes collapse the decision table, combining columns, to achieve a more concise—and in some cases sensible—decision table. In any situation where the value of one or more particular conditions can't affect the actions for two or more combinations of conditions, we can collapse the decision table.

This involves combining two or more columns where, as I said, one or more of the conditions don't affect the actions. As a hint, combinable columns are often **but not always** next to each other. You can at least start by looking at columns next to each other.

To combine two or more columns, look for two or more columns that result in the same combination of actions. Note that the actions must be the same for all of the actions in the table, not just some of them. In these columns, some of the conditions will be the same, and some will be different. The ones that are different obviously don't affect the outcome. So, we can replace the conditions that are different in those columns with a dash. The dash usually means I don't care, it doesn't matter, or it can't happen, given the other conditions.

Now, repeat this process until the only further columns that share the same combination of actions for all the actions in the table are ones where you'd be combining a dash with a yes or no value and thus wiping out an important distinction for cause of action. What I mean by this will be clear in the example on the next page, if it's not clear already.

Another word of caution at this point: be careful when dealing with a table where more than one rule can apply at one single point in time. These tables have non-exclusive rules. We'll discuss that further later in this section.

Example: Decision Table (Collapsed)

Table 3–13 shows the same decision table as before, but collapsed to eliminate extraneous columns. Most notably, you can see that what were columns 9 through 16 in the original decision table, collapsed into a single column.

Table 3–13   *Decision table (collapsed)*

Conditions	1	2	3	5	6	7	9
Real account?	Y	Y	Y	Y	Y	Y	N
Active account?	Y	Y	Y	N	N	N	-
Within limit?	Y	Y	N	Y	Y	N	-
Location okay?	Y	N	-	Y	N	-	-
Actions							
Approve?	Y	N	N	N	N	N	N
Call cardholder?	N	Y	Y	N	Y	Y	N
Call vendor?	N	N	N	Y	Y	Y	Y

I've kept the original column numbers for ease of comparison. Again, take a minute to study the table to see how I did this. Look carefully at columns 1, 2, and 3. Notice that we can't collapse columns 2 and 3 because that would result in a dash for both within limit and location okay. If you study this table or the full one, you can see that one of these conditions must not be true for the cardholder to receive a call. The collapse of rule 4 into rule 3 says that, if the card is over limit, the cardholder will be called, regardless of location.

The same logic applies to the collapse of rule 8 into rule 7.

Notice that the format is unchanged. The conditions are listed at the top left of the table, and the actions at the bottom left. Each column to the right of this leftmost column contains a business rule. Each rule says, "Under this particular combination of conditions (shown at the top of the rule, some of which might not be applicable), carry out this particular combination of actions (shown at the bottom of the rule, all of which are fully specified)."

Notice that the number of columns is no longer equal to 2 raised to the power of the number of conditions. This makes sense, right, since otherwise no collapsing would have occurred. If you are concerned that you might miss something important, you can always start with the full decision table. In a full table, because of the way you generate it, it is guaranteed to have all the combinations of conditions. You can mathematically check if it does. Then, carefully collapse the table to reduce the number of tests you create.

Also, notice that, when you collapse the table, that pleasant pattern of Yes and No columns present in the full table goes away. This is yet another reason to be very careful when collapsing the columns, because you can't count on the pattern or the mathematical formula to check your work.

Equivalence Partitions, Boundary Values, and Decision Tables

Okay, let's address an issue I brought up earlier, the possibility of multiple tests per column in the decision table via the combination of equivalence partitioning with the decision table technique. Let's refer back to our example decision table, specifically column 9 as shown in Figure 3–23.

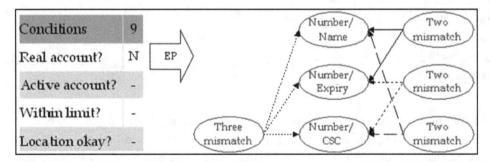

Figure 3–23   *Column 9 of collapsed decision table*

We can apply equivalence partitioning to the question of, "How many interesting—from a test point of view—ways are there to have an account not be real?" As you can see from Figure 3–23, this could happen six potentially interesting ways:

- Card number and cardholder mismatch
- Card number and expiry mismatch
- Card number and CSC mismatch
- Two of the above mismatches (three possibilities)
- All three mismatches.

So, there could be seven tests for that column.

How about boundary value analysis? Yes, that too can be applied to decision tables to find new and interesting tests. For example, "How many interesting test values are there that relate to the credit limit?"

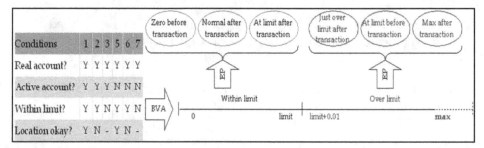

Figure 3–24 *Applying boundary values to decision tables*

As you can see in Figure 3–24, equivalence partitioning and boundary value analysis show us six interesting possibilities:

1. The account starts at zero balance.
2. The account would be at a normal balance after the transaction.
3. The account would be exactly at the limit after the transaction.
4. The account would be exactly over the limit after the transaction.
5. The account was at exactly the limit before the transaction (which would ensure going over if the transaction concluded).
6. The account would be at the maximum overdraft value after the transaction (which might not be possible).

Combining this with the decision table, we can see that we would again end up with more "over limit" tests than we have columns—one more, to be exact—so we'd increase the number of tests just slightly. In other words, there would be four within-limit tests and three over-limit tests. That's true unless you wanted to make sure that each within-limit equivalence class was represented in an approved transaction, in which case column 1 would go from one test to three.

Example: Nonexclusive Rules

Let's finish our discussion about decision tables by looking at the issue of nonexclusive rules I mentioned earlier.

Sometimes more than one rule can apply to a transaction. In Table 3–14 you see a table that shows the calculation of credit card fees. There are three conditions, and notice that zero, one, two, or all three of those conditions could be met in a given month. How does this situation affect testing?

Table 3–14   *Nonexclusive rules*

Conditions	1	2	3
Foreign exchange?	Y	-	-
Balance forward?	-	Y	-
Late payment?	-	-	Y
Actions			
Exchange fee?	Y	-	-
Charge interest?	-	Y	-
Charge late fee?	-	-	Y

It complicates the testing a bit, but we can use a methodical approach and risk-based testing to avoid the major pitfalls.

To start, test the decision table like a normal one, one rule at a time, making sure that no conditions not related to the rule you are testing are met. This allows you to test rules in isolation—just like you are forced to do in situations where the rules are exclusive.

Next, consider testing combinations of rules. Notice I said, "consider testing," not "test all possible combinations of rules." You'll want to avoid combinatorial explosions, which is what happens when testers start to test combinations of factors without consideration of the value of those tests. Now, in this case, there are only eight possible combinations—three factors, two options for each factor, 2 times 2 times 2 is 8. However, if you have six factors with five options each, you now have 15,625 combinations.

One way to avoid combinatorial explosions is to identify the possible combinations and then use risk to weight those combinations. Try to get to the important combinations and don't worry about the rest.

Another way to avoid combinatorial explosions is to use techniques like classification trees and pairwise testing, which we'll cover later in this section.

3.2.4 Cause-Effect Graphs

Cause-effect graphs are simply pictorial representations of the same business logic that is shown in a decision table. We can always convert one to the other. It is applied in the same way and to the same situations as a decision table. However, it can require tools to create the graphs, and you have to be able to learn the notation. Coverage is measured through the lines connecting causes to effects, which has the same result of covering every column in a decision table. Cause-effect graph tests find the same types of bugs as decision tables.

Example: Cause-Effect Graph

In Figure 3–25 you see the cause-effect graph that corresponds to the example decision tables we've looked at so far. You might ask, "Which one, the full or collapsed?" Both. The full and the collapsed table are logically equivalent, unless there's something wrong with the collapsed version.

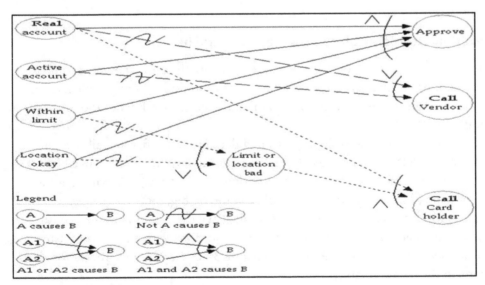

Figure 3–25 *Cause-effect graph*

At the bottom left of this figure, you see the legend that tells you how to read the operations. Let's go clockwise from the top left of the legend.

We have simple causality:	If A is true, B will occur, or, in other words, A causes B.
We have negation:	When A is not true, B will occur, or, not A causes B.
We have AND operation:	When A1 and A2 are both true, B will occur, or A1 and A2 causes B.
We have OR operation:	When A1 or A2 is true, B will occur, or A1 or A2 causes B.

Let's look at the connection between conditions and actions. The solid causality lines, together with an AND operator, show that all four conditions must be met for the transaction to be approved.

The dashed causality lines, together with negation operators and an OR operator, show that, if the account is not real or the account is not active, we will call the vendor.

The dotted causality lines are a bit more complicated. First, we combine the "within limit" and "location okay" conditions, with negation operators and an OR operator, to create an intermediate condition of "Limit or location bad." Now, we combine that with the "real account" condition to say that, if we have an over-limit or bad location situation, and the account is real, we will call the cardholder.

Converting Decision Tables and Cause-Effect Graphs

When collapsing a decision table, a cause-effect graph can be helpful to make sure you don't accidentally collapse columns you shouldn't. Some people like to use them for test design directly, but, as I mentioned earlier, I'm not too fond of trying to do that.

So, to create a cause-effect graph from a decision table, first list all the conditions on the left of a blank page. Next, list all the actions on the right of a blank page. Obviously, if there are a lot of conditions and actions, this will be a big page of paper, but then your decision table would be big, too.

Now, for each action, read the table to identify how combinations of conditions cause an action. Connect one or more conditions with each action using Boolean operators, which were shown in Figure 3–25. Repeat this process for all actions in the decision table.

If you happen to be given a cause-effect graph and want to create a decision table, first list all the conditions on the top left of a blank decision table. Next, list all the actions on the bottom left of the decision table, under the conditions. Following the pattern shown earlier, generate all possible combinations of conditions. Now, referring to the cause-effect graph, determine the actions taken and not taken for each combination of conditions. Once the actions section is fully populated, you can collapse the table if you'd like.

Home Equity Loan Insurance Exercise

During development, the HELLOCARMS project team adds a feature to the HELLOCARMS system. This feature allows the system to sell a life insurance policy to cover the amount of a home equity loan so that, should the borrower die, the policy will pay off the loan. The premium is calculated annually, at the beginning of each annual policy period, based on the loan balance at that time. The base annual premium will be $1 for $10,000 in loan balance. The insurance policy is not available for lines of credit or for reverse mortgages.

The system will increase the base premium by a certain percentage based on some basic physical and health questions that the telephone banker will ask during the interview.

A yes answer to any of the following questions will trigger a 50% increase to the base premium.

1. Have you smoked cigarettes in the past twelve months?
2. Have you ever been diagnosed with cancer, diabetes, high cholesterol, high blood pressure, a heart disorder, or stroke?
3. Within the last five years, have you been hospitalized for more than seventy-two hours except for childbirth or broken bones?
4. Within the last five years, have you been completely disabled from work for a week or longer due to a single illness or injury?

The telephone banker will also ask about age, weight, and height. (Applicants cannot be under eighteen.) The weight and height are combined to calculate the body mass index (BMI). Based on that information, the telephone banker will apply Table 3–15 to decide whether to increase the rate or even decline to issue the policy, based on possible weight-related illnesses in the person's future.

Table 3–15   *BMI/age policy increase*

	Body Mass Index (BMI)			
Age	<17	34–36	37–39	>39
18–39	Decline	75%	100%	Decline
40–59	Decline	50%	75%	Decline
>59	Decline	25%	50%	Decline

The increases are cumulative. For example, if the person has normal weight, smokes cigarettes, and has high blood pressure, the annual rate is increased from $1 per $10,000 to $2.25 per $10,000. If the person is a 45-year-old male diabetic with a body mass index of 39, the annual rate is increased from $1 per $10,000 to $2.625 per $10,000.

The exercise consists of four steps:

1. Create a decision table that shows the effect of the four health questions and the body mass index.
2. Translate the decision table into a cause-effect graph.
3. Show the boundary values for body mass index and age.
4. Create test cases to cover the decision table and the boundary values, keeping in mind the rules about testing nonexclusive rules.

The answers to the four parts are shown on the next pages. You should review the answer to each part (and, if necessary, revise your answer to the next parts) before reviewing the answer to the next part.

Note: If you prefer, you can reverse the order of steps 1 and 2.

Home Equity Loan Insurance Debrief

First, I created the decision table from the four health questions and the BMI/age table. The answer is shown in Table 3–16. Note that the increases are shown in percentages.

Table 3–16   *Decision table for life insurance rate increases*

Conditions	1	2	3	4	5	6	7	8	9	10	11	12
Smoked?	Y	-	-	-	-	-	-	-	-	-	-	-
Diagnosed?	-	Y	-	-	-	-	-	-	-	-	-	-
Hospitalized?	-	-	Y	-	-	-	-	-	-	-	-	-
Disabled?	-	-	-	Y	-	-	-	-	-	-	-	-
BMI	-	-	-	-	34–36	34–36	34–36	37–39	37–39	37–39	<17	>39
Age	-	-	-	-	18–39	40–59	>59	18–39	40–59	>59	-	-
Actions												
Increase	50	50	50	50	75	50	25	100	75	50	-	-
Decline	-	-	-	-	-	-	-	-	-	-	Y	Y

It's important to notice that rules 1 through 4 are nonexclusive, though rules 5 through 12 are exclusive.

In addition, there is an implicit rule that the age must be greater than 17, or the applicant will be denied not only insurance, but the loan itself. I could have put that here in the decision table, but my focus is primarily on test business functionality, not input validation. I'll cover those tests with boundary values.

Next, I created the cause-effect graph shown in Figure 3–26.

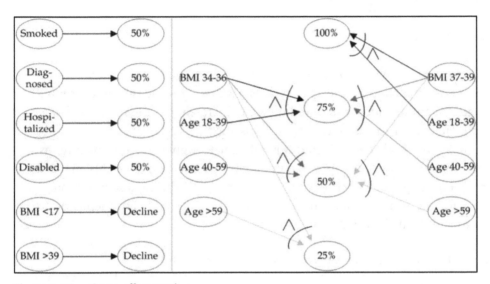

Figure 3–26   *Cause-effect graph*

Note on the left side of the graph that each nonexclusive rule is shown on its own, not as combining with an OR operator on the 50% action. Why? Because if I had shown it as combining with an OR operator, then the cumulative increase would not occur. I've also shown the two BMI conditions that can result in a decline action here.

Now, let's look at the boundary values for body mass index and age, shown in Figure 3–27.

Three important testing notes relate to the body mass index. First, the body mass index is not entered directly but rather by entering height and weight. Depending on the range and precision of these two fields, there could be dozens of ways to enter a given body mass index. Second, the maximum body mass index is achieved by entering the smallest possible height and the largest possible weight. Third, we'd need to separately understand the boundary values for these two fields and make sure those were tested properly.

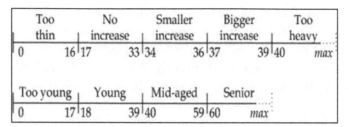

Figure 3–27   *Boundary values*

An important testing note relates to the age. You can see that I omitted equivalence classes related to invalid ages, such as negative ages and non-integer input for ages. Again, my idea is that we'd need to separately test the input field validation. Here, my focus is on testing business logic.

Finally, for both fields, I omit any attempt to figure out the maximums. Either someone will give me a requirements specification that tells me that during test design, or I'll try to ascertain it empirically during test execution.

So, for the BMI, we can show the boundary values and equivalence partitions as shown in Table 3–17

Table 3–17   *Boundary values and equivalence partitions for the BMI*

#	Partition	Boundary Value
1	Too thin	0
2	Too thin	16
3	No increase	17
4	No increase	33
5	Smaller increase	34
6	Smaller increase	36
7	Bigger increase	37
8	Bigger increase	39
9	Too heavy	40
10	Too heavy	max

So, for the age, we can show the boundary values and equivalence partitions as shown in Table 3–18

Table 3–18   *Boundary values and equivalence partitions for the age*

#	Partition	Boundary Value
1	Too young	0
2	Too young	17
3	Young	18
4	Young	39
5	Middle-aged	40
6	Middle-aged	59
7	Senior	60
8	Senior	max

Finally, Table 3–19 shows the test cases. They are much like the decision table, but note that I have shown the rate (in dollars per $10,000 of loan balance) rather than the percentage increase.

Table 3–19   *Test cases: rate in dollars per $10,000 of loan balance*

	Test case											
Conditions	1	2	3	4	5	6	7	8	9	10	11	12
Smoked?	Y	N	N	N	N	N	N	N	N	N	N	N
Diagnosed?	N	Y	N	N	N	N	N	N	N	N	N	N
Hospitalized?	N	N	Y	N	N	N	N	N	N	N	N	N
Disabled?	N	N	N	Y	N	N	N	N	N	N	N	N
BMI	20	24	28	32	34	36	35	34	36	35	37	39
Age	30	40	50	60	18	39	40	59	60	max	20	30
Actions												
Rate	1.5	1.5	1.5	1.5	1.75	1.75	1.5	1.5	1.25	1.25	2	2
Decline	N	N	N	N	N	N	N	N	N	N	N	N

	Test case											
Conditions	13	14	15	16	17	18	19	20	21	22	23	24
Smoked?	N	N	N	N	N	N	N	N	N	N	N	N
Diagnosed?	N	N	N	N	N	N	N	N	N	N	N	N
Hospitalized?	N	N	N	N	N	N	N	N	N	N	N	N
Disabled?	N	N	N	N	N	N	N	N	N	N	N	N
BMI	38	37	39	38	16	40	0	max	17	33	20	30
Age	45	55	65	75	35	50	25	70	37	47	0	17

Actions												
Rate	1.75	1.75	1.50	1.50	N/A	N/A	N/A	N/A	1	1	N/A	N/A
Decline	N	N	N	N	Y	Y	Y	Y	N	N	Y	Y

					Test case							
Conditions	25	26	27	28	29	30	31	32	33	34	35	36
Smoked?	Y	N	N	N	Y							
Diagnosed?	N	Y	N	N	Y							
Hospitalized?	N	N	Y	N	Y							
Disabled?	N	N	N	Y	Y							
BMI	35	36	34	38	37							
Age	20	50	70	30	35							
Actions												
Rate	2.625	2.25	1.875	3	10.125							
Decline	N	N	N	N	N							

Notice my approach to testing the nonexclusive rules. First, I tested every rule, exclusive and nonexclusive, in isolation. Then, I tested the remaining untested boundary values. Next, I tested combinations of only one nonexclusive rule with one exclusive rule, making sure each nonexclusive rule had been tested once in combination (but not all the exclusive rules were tested in combination). Finally, I tested a combination of all four nonexclusive rules with one exclusive rule. I did not use combinations with the "decline" rules, since presumably there's no way to check whether the increase was correctly calculated.

You might also have noticed that I managed to sneak in covering the minimum and maximum increases. However, I probably didn't cover every possible increase. Since I didn't test every possible pair, triple, and quadruple combination of rules, I certainly didn't test every way an increase could be calculated by that table. I'll spend more time on that topic in the material on classification trees and pairwise testing.

For the decision table and the boundary values, I've captured test coverage in Table 3–20, Table 3–21, and Table 3–22 to make sure I missed nothing. Table 3–20 shows decision table coverage, using three coverage metrics:

Table 3–20   *Decision table coverage using three coverage metrics*

Conditions	1	2	3	4	5	6	7	8	9	10	11	12
Smoked?	Y	-	-	-	-	-	-	-	-	-	-	-
Diagnosed?	-	Y	-	-	-	-	-	-	-	-	-	-
Hospitalized?	-	-	Y	-	-	-	-	-	-	-	-	-
Disabled?	-	-	-	Y	-	-	-	-	-	-	-	-
BMI	-	-	-	-	34–36	34–36	34–36	37–39	37–39	37–39	<17	>39
Age	-	-	-	-	18–39	40–59	>59	18–39	40–59	>59	-	-
Actions												
Increase	50	50	50	50	75	50	25	100	75	50	-	-
Decline	-	-	-	-	-	-	-	-	-	-	Y	Y
Single Rule Coverage												
Test case(s)	1	2	3	4	5, 6	7, 8	9, 10	11, 12	13, 14	15, 16	17, 19	18, 20
Pairs of Rules Coverage												
Test case(s)	25	26	27	28	25	26	27	28				
Maximum Combination of Rules Coverage												
Test case(s)	29	29	29	29				29				

Table 3–21 shows BMI coverage:

#	Partition	Boundary Value	Test Case
1	Too thin	0	19
2	Too thin	16	17
3	No increase	17	21
4	No increase	33	22
5	Smaller increase	34	5
6	Smaller increase	36	6
7	Bigger increase	37	11
8	Bigger increase	39	12
9	Too heavy	40	18
10	Too heavy	max	20

Table 3–21   *BMI coverage*

Table 3–22 shows age coverage:

#	Partition	Boundary Value	Test Case
1	Too young	0	23
2	Too young	17	24
3	Young	18	5
4	Young	39	6
5	Mid-aged	39	7
6	Mid-aged	59	8
7	Senior	60	9
8	Senior	max	10

Table 3–22   *Age coverage*

3.2.5   Use Case Testing

Like decision tables, use cases also focus on transactional situations, but they are more about end-to-end usage scenarios, where someone (referred to as the actor) uses the system to get something done. It can be used at any level, but is most common at system test and acceptance test levels. It is important that the system be complete enough for the intended usage, which can happen during integration testing, and does happen during integration testing in Agile projects. In addition, the realistic usage of the system, including the atypical usages, must be well understood, or gaps will occur in the testing. Testing must cover the typical usage, called the *main path* or *happy path*, as well as each of the atypical usages, called the *alternate paths* or *exception paths*. This technique can validate the software by checking for improper processing of main or alternate paths, missing alternate paths, and problems with error reporting.

Conceptually, use case testing is a way to ensure that we have tested typical and exceptional workflows and scenarios for the system, from the point of view of the various actors who directly interact with the system and from the point of view of the various stakeholders who indirectly interact with the system. If we (as test analysts) receive use cases from business analysts or system designers, then these can serve as easy frameworks for creating logical tests.

Remember that, with decision tables, we were focused on transactional situations, where the conditions—inputs, preconditions, and so forth—that exist at a given moment in time for a single transaction are sufficient by themselves to determine the actions the system should take. Use cases aren't quite as rigid on this point, but, generally, the assumption is that the typical workflows are independent of each other. An exceptional workflow occurs when a typical workflow can't occur, but usually we have independence from one workflow to the next. This is ensured—at least for formal use cases—by clearly defined preconditions and postconditions, which guarantee certain things are true at the beginning and end of the workflow. These act to insulate one workflow from the next. Again, if we have heavy interaction of past events and conditions with the way current events and conditions should be handled, we'll want to use state-based testing.

The model is less formal than what we've seen with equivalence partitions, boundary values, and decision tables. Indeed, the concept of a use case itself can vary considerably in formality and presentation. The basic idea is that we have some numbered (or at least sequential) list of steps that describes how an actor interacts with the system. The steps can be shown in text or as part of a flow-chart.

The use case should also show the results obtained at the end of that sequence of steps. The results obtained should be of some benefit to some party, either the actor interacting directly with the system or some other stakeholder who indirectly receives the value of the results.

At the very least, the set of steps should show a typical workflow, the normal processing. This normal processing is sometimes called the primary scenario, the normal course, the basic course, the main path, the normal flow, or the happy path. However, since things are not always happy, the set of steps should also show abnormal processing, sometimes called exceptions, exceptional processing, or alternative workflows.

More formal approaches to documenting use cases cover not only typical and exceptional workflows, but also explicit identification of the actor, the preconditions, the postconditions, the priority, the frequency of use, special requirements, assumptions, and potentially more. The formal approach might also entail the creation of a use case diagram that shows all the actors, all the use cases, and the relationship between the actors and the use cases.

Now, an assumption that I'm making here—in fact, it's an assumption implicitly embedded within the ISTQB syllabi—is that you are going to receive use cases, not create them. If you look at the Advanced Test Analyst and Foundation syllabi, they talk about use cases as something that test analysts receive, upon which they base their tests. So, rather then try to cover the entire gamut of use case variation that might exist in the wild and wooly world of software development, I'm going to talk about using basic, informal use cases for test design, and talk about using more formalized use cases for test design, and leave out too much discussion of the variations.

So, assuming we receive a use case, how do we derive tests? Well, at the very least, we should create a test for every workflow, including both the typical and exceptional workflows. If the exceptional workflows were omitted, then you'll need to figure those out, possibly from requirements or some other source. Failing to test exceptions is a common testing mistake when using informal use cases.

Creating tests can involve applying equivalence partitioning and boundary value analysis along the way. In fact, if you find a situation where combinations of conditions are determining actions, then you might have found an embedded, implied decision table. Covering the partitions, boundaries, and business rules you discover in the use case might result in two, five, ten, twenty, or more test cases per workflow when you're all done.

Remember that I said that a use case has a tangible result. So, part of evaluating the results of the test is verifying that result. That's above and beyond verifying proper screens, messages, input validation, and the like as you proceed through the workflow.

Note the coverage criterion implied above: At least one test per workflow, including both typical and exceptional workflows. That's not a formal criterion, but it's a good one to remember as a rule of thumb.

What is our underlying bug hypothesis? Remember, in decision tables we were looking for combinations of conditions that result in the wrong action occurring or the right action not occurring. With use cases, we're a bit more coarse grained. Here, we are looking for a situation where the system interacts improperly with the user or delivers an improper result.

Example: Informal Use Case

Next, we see an example of an informal use case describing purchases from an e-commerce site, like the rbcs-us.com example shown for decision tables.

At the top, we have the website purchasing normal workflow. This is the happy path.

Note that the final result is that the order is in the system for delivery. Presumably another use case, perhaps called order fulfillment, describes how this order ends up arriving at the customer's home or place of business.

We also see some exception workflows defined. These include trying to check out with an empty shopping cart; providing invalid address, payment, or shipping information; or abandoning the transaction.

Let's look at deriving tests for this use case. In Table 3–23 you see the body of the test to cover the typical workflow. For brevity's sake, I've left off the typical header and footer information found on a test.

As you can see, each step in the workflow has mapped into a step in the test. You can also see that I did some equivalence partitioning and boundary value analysis on the number of items, the payment type, and the delivery address. Because all of these selections are valid, I've combined them. Note the space-saving approach of describing how to repeat the core steps of the test with variations, rather than a complete restatement of the test procedure, at the bottom.

Table 3–23   *Deriving tests (typical)*

#	Test Step	Expected Result
1	Place one item in cart	Item in cart
2	Click check out	Checkout screen
3	Input valid US address, valid payment using American Express, and valid shipping method information	Each screen displays correctly, and valid inputs are accepted
4	Verify order information	Shown as entered
5	Confirm order	Order in system
6	Repeat steps 1–5, but place two items in cart, pay with Visa, and ship internationally	As shown in 1–5
7	Repeat steps 1–5, but place the maximum number of items in cart and pay with MasterCard	As shown in 1–5
8	Repeat steps 1–5, but pay with Discover	As shown in 1–5

In Table 3–24 you see the body of the test to cover the exception flows. You can see that I did equivalence partitioning of the points at which the customer could abandon a transaction.

Table 3–24   *Deriving tests (exception)*

#	Test Step	Expected Result
1	Do not place any items in cart	Cart empty
2	Click check out	Error message
3	Place item in cart, click check out, enter invalid address, then invalid payment, then invalid shipping information	Error messages, can't proceed to next screen until resolved
4	Verify order information	Shown as entered
5	Confirm order	Order in system
6	Repeat steps 1–3, but stop activity and abandon transaction after placing item in cart	User logged out exactly ten minutes after last activity
7	Repeat steps 1–3, but stop activity and abandon transaction on each screen	As shown in 6
8	Repeat steps 1–4; do not confirm order	As shown in 6

Logical and Concrete Tests

This is a good point to review an important distinction, that between logical and concrete tests, that we discussed earlier in Chapter 1.

Now, for the ISTQB exam, you'll want to make sure you know the Glossary definitions for these terms. For our purposes here, we can say that a logical or high-level test describes the test conditions and results. A concrete or low-level test gives the input data to create the test conditions and the output data observed in the results.

As you just saw in Table 3–23 and Table 3–24, you can easily translate a use case into one or more logical tests. However, translation of the logical tests into concrete tests can require additional documentation.

For example, what was the maximum number of items we could put in the shopping cart? We'd need some further information, ideally a requirements specification, to know that. What items can we put in shopping cart? Some description of the store inventory is needed.

Is it cheating to define logical tests rather than concrete tests? No, absolutely not. However, notice that, at some point, a test must become concrete. You have to enter specific inputs. You have to verify specific outputs. This translation from logical test to concrete test is considered an implementation activity in the ISTQB fundamental test process. If you choose to leave implementation of concrete tests for the testers to handle during test execution, that's fine, but you'll need to make sure that adequate information is at hand during test execution to do so. Otherwise, you risk delays.

Elements of a Formal Use Case

So, what's different or additional in a formal use case?

Usually, a formal use case contains more information than an informal one. For example, a formal use case might contain:

- ID—some use case identifier number
- Name—a short name, like E-commerce Purchase
- Actor—the actor, such as customer
- Description—a short description of the use case
- Priority—the priority, from an implementation point of view
- Frequency of use—how often this will occur
- Preconditions—what must be true to start the use case normally
- Typical workflow—often like the informal use case, but sometimes broken into two columns, one for the actor actions and one for the system response
- Exception workflows—one for each exception, often also with actor action and system response columns
- Postconditions—what should be true about the state of the system after the use case completes normally

Notice that some of this information can be useful to you as a test analyst. Some, like the priority and frequency of use, might not be so useful, except during the risk analysis process.

Notice that the breakdown on the workflows, especially the exception workflows, is finer grained, so your test traceability can be finer grained, too.

Example: Formal Use Case

Table 3–25 shows the header information on a formal version of the informal use case we saw earlier.

Table 3–25   *Formal use case (part 1)*

ID	02.001
Name	E-commerce Purchase
Actor	Customer
Description	Allow customer to complete a transaction by purchasing the item(s) in her shopping cart
Priority	Very high
Frequency of use	25% of customers, up to 1,000 customers per day
Preconditions	1. One or more items in shopping cart 2. Customer is logged in 3. Customer has clicked on check out

Notice that some of the steps of the informal use case became preconditions. This means that the shopping portion of the use case would become its own use case, allowing this use case to focus entirely on the purchase aspects of the e-commerce site.

Notice also that we didn't know about that "logged in" requirement before. That's important information for our testing.

Table 3–26 shows the main body of the formal use case, the normal workflow, and the three exceptions. Notice the normal workflow is a bit shorter now because some of its steps became preconditions. Also, each exception is its own row in the table. Finally, notice that the postcondition is true only if the normal workflow ultimately completed.

Table 3–26   *Formal use case (part 2)*

Typical workflow	1. System gathers address, payment, and shipping information from customer. 2. System displays all information for user confirmation. 3. User confirms order to system for delivery.
Exception 1	Customer attempts to check out with empty shopping cart. System gives error message.
Exception 2	Customer provides invalid address, payment, or shipping information. System gives error messages as appropriate.
Exception 3	Customer abandons transaction before or during checkout. System logs customer out after ten minutes of inactivity.
Postconditions	Order is active in system.

Use Case Exercise

Refer to section 001 of the HELLOCARMS system requirements document. Assume that the life insurance discussed in the previous exercise is offered during step 5 of that use case.

The exercise consists of two steps:

1. Translate the informal use case given in section 001 into a slightly more formal version that shows the actor, the preconditions, the exception workflows, and the postconditions. Include the insurance offering.
2. Create logical test cases in a test procedure to cover the use case, applying equivalence partitioning and boundary value analysis as appropriate.

The answers to the two parts are shown on the next pages. You should review the answer to the first part (and, if necessary, revise your answer to the second part) before reviewing the answer to the second part.

Use Case Debrief

For ease of reference, here is the informal use case from section 001 again.

The following informal use case applies for typical transactions in the HELLOCARMS system:

1. A Globobank telephone banker in a Globobank call center receives a phone call from a customer.
2. The telephone banker interviews the customer, entering information into the HELLOCARMS system through a web browser interface on their desktop. If the customer is requesting a large loan or borrowing against a high-value property, the telephone banker escalates the application to a senior telephone banker who decides whether to proceed with the application.
3. Once the telephone banker has gathered the information from the customer, the HELLOCARMS system determines the creditworthiness of the customer using the scoring mainframe.
4. Based on all of the customer information, the HELLOCARMS system displays various home equity products (if any) that the telephone banker can offer to the customer.
5. If the customer chooses one of these products, the telephone banker will conditionally confirm the product.
6. The interview ends. The telephone banker directs the HELLOCARMS system to transmit the loan information to the Loan Document Printing System (LoDoPS) in the Los Angeles data center for origination.
7. The HELLOCARMS system receives an update from the LoDoPS when the following events occur:
   a. LoDoPS sends documents to customer.
   b. Globobank Loan Servicing Center receives signed documents from customer.
   c. Globobank Loan Servicing Center sends check or other materials as appropriate to the customer's product selection.

Notice that step 7 actually belongs in another use case, because, at the end of step six 6, a tangible, useful result has been produced—namely the submitted application.

So, I've moved steps 1 through 6 into a semi-formalized use case, shown in Table 3–27. I've added the life insurance offering in step 5.

Table 3–27 *Semiformal HELLOCARMS use case*

Actor	Telephone Banker
Preconditions	The Globobank telephone banker is logged in to HELLOCARMS system.
Normal Workflow	1. The telephone banker receives a phone call from a customer. 2. The telephone banker interviews the customer, entering information into the HELLOCARMS system through a web browser interface on their desktop. 3. Once the telephone banker has gathered the information from the customer, the HELLOCARMS system determines the creditworthiness of the customer using the scoring mainframe. 4. Based on all of the customer information, the HELLOCARMS system displays various home equity products that the telephone banker can offer to the customer. 5. If the customer chooses one of these products, the telephone banker will conditionally confirm the product. 6. The interview ends. The telephone banker directs the HELLOCARMS system to transmit the loan information to the Loan Document Printing System (LoDoPS) in the Los Angeles data center for origination.
Exception Workflow 1	During step 2 of the normal workflow, if the customer is requesting a large loan or borrowing against a high-value property, the telephone banker escalates the application to a senior telephone banker who decides whether to proceed with the application. If the decision is to proceed, then the telephone banker completes the remainder of step 2 and proceeds normally. If the decision is not to proceed, the telephone banker informs the customer that the application is declined, and the interview ends.
Exception Workflow 2	During step 4 of the normal workflow, if the system does not display any home equity products as available, the telephone banker informs the customer that the application is declined, and the interview ends.

Exception Workflow 3	During step 5 of the normal workflow, if the product chosen by the customer was a home equity loan, the telephone banker offers the customer the option of applying for life insurance to cover the loan. If the customer wants to apply, the following steps occur:
	1. The telephone banker interviews the customer, entering health information into the HELLOCARMS system through a web browser interface on their desktop.
	2. The HELLOCARMS system processes the information as described in the previous exercise. One of two outcomes will occur:
	  a. The HELLOCARMS system declines to offer insurance based on the health information given. The telephone banker informs the customer that the insurance application was denied. This exception workflow is over, and processing returns to step 5.
	  b. The HELLOCARMS system offers insurance at a rate based on the loan size and the health information given. The telephone banker informs the customer of the offer.
	3. The customer makes one of two decisions:
	  a. Accept the offer. The telephone banker makes the life insurance purchase part of the overall application. This exception workflow is over, and processing returns to step 5.
	  b. Reject the offer. The telephone banker excludes the life insurance purchase from the overall application. This exception workflow is over, and processing returns to step 5.

Exception Workflow 4	During any of steps 1 through 5 of the normal workflow, if the customer chooses to end the interview without continuing the process or selecting a product, the application is canceled, and the interview ends.

Exception Workflow 5	If no telephone banker is logged in to the system (e.g., because the system is down) and step 1 of the normal workflow begins, the following steps occur:
	 1. The telephone banker takes the information manually. At the end of the interview, the telephone banker informs the customer that a telephone banker will call back shortly with the decision on the application.
	 2. Once a telephone banker is logged in to the system, the application information is entered into HELLOCARMS, and normal processing resumes at step 2.
	 3. The telephone banker calls the customer once one of the following outcomes has occurred:
	    a. Step 5 of normal processing is reached. Processing continues at step 5.
	    b. At step 2 of normal processing, exception workflow 1 was triggered. Processing continues at step 2.
	    c. At step 4 of normal processing, exception workflow 2 was triggered. No processing remains to be done.

Postconditions	Loan application is in LoDoPS for origination.

Now, I'll create logical tests to cover this use case. I'm going to follow the pattern I've used in the book where I broke the test into a normal workflow test (see Table 3–29) and an exception test for each exception workflow (see Table 3–30, Table 3–31, Table 3–32, Table 3–33, and Table 3–34).

Table 3–28   *Normal workflow test*

#	Test Step	Expected Results
1	Enter a home equity loan application for a creditworthy customer into the HELLOCARMS system.	Validate screens and messages.
2	Submit the customer information for processing of the creditworthiness via the scoring mainframe.	Verify communication with scoring mainframe.
3	Check the various home equity products that can be offered.	Verify appropriate products offered. Validate screen and messages.
4	Choose the home equity loan.	Validate screens and messages.
5	Direct the HELLOCARMS system to transmit the loan information to the Loan Document Printing System (LoDoPS).	Verify communication with LoDoPS.
6	Repeat steps 1–5, but select a home equity line of credit in step 4.	As shown in steps 1–5.
7	Repeat steps 1–5, but select a reverse mortgage in step 4.	As shown in steps 1–5.

Table 3–29   *Exception 1 workflow test*

#	Test Step	Expected Results
1	Enter a home equity loan application for a creditworthy customer into the HELLOCARMS system.	Validate screens and messages.
2	When entering the loan amount, enter a requested loan amount that exceeds the maximum.	Verify escalation screens.
3	Enter the "Proceed" authorization code.	Verify processing resumes at step 2 of the normal workflow.
4	Complete the normal workflow.	Verify loan is properly submitted to LoDoPS.
5	Repeat steps 1–2, but enter a property value that exceeds the maximum, and in step 3 enter the "Decline" authorization code.	Verify that the Decline script shows and that this application is terminated.
6	Repeat steps 1–4, but enter a property value and a loan amount that both exceed the maximum.	As shown in steps 1–4.

Table 3–30   *Exception 2 workflow test*

#	Test Step	Expected Results
1	Enter a home equity loan application for a non-creditworthy customer into the HELLOCARMS system.	Validate screens and messages.
2	Submit the customer information for processing of the creditworthiness via the scoring mainframe.	Verify communication with scoring mainframe.
3	Check the various home equity products that can be offered.	Verify no products offered. Validate screens and messages. Verify that the Decline script shows and that this application is terminated.

Table 3–31   *Exception 3 workflow test*

#	Test Step	Expected Results
1	Enter a home equity loan application for a creditworthy and insurance-qualified customer into the HELLOCARMS system.	Validate screens and messages.
2	Submit the customer information for processing of the credit-worthiness via the scoring mainframe.	Verify communication with scoring mainframe.
3	Check the various home equity products that can be offered. Select the home equity loan. Indicate customer wants to apply for insurance.	Verify appropriate products offered. Validate screens and messages.
4	Enter customer health information.	Validate screens and messages.
5	Check insurance offer, accept the offer, and complete the application, including sending to LoDoPS.	Verify amount of offer. Verify that life insurance application is included in LoDoPS information.
6	Repeat steps 1–5, but decline the offer.	As shown in steps 1–5, but verify that life insurance application is not included in LoDoPS information.
7	Repeat steps 1–5, but use a non-insurance-qualified customer.	As shown in steps 1–5, but verify that no life insurance is offered and that no life insurance application is included in LoDoPS information.

Table 3–32   *Exception 4 workflow test*

#	Test Step	Expected Results
1	Enter a home equity loan application for a creditworthy customer into the HELLOCARMS system.	Validate screens and messages.
2	Submit the customer information for processing of the creditworthiness via the scoring mainframe.	Verify communication with scoring mainframe.
3	Check the various home equity products that can be offered.	Verify appropriate products offered. Validate screens and messages.
4	Indicate that the customer canceled the application.	Validate the screen that displays. Verify that the application is cancelled.
5	Repeat steps 1–2, but cancel on the penultimate screen.	As show in step 4.
6	Repeat step 5, canceling on each of the possible screens including the first screen.	As shown in steps 1–5.
7	Repeat steps 1–5, but select a home equity line of credit in step 4.	As shown in steps 1–5.

Table 3–33   *Exception 5 workflow test*

#	Test Step	Expected Results
1	Activate the "Manual Application Entry" mode. Enter a home equity loan application for a normal loan amount and property value and a creditworthy customer into the HELLOCARMS system.	Validate screens and messages. Verify directive to call customer at step 5 of the normal workflow. Verify normal processing and submission from that point.
2	Repeat step 1, but using a high-loan-amount application. Enter the "Proceed" authorization code when requested.	Validate screens and messages. Verify directive to call customer at step 2 of the normal workflow. Verify normal processing and submission from that point.
3	Repeat step 1, but using a non-creditworthy customer.	Validate screens and messages. Verify directive to call customer at step 4 of the normal workflow. Verify that application is declined.

Notice that I equivalence partitioned the customer as follows:

- Creditworthy
- Not creditworthy

You might also have decided to use boundary value analysis here, based on credit scores, to test customers who were just barely creditworthy and those who were almost creditworthy. I equivalence partitioned the products as follows:

- Home equity loan
- Home equity line of credit
- Reverse mortgage

Again, you might have decided to use boundary value analysis to apply for the largest and smallest possible product in each category. I equivalence partitioned the senior telephone banker decline as follows:

- Property value too high
- Loan too high

I would also want to test the boundary values and equivalence partitions previously identified for this situation in the second exercise for this section.

3.2.6 State Transition Testing

Let's move to the next test technique focused on testing business logic, state-based testing. State-based testing is ideal when we have sequences of events that occur and conditions that apply to those events, and the proper handling of a particular event/condition situation depends on the events and conditions that have occurred in the past. In some cases, the sequences of events can be potentially infinite, which of course exceeds our testing capabilities, but we want to have a test design technique that allows us to handle arbitrarily long sequences of events.

This technique can be applied to any level at testing, in any situation where software exhibits state-based behavior. There are various levels of coverage, which we'll discuss in this section, with the higher levels of coverage associated with higher levels of risk. These levels of coverage can be difficult to achieve in part because properly constructing the state-based models—which are both graphs and tables—can be hard to learn. However, when properly applied, this technique is very powerful, and can find defects in processing, reliability, missing behaviors, and other state-related bugs.

The underlying model is a state transition diagram or table. The diagram or table connects beginning states, events, and conditions with resulting states and actions.

In other words, some status quo prevailed and the system was in a current state. Then some event occurs, some event that the system must handle. The handling of that event might be influenced by one or more conditions. The event/condition combination triggers a state transition, either from the current state to a new state or from the current state back to the current state again. In the course of the transition, the system takes one or more actions.

Given this model, we generate tests that traverse the states and transitions. The inputs trigger events and create conditions, while the expected results of the test are the new states and actions taken by the system.

Differing coverage criteria apply for state-based testing. The weakest criterion requires that the tests visit every state and traverse every transition. This criterion can be applied to state transition diagrams. A higher coverage criterion is at least one test covering every row in a state transition table. Achieving every-row coverage will also achieve every state and transition coverage, which is why I said it was a high coverage criterion.

Another potentially higher coverage criterion requires at least one test covering each transition sequence of N or less length. The N can be 1, 2, 3, 4, or higher. This is called alternatively *Chow's switch coverage*—after the Professor Chow who developed it—or *N-1 switch coverage*, after the level given to the degree of coverage. If you cover all transitions of length one, then N-1 switch coverage means 0-switch coverage. Notice that this is the same as the lowest level of coverage discussed. If you cover all transitions of length one and two, then N-1 switch coverage means 1-switch coverage. This is a higher level of coverage than the lowest level, of course.

Now, 1-switch coverage is not necessarily a higher level of coverage than every-row coverage. This is because the state transition table forces testing of state and event/condition combinations that do not occur in the state transition diagram. The switches in N-1 switch coverage are derived from the state transition diagram, not the state transition table.

All this might be a bit confusing if you're fuzzy on the test design material covered at the Foundation level. This is a common problem for those who took brain cram courses rather than hands-on courses to prepare for the Foundation exam. Don't worry, though; it will be clear to you shortly.[3]

So, what is the bug hypothesis in state-based testing? We're looking for situations where the wrong action or the wrong new state occur in response to a particular event under a given set of conditions based on the history of event/condition combinations so far.

Example: State Transition Diagram

Figure 3–28 shows the state transition diagram for shopping and buying items online from an e-commerce application. It shows the interaction of the system with a customer, from the customer's point of view. Let's walk through it, and I'll point out the key elements of state transition diagrams in general and the features of this one in particular.

First, notice that we have at the leftmost side a small dot-and-arrow element labeled "initial state indicator." This notation shows that, from the customer's point of view, the transaction starts when she starts browsing the website. We can click on links and browse the catalog of items, remaining in a browsing state. Notice the looping arrow above the browsing state. The nodes or bubbles represent states, as shown by the label below the browsing state. The arrows represent transitions, as shown by the label above the looping arrow.

---

3. You can find different explanations of state-based testing in Graham Bath and Judy McKay's *The Software Test Engineer's Handbook* and my own *Pragmatic Software Testing*.

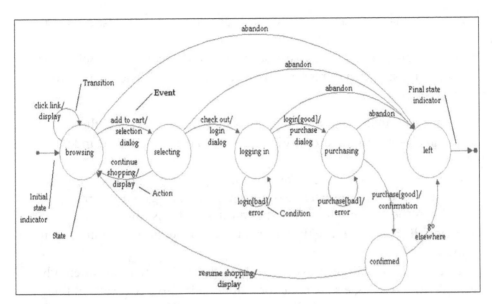

Figure 3–28   *State transition diagram*

Next, we see that we can enter a "selecting" state by adding an item to the shopping cart. The event is "add to cart," as shown by the label above. The system will display a "selection dialog" where we ask the customer to tell us how many of the item she wants, along with any other information we need to add the item to the cart. Once that's done, the customer can tell the system she wants to continue shopping—in which case, the system displays the home screen again, and the customer is back in a browsing state. From a notation point of view, notice that the actions taken by the system are shown under the event and after the slash symbol, on the transition arrow, as shown by the label below.

Alternatively, the customer can choose to check out. At this point, she enters a logging-in state. She enters login information. A condition applies to that login information: either it was good or it was bad. If it was bad, the system displays an error and the customer remains in the logging-in state. If it was good, the system displays the first screen in the purchasing dialog. Notice that the "bad" and "good" shown in brackets are notationally conditions.

While in the purchasing state, the system will display screens, and the customer will enter payment information. That information is either good or bad—conditions again—and determines whether we can complete and confirm the transaction. Once the transaction is confirmed, the customer can either resume shopping or go somewhere else.

Notice also that the user can always abandon the transaction and go elsewhere.

When we talk about state-based testing during our courses, people often ask, "How do I distinguish a state, an event, and an action?" The main distinctions are as follows:

- A state persists, until something happens—something external to the system itself, usually—to trigger a transition. A state can persist for an indefinite period.
- An event occurs, either instantly or in a limited, finite period. It is the something that happened—the external occurrence—that triggered the transition.
- An action is the response the system has during the transition.
- An action, like an event, is either instantaneous or requires a limited, finite period.
- That said, it is sometimes possible to draw the same situation differently, especially when a single state or action can be split into a sequence of finer-grained states, events, and actions. We'll see an example of that in a moment, splitting the purchase state into substates.
- Finally, notice that, at the outset, I said this chart is shown from the customer's point of view. If we drew the diagram from the system's point of view, it would look different. Maintaining a consistent point of view is critical when drawing these diagrams; otherwise nonsensical things will happen.

Deriving Tests (State/Transition Cover)

State-based testing uses a formal model, so we can have a formal procedure for deriving tests from the model. The following is a procedure that will work to derive tests that achieve state/transition coverage (i.e., 0-switch coverage):

1. Adopt a rule for where a test must start and where it may or must end. An example is to say that a test must start in an initial state and may only end in a final state. The reason for the "may" or "must" wording on the ending part is because, in situations where the initial and final states are the same, you might want to allow sequences of states and transitions that pass through the initial state more than once.
2. From an allowed test starting state, define a sequence of event/condition combinations that leads to an allowed test-ending state. For each transition that will occur, capture the expected action that the system should take. This is the expected result.

3. As you visit each state and traverse each transition, mark it as covered. The easiest way to do this is to print the state transition diagram and then use a marker to highlight each node and arrow as you cover it.

4. Repeat steps 2 and 3 until all states have been visited and all transitions traversed. (In other words, every node and arrow has been marked with the marker.)

This procedure will generate logical tests. To create concrete tests, you'd have to generate the actual input values and the actual output values. For this book, I intend to generate logical tests to illustrate the techniques, but remember, as I mentioned before, at some point before execution, the implementation of concrete tests must occur.

Example: Deriving Tests

Let's apply this process to the example e-commerce application we've just looked at. In Figure 3–29 we see two things:

⊕   Rule: A test must start in the initial state and must end in the final state

1.   Generate the first test: (browsing, click link, display, add to cart, selection dialog, continue shopping, display, add to cart, selection dialog, checkout, login dialog, login[bad], error, login[good], purchase dialog, purchase[bad], error, purchase[good], confirmation, resume shopping, display, abandon, left)
     Check completeness of coverage

Figure 3–29   *Deriving tests 1*

1. First, we have the rule that says that a test must start in the initial state and must end in the final state.

2. Next, we generate the first test. (browsing, click link, display, add to cart, selection dialog, continue shopping, display, add to cart, selection dialog, checkout, login dialog, login[bad], error, login[good], purchase dialog, purchase[bad], error, purchase[good], confirmation, resume shopping, display, abandon, left)

At this point, we check completeness of coverage, which we've been keeping track of on our state transition diagram that's shown in Figure 3–30.

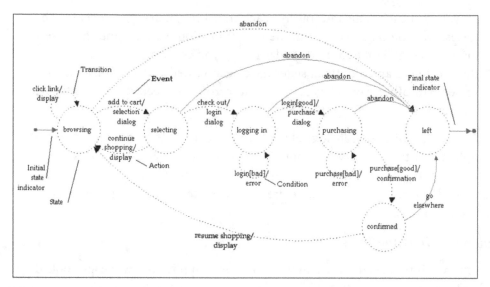

Figure 3–30   *Coverage check 1*

As you can see, we covered all of the states and most transitions, but not all of the transitions. We need to create some more tests.

In Figure 3–31 we see all the tests that were defined to cover the state transition diagram.

1. (browsing, click link, display, add to cart, selection dialog, continue shopping, display, add to cart, selection dialog, checkout, login dialog, login[bad], error, login[good], purchase dialog, purchase[bad], error, purchase[good], confirmation, resume shopping, display, abandon, left)

2. (browsing, add to cart, selection dialog, abandon, <no action>, left)

3. (browsing, add to cart, selection dialog, checkout, login dialog, abandon, <no action>, left)

4. (browsing, add to cart, selection dialog, checkout, login dialog, login[good], purchase dialog, abandon, <no action>, left)

5. (browsing, add to cart, selection dialog, continue shopping, display, add to cart, selection dialog, checkout, login dialog, login[good], purchase dialog, purchase[good], confirmation, go elsewhere, <no action>, left)

Figure 3–31   *Deriving tests 2*

Figure 3–32 shows the coverage tracing for the states and transitions. You're not done generating tests until every state and every transition has been highlighted, as shown here.

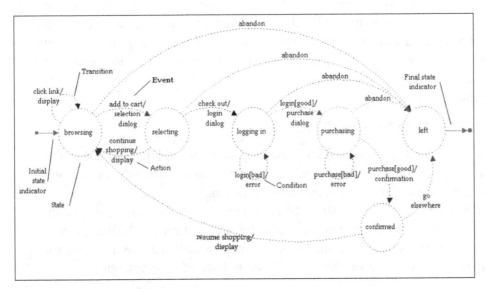

Figure 3–32 *Coverage check 2*

Example: Superstates and Substates

In some cases, it makes sense to unfold a single state into a superstate consisting of two or more substates.

In Figure 3–33 you see that I've taken the purchasing state from the e-commerce example and expanded it into three substates.

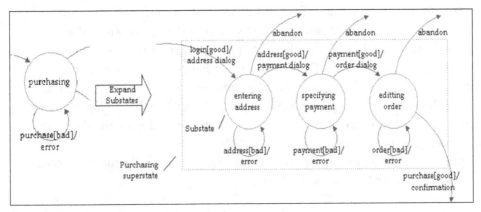

Figure 3–33 *Example: Superstates and substates*

The rule for basic coverage here follows simply. Cover all transitions into the superstate, all transitions out of the superstate, all substates, and all transitions within the superstate.

Notice that, in our example, this would increase the number of tests, because we now have three "abandon" transitions to the "left" state out of the purchasing superstate, rather than just one transition from the purchasing state. This would also add a finer-grained element to our tests—i.e., more events and actions—as well as making sure we tested at least three different types of bad purchasing entries.

Example: State Transition Table

State transition tables are useful because they force us—and the business analysts and the system designers—to consider combinations of states with event/condition combinations that they might have forgotten.

To construct a state transition table, you first list all the states from the state transition diagram. Next, you list all the event/condition combinations shown on the state transition diagram. Then, you create a table that has a row for each state with every event/condition combination. Each row has four fields:

1. Current state
2. Event/condition
3. Action
4. New state

For those rows where the state transition diagram specifies the action and new state for the given combination of current state and event/condition, we can populate those two fields from the state transition diagram. However, for the other rows in the table, we have found undefined situations.

We can now go to the business analysts, system designers, and other such people and ask, "So, what exactly should happen in each of these situations?"

You might hear them say, "Oh, that can never happen!" As a test analyst, you know what that means. Your job now is to figure out how to make it happen.

You might hear them say, "Oh, well, I'd never thought of that." That probably means you just prevented a bug from ever happening, if you are doing test design during system design.

Figure 3–34 shows an excerpt of the table we would create for the e-commerce example we've been looking at so far.

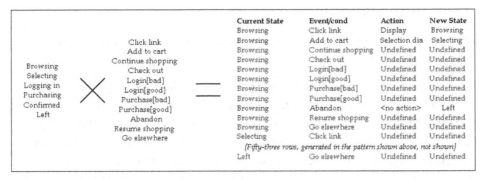

		Current State	Event/cond	Action	New State
	Click link	Browsing	Click link	Display	Browsing
	Add to cart	Browsing	Add to cart	Selection dia	Selecting
Browsing	Continue shopping	Browsing	Continue shopping	Undefined	Undefined
Selecting	Check out	Browsing	Check out	Undefined	Undefined
Logging in	Login[bad]	Browsing	Login[bad]	Undefined	Undefined
Purchasing	Login[good]	Browsing	Login[good]	Undefined	Undefined
Confirmed	Purchase[bad]	Browsing	Purchase[bad]	Undefined	Undefined
Left	Purchase[good]	Browsing	Purchase[good]	Undefined	Undefined
	Abandon	Browsing	Abandon	<no action>	Left
	Resume shopping	Browsing	Resume shopping	Undefined	Undefined
	Go elsewhere	Browsing	Go elsewhere	Undefined	Undefined
		Selecting	Click link	Undefined	Undefined
		{Fifty-three rows, generated in the pattern shown above, not shown}			
		Left	Go elsewhere	Undefined	Undefined

Figure 3–34   *Example: State transition table*

We have six states:

1. Browsing
2. Selecting
3. Logging in
4. Purchasing
5. Confirmed
6. Left

We have eleven event/condition combinations:

1. Click link
2. Add to cart
3. Continue shopping
4. Check out
5. Login[bad]
6. Login[good]
7. Purchase[bad]
8. Purchase[good]
9. Abandon
10. Resume shopping
11. Go elsewhere

That means our state transition table would have sixty-six rows, one for each possible pairing of a specific state with a specific event/condition combination.

Deriving Tests (Row Cover)

To derive a set of tests that covers the state transition table, we can follow the procedure here:

1. Start with a set of tests (including the starting and stopping state rule), derived from a state transition diagram that achieves state/transition cover.
2. Construct the state transition table, and confirm that the tests cover all the defined rows. If they do not, then either you didn't generate the existing set of tests properly, or you didn't generate the table properly, or the state transition diagram is screwed up. Do not proceed until you have identified and resolved the problem, including re-creating the state transition table or the set of tests, if necessary.
3. Select a test that visits a state for which one or more undefined rows exists in the table. Modify that test to attempt to introduce the undefined event/condition combination for that state. Notice that the action in this case is undefined.
4. As you modify the tests, mark the row as covered. The easiest way to do this is to take a printed version of the table and use a marker to highlight each row as covered.
5. Repeat steps 3 and 4 until all rows have been covered.

Notice that we build on an existing set of tests created from the state transition diagram to achieve state/transition or 0-switch cover. Again, this procedure will generate logical tests.

Example: Deriving Tests

Let's look at an example of deriving table-based tests, building on the e-commerce example already shown. We start with an existing test from the larger set of tests derived before:

(browsing, add to cart, selection dialog, checkout, login dialog, login[good], purchase dialog, abandon, <no action>, left)

Now, from here I started to create modified tests to cover undefined browsing event/conditions, and those undefined conditions only:

(browsing, *attempt:* continue shopping, *action undefined*, add to cart, selection dialog, checkout, login dialog, login[good], purchase dialog, abandon, <no action>, left) (browsing, *attempt:* check out, *action undefined*, add to cart, selection dialog, checkout, login dialog, login[good], purchase dialog, abandon, <no action>, left)

There are six other modified tests for browsing. As you can see, it's a mechanical process to generate these tests. As long as you are careful to keep track of which rows you've covered—using the marker trick I mentioned earlier, for example—it's almost impossible to forget a test.

Now, you'll notice that I only included one undefined event/condition combination in each test step. Why? This is a variant of the equivalence partitioning rule that we should not create invalid tests that combine multiple invalids. In this case, each row corresponds to an invalid. If we try to cover two rows in a single test step, we can't be sure the system will remain testable after the first invalid.

Notice that I indicated that the action is undefined. What is the ideal system behavior under these conditions? Well, the best-case scenario is that the undefined event/condition combination is ignored or—better yet—rejected with an intelligent error message. At that point, processing continues normally from there. In the absence of any meaningful input from business analysts, the requirements specification, system designers, or any other authority, I would take the position that any other outcome is a bug, including some inscrutable error message like, "What just happened can't happen." (No, I'm not making that up; an RBCS course attendee once told me she had seen exactly that message when inputting an unexpected value.)

- Existing test
  - (browsing, add to cart, selection dialog, checkout, login dialog, login[good], purchase dialog, abandon, <no action>, left)
- Modified tests (to cover undefined browsing event/conditions only)
  - (browsing, *attempt:* continue shopping, *action undefined*, add to cart, selection dialog, checkout, login dialog, login[good], purchase dialog, abandon, <no action>, left)
  - (browsing, *attempt:* check out, *action undefined*, add to cart, selection dialog, checkout, login dialog, login[good], purchase dialog, abandon, <no action>, left)
  - There are six other modified tests for browsing, not shown...
- Don't try to cover undefined event/conditions combinations for more than one state in any test, because you don't know whether the system will remain testable!
- Best case scenario is that the undefined event/condition combination is ignored or rejected with an intelligent error message, and processing continues normally from there

Figure 3–35 *Example: Deriving tests*

Example: N-1 Switch Coverage

In Figure 3–35 you see the same state transition diagram as before, except that I have replaced the state labels with letters, and the transition labels with numbers. Now, a state/transition pair can be specified as a letter followed by a number. Notice that I'm not bothering to list, in the table below, a letter after the number, because it's unambiguous from the diagram what state we'll be in after the given transition. There is only one arrow labeled with a given number that leads out of a state labeled with a given letter, and that arrow lands on exactly one state.

Table 3–34 contains two types of columns. The first is the state/transition pairs that we must cover to achieve 0-switch coverage. Study this for a moment, and assure yourself that, by designing tests that cover each state/transition pair in the 0-switch columns, you'll achieve state/transition coverage as discussed previously.

Table 3–34   *0-switch and 1-switch table*

0-switch			1-switch								
A1	A2	A9	A1A1	A1A2	A1A9				A9B10	A9B8	A9B3
B10	B8	B3	B10C14	B10C11	B10C4	B8A1	B8A2	B8A9			
C14	C11	C4	C14C14	C14C11	C14C4	C11D13	C11D12	C11D5			
D13	D12	D5	D13D13	D13D12	D13D5	D12F6	D12F7				
F6	F7					F7A1	F7A2	F7A9			

Constructing the 0-switch columns is easy. The first row consists of the first state, with a column for each transition leaving that state. There are at most three transitions from the A state. Repeat that process for each state for which there is an outbound transition. Notice that the E state doesn't have a row, because E is a final state and there's no outbound transition. Notice also that, for this example, there are at most three transitions from any given state. Hence there are three 0-switch columns.

The 1-switch columns are a little trickier to construct, but there's a regularity here that makes it mechanical if you are meticulous. Notice, again, that after each transition occurs in the 0-switch situation, we are left in a state, which is implicit in the 0-switch cells. As mentioned above, there are at most three transitions from any given state. So, that means that, for this example, each 0-switch cell can expand to at most three 1-switch cells.

So, we can take each 0-switch cell for the A row and copy it into three cells in the 1-switch columns, for nine cells for the A row. Now, we ask ourselves, for each triple of cells in the A row of the 1-switch columns, what implicit state did we end up in? We can then refer to the appropriate 0-switch cells to populate the remainder of the 1-switch cell.

Notice that the blank cells in the 1-switch columns indicate situations where we entered a state in the first transition from which there was no outbound transition. In this example, that is the state labeled "E" here in Table 3–35, which was labeled "Left" on the full-size diagram.

So, given a set of state/transition sequences like those shown—whether 0-switch, 1-switch, 2-switch, or even higher—how do we derive tests to cover those sequences and achieve the desired level of coverage? Again, I'm going to build on an existing set of tests created from the state transition diagram to achieve state/transition or 0-switch cover, using the following procedure:

1. Start with a set of tests (including the starting and stopping state rule), derived from a state transition diagram that achieves state/transition cover.
2. Construct the switch table using the technique shown previously. Once you have, confirm that the tests cover all of the cells in the 0-switch columns. If they do not, then either you didn't generate the existing set of tests properly, or you didn't generate the switch table properly, or the state transition diagram is screwed up. Do not proceed until you have identified and resolved the problem, including re-creating the switch table or the set of tests, if necessary. Once you have that done, check for higher-order switches already covered by the tests.
3. Now, using 0-switch sequences as needed, construct a test that reaches a state from which an uncovered higher-order switch sequence originates. Include that switch sequence in the test. Check to see what state this left you in. Ideally, another uncovered higher-order switch sequence originates from this state, but, if not, see if you can use 0-switch sequences to reach such a state. You're crawling around in the state transition diagram looking for ways to cover higher-order sequences. Repeat this for the current test until the test must terminate.
4. As you construct tests, mark the switch sequences as covered once you include them in a test. The easiest way to do this is to take a printed version of the switch table and use a marker to highlight each cell as covered.
5. Repeat steps 3 and 4 until all switch sequences have been covered.

Again, this procedure will generate logical tests.

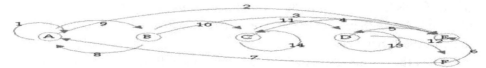

Figure 3–36   *State transition diagram*

In Figure 3–36 and Table 3–35 we see the application of the derivation technique just described to the e-commerce example we've used. After finishing the second step, that of assessing coverage already attained via 0-switch coverage, we can see that most of the table as shown in Table 3–35 is already shaded. Those are the dark grey–shaded cells, which are covered by the five existing state/transition cover tests.

Table 3–35   *0-switch and 1-switch table*

0-switch			1-switch								
A1	A2	A9	A1A1	A1A2	A1A9				A9B10	A9B8	A9B3
B10	B8	B3	B10C14	B10C11	B10C4	B8A1	B8A2	B8A9			
C14	C11	C4	C14C14	C14C11	C14C4	C11D13	C11D12	C11D5			
D13	D12	D5	D13D13	D13D12	D13D5	D12F6	D12F7				
F6	F7					F7A1	F7A2	F7A9			

Now, we generate five new tests to achieve 1-switch cover. Those are shown in Table 3–35. The light grey–shaded cells are covered by five new 1-switch cover tests.

Let me mention something about this algorithm for deriving higher-order switch coverage tests, as well as the one given previously for row coverage tests. Both build on an existing set of tests that achieve state/transition cover. That is efficient from a test design point of view. It's also conservative from a test execution point of view, because we cover the less challenging stuff first, then move on to the more difficult tests.

However, it is quite possible that, starting from scratch, a smaller set of tests could be built, both for the row coverage situation and for the 1-switch coverage situation. If the most important thing is to create the minimum number of tests, then you should look for ways to reduce the tests created, or modify the derivation procedures given here to start from scratch rather than to build on an existing set of 0–switch tests.

Equivalence Partitions, Boundary Values, Decision Tables, and State-Based Testing

Let's finish our discussion on state-based testing by looking at a couple interesting questions. First, how might equivalence partitioning and boundary value analysis combine with state-based testing? The answer is quite well.

From the e-commerce example, suppose that the minimum purchase is $10 and the maximum is $10,000. In that case, we can perform boundary value analysis as shown in Figure 3–37 performed on the purchase[good] and purchase[bad] event/condition combinations. By covering not only transitions, or rows, or transitions sequence, but also boundary values, this forces us to try different purchase amounts.

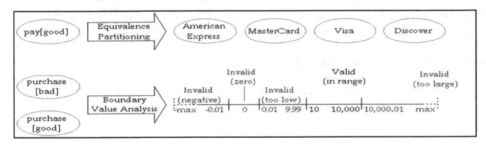

Figure 3–37   *Equivalence partitions and boundary values*

We can also apply equivalence partitioning to the pay[good] event/condition combination. For example, suppose we accept four different types of credit cards. By covering not only transitions, or rows, or transition sequences, but also equivalence partitions, this forces us to try different payment types.

Now, to come full circle on a question I brought up at the start of the discussion on these three business-logic test techniques: When do we use decision tables, and when do we use state diagrams?

This can be, in some cases, a matter of taste. The decision table is nice and compact. If we're not too worried about the higher-order coverage, or the effect of states on the tests, many state-influenced situations can be modeled as decision tables, using conditions to model states. However, if the decision table's conditions section starts to become very long, you're probably stretching the technique. Also, keep in mind that test coverage is usually more thorough using state-based techniques.

In most cases, one technique or the other will clearly fit better. If you are at a loss, try both and see which feels most appropriate.

Telephone Banker States Exercise

This exercise consists of four parts.

1. Using the semiformal use case you developed in the home equity loan insurance exercise, translate that use case into a state transition diagram, shown from the point of view of the telephone banker.
2. Generate test cases to cover the states and transitions (0-switch coverage).
3. Generate a state transition table from the state transition diagram, and create additional error-handling test cases using the state transition table.
4. Generate a switch table to the 1-switch level, and create additional test cases to achieve 1-switch coverage.

The answers to the four parts are shown on the next pages. You should review the answer to each part (and, if necessary, revise your answer to the next part) before reviewing the answer to the next part.

Telephone Banker States Debrief

Figure 3–38 shows the state transition diagram I generated based on the semiformal use case shown in Table 3–28.

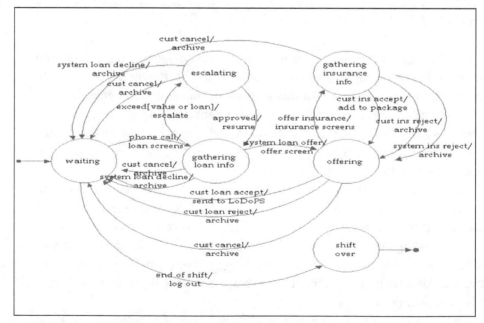

Figure 3–38   *HELLOCARMS state transition diagram*

Let's adopt a rule that says that any test must start in the initial waiting state and may only end in the waiting state or the shift over state. To achieve state and transition coverage, the following tests will suffice:

1. (waiting, phone call, loan screens, exceed[value], escalate, approved, resume, system loan offer, offer screen, offer insurance, insurance screens, cust ins accept, add to package, cust loan accept, send to LoDoPS, waiting)
2. (waiting, phone call, loan screens, exceed[loan], escalate, approved, resume, system loan offer, offer screen, offer insurance, insurance screens, cust ins reject, archive, cust loan accept, send to LoDoPS, waiting)
3. (waiting, phone call, loan screens, system loan offer, offer screen, offer insurance, insurance screens, system ins reject, archive, cust loan reject, archive, waiting)
4. (waiting, phone call, loan screens, exceed[loan], escalate, system loan decline, archive, waiting)
5. (waiting, phone call, loan screens, system loan decline, archive, waiting)
6. (waiting, phone call, loan screens, cust cancel, archive, waiting)
7. (waiting, phone call, loan screens, exceed[loan], escalate, cust cancel, archive, waiting)
8. (waiting, phone call, loan screens, system loan offer, offer screen, cust cancel, archive, waiting)
9. (waiting, phone call, loan screens, system loan offer, offer screen, offer insurance, insurance screens, cust cancel, archive, waiting)
10. (waiting, end of shift, log out, shift over)

Notice that I didn't do an explicit boundary value or equivalence partitioning testing of, say, the loan amount or the property value, though I certainly could have.

Next, let's generate the state transition table. Notice that there are six distinct states:

1. Waiting
2. Gathering loan info
3. Escalating
4. Offering
5. Gathering insurance info
6. Shift over

There are thirteen distinct event/condition combinations:

1. Phone call
2. Exceed[value or loan]
3. Approved
4. System loan decline
5. System loan offer
6. Offer insurance
7. Cust ins accept
8. Cust ins reject
9. System ins reject
10. Cust loan accept
11. Cust loan reject
12. Cust cancel
13. End of shift

Therefore, there are seventy-eight rows in the state transition table, shown in Table 3–36.

Table 3–36   *HELLOCARMS state transition table*

#	Current State	Event/Condition	Action	New State
1.	waiting	phone call	loan screens	gathering loan info
2.		exceed[value or loan]	undefined	undefined
3.		approved	undefined	undefined
4.		system loan decline	undefined	undefined
5.		system loan offer	undefined	undefined
6.		offer insurance	undefined	undefined
7.		cust ins accept	undefined	undefined
8.		cust ins reject	undefined	undefined
9.		system ins reject	undefined	undefined
10.		cust loan accept	undefined	undefined
11.		cust loan reject	undefined	undefined
12.		cust cancel	undefined	undefined
13.		end of shift	undefined	undefined

#	Current State	Event/Condition	Action	New State
14.	gathering loan info	phone call	undefined	undefined
15.		exceed[value or loan]	escalate	escalating
16.		approved	undefined	undefined
17.		system loan decline	archive	waiting
18.		system loan offer	offer screen	offering
19.		offer insurance	undefined	undefined
20.		cust ins accept	undefined	undefined
21.		cust ins reject	undefined	undefined
22.		system ins reject	undefined	undefined
23.		cust loan accept	undefined	undefined
24.		cust loan reject	undefined	undefined
25.		cust cancel	archive	waiting
26.		end of shift	undefined	undefined
27.	escalating	phone call	undefined	undefined
28.		exceed[value or loan]	undefined	undefined
29.		approved	resume	gathering loan info
30.		system loan decline	archive	waiting
31.		system loan offer	undefined	undefined
32.		offer insurance	undefined	undefined
33.		cust ins accept	undefined	undefined
34.		cust ins reject	undefined	undefined
35.		system ins reject	undefined	undefined
36.		cust loan accept	undefined	undefined
37.		cust loan reject	undefined	undefined
38.		cust cancel	archive	waiting
39.		end of shift	undefined	undefined

#	Current State	Event/Condition	Action	New State
40.	offering	phone call	undefined	undefined
41.		exceed[value or loan]	undefined	undefined
42.		approved	undefined	undefined
43.		system loan decline	undefined	undefined
44.		system loan offer	undefined	undefined
45.		offer insurance	insurance screens	gather insurance info
46.		cust ins accept	undefined	undefined
47.		cust ins reject	undefined	undefined
48.		system ins reject	undefined	undefined
49.		cust loan accept	send to LoDoPS	Waiting
50.		cust loan reject	archive	waiting
51.		cust cancel	archive	waiting
52.		end of shift	undefined	undefined
53.	gathering insurance info	phone call	undefined	undefined
54.		exceed[value or loan]	undefined	undefined
55.		approved	undefined	undefined
56.		system loan decline	undefined	undefined
57.		system loan offer	undefined	undefined
58.		offer insurance	undefined	undefined
59.		cust ins accept	add to package	offering
60.		cust ins reject	archive	offering
61.		system ins reject	archive	offering
62.		cust loan accept	undefined	undefined
63.		cust loan reject	undefined	undefined
64.		cust cancel	archive	waiting
65.		end of shift	undefined	undefined

#	Current State	Event/Condition	Action	New State
66.	shift over	phone call	undefined	undefined
67.		exceed[value or loan]	undefined	undefined
68.		approved	undefined	undefined
69.		system loan decline	undefined	undefined
70.		system loan offer	undefined	undefined
71.		offer insurance	undefined	undefined
72.		cust ins accept	undefined	undefined
73.		cust ins reject	undefined	undefined
74.		system ins reject	undefined	undefined
75.		cust loan accept	undefined	undefined
76.		cust loan reject	undefined	undefined
77.		cust cancel	undefined	undefined
78.		end of shift	undefined	undefined

To achieve row coverage, I add the following tests:

11. (waiting, *attempt*: exceed[value or loan], *action undefined*, end of shift, log out, shift over)
12. (waiting, *attempt*: approved, *action undefined*, end of shift, log out, shift over)
13. (waiting, *attempt*: system loan decline, *action undefined*, end of shift, log out, shift over)
14. (waiting, *attempt*: system loan offer, *action undefined*, end of shift, log out, shift over)
15. (waiting, *attempt*: offer insurance, *action undefined*, end of shift, log out, shift over)
16. (waiting, *attempt*: cust ins accept, *action undefined*, end of shift, log out, shift over)
17. (waiting, *attempt*: cust ins reject, *action undefined*, end of shift, log out, shift over)
18. (waiting, *attempt*: system ins reject, *action undefined*, end of shift, log out, shift over)
19. (waiting, *attempt*: cust loan accept, *action undefined*, end of shift, log out, shift over)
20. (waiting, *attempt*: cust loan reject, *action undefined*, end of shift, log out, shift over)

21. (waiting, *attempt*: cust cancel, *action undefined*, end of shift, log out, shift over)

22. (waiting, *attempt*: end of shift, *action undefined*, end of shift, log out, shift over)

23. (waiting, phone call, loan screens, *attempt*: phone call, *action undefined*, cust cancel, archive, end of shift, log out, shift over)

24. (waiting, phone call, loan screens, *attempt*: exceed[value or loan], *action undefined*, cust cancel, archive, end of shift, log out, shift over)

25. (waiting, phone call, loan screens, *attempt*: approved, *action undefined*, cust cancel, archive, end of shift, log out, shift over)

26. (waiting, phone call, loan screens, *attempt*: offer insurance, *action undefined*, cust cancel, archive, end of shift, log out, shift over)

27. (waiting, phone call, loan screens, *attempt*: cust ins accept, *action undefined*, cust cancel, archive, end of shift, log out, shift over).

28. (waiting, phone call, loan screens, *attempt*: cust ins reject, *action undefined*, cust cancel, archive, end of shift, log out, shift over)

29. (waiting, phone call, loan screens, *attempt*: system ins reject, *action undefined*, cust cancel, archive, end of shift, log out, shift over)

30. (waiting, phone call, loan screens, *attempt*: cust loan accept, *action undefined*, cust cancel, archive, end of shift, log out, shift over)

31. (waiting, phone call, loan screens, *attempt*: cust loan reject, *action undefined*, cust cancel, archive, end of shift, log out, shift over)

32. (waiting, phone call, loan screens, *attempt*: end of shift, *action undefined*, cust cancel, archive, end of shift, log out, shift over)

33. (waiting, phone call, loan screens, exceed[loan], escalate, *attempt*: phone call, *action undefined*, cust cancel, archive, end of shift, log out, shift over)

34. (waiting, phone call, loan screens, exceed[value], escalate, *attempt*: exceed[value], *action undefined*, cust cancel, archive, end of shift, log out, shift over)

35. (waiting, phone call, loan screens, exceed[value], escalate, *attempt*: system loan offer, *action undefined*, cust cancel, archive, end of shift, log out, shift over)

36. (waiting, phone call, loan screens, exceed[value], escalate, *attempt*: offer insurance, *action undefined*, cust cancel, archive, end of shift, log out, shift over)

37. (waiting, phone call, loan screens, exceed[value], escalate, *attempt*: cust ins accept, *action undefined*, cust cancel, archive, end of shift, log out, shift over)

38. (waiting, phone call, loan screens, exceed[value], escalate, *attempt*: cust ins reject, *action undefined*, cust cancel, archive, end of shift, log out, shift over)

39. (waiting, phone call, loan screens, exceed[value], escalate, *attempt*: system ins reject, *action undefined*, cust cancel, archive, end of shift, log out, shift over)

40. (waiting, phone call, loan screens, exceed[value], escalate, *attempt*: cust loan accept, *action undefined*, cust cancel, archive, end of shift, log out, shift over)

41. (waiting, phone call, loan screens, exceed[value], escalate, *attempt*: cust loan reject, *action undefined*, cust cancel, archive, end of shift, log out, shift over)

42. (waiting, phone call, loan screens, exceed[value], escalate, *attempt*: end of shift, *action undefined*, cust cancel, archive, end of shift, log out, shift over)

43. (waiting, phone call, loan screens, system loan offer, offer screen, *attempt*: phone call, *action undefined*, cust cancel, archive, end of shift, log out, shift over)

44. (waiting, phone call, loan screens, system loan offer, offer screen, *attempt*: exceed[loan], *action undefined*, cust cancel, archive, end of shift, log out, shift over)

45. (waiting, phone call, loan screens, system loan offer, offer screen, *attempt*: approved, *action undefined*, cust cancel, archive, end of shift, log out, shift over)

46. (waiting, phone call, loan screens, system loan offer, offer screen, *attempt*: system loan decline, *action undefined*, cust cancel, archive, end of shift, log out, shift over)

47. (waiting, phone call, loan screens, system loan offer, offer screen, *attempt*: system loan offer, *action undefined*, cust cancel, archive, end of shift, log out, shift over)

48. (waiting, phone call, loan screens, system loan offer, offer screen, *attempt*: cust ins accept, *action undefined*, cust cancel, archive, end of shift, log out, shift over)

49. (waiting, phone call, loan screens, system loan offer, offer screen, *attempt*: cust ins reject, *action undefined*, cust cancel, archive, end of shift, log out, shift over)

50. (waiting, phone call, loan screens, system loan offer, offer screen, *attempt*: system ins reject, *action undefined*, cust cancel, archive, end of shift, log out, shift over)

51. (waiting, phone call, loan screens, system loan offer, offer screen, *attempt*: end of shift, *action undefined*, cust cancel, archive, end of shift, log out, shift over)

52. (waiting, phone call, loan screens, system loan offer, offer screen, offer insurance, insurance screens, *attempt*: phone call, *action undefined*, cust cancel, archive, end of shift, log out, shift over)

53. (waiting, phone call, loan screens, system loan offer, offer screen, offer insurance, insurance screens, *attempt*: exceed[loan], *action undefined*, cust cancel, archive, end of shift, log out, shift over)

54. (waiting, phone call, loan screens, system loan offer, offer screen, offer insurance, insurance screens, *attempt*: approved, *action undefined*, cust cancel, archive, end of shift, log out, shift over)

55. (waiting, phone call, loan screens, system loan offer, offer screen, offer insurance, insurance screens, *attempt*: system loan decline, *action undefined*, cust cancel, archive, end of shift, log out, shift over)

56. (waiting, phone call, loan screens, system loan offer, offer screen, offer insurance, insurance screens, *attempt*: system loan offer, *action undefined*, cust cancel, archive, end of shift, log out, shift over)

57. (waiting, phone call, loan screens, system loan offer, offer screen, offer insurance, insurance screens, *attempt*: offer insurance, *action undefined*, cust cancel, archive, end of shift, log out, shift over)

58. (waiting, phone call, loan screens, system loan offer, offer screen, offer insurance, insurance screens, *attempt*: cust loan accept, *action undefined*, cust cancel, archive, end of shift, log out, shift over)

59. (waiting, phone call, loan screens, system loan offer, offer screen, offer insurance, insurance screens, *attempt*: cust loan reject, *action undefined*, cust cancel, archive, end of shift, log out, shift over)

60. (waiting, phone call, loan screens, system loan offer, offer screen, offer insurance, insurance screens, *attempt*: end of shift, *action undefined*, cust cancel, archive, end of shift, log out, shift over)

61. (waiting, end of shift, log out, *attempt*: phone call, *action undefined*, shift over)

62. (waiting, end of shift, log out, *attempt*: exceed[value], *action undefined*, shift over)

63. (waiting, end of shift, log out, *attempt*: approved, *action undefined*, shift over)

64. (waiting, end of shift, log out, *attempt*: system loan decline, *action undefined*, shift over)

65. (waiting, end of shift, log out, *attempt*: system loan offer, *action undefined*, shift over)

66. (waiting, end of shift, log out, *attempt*: offer insurance, *action undefined*, shift over)

67. (waiting, end of shift, log out, *attempt*: cust ins accept, *action undefined*, shift over)

68. (waiting, end of shift, log out, *attempt*: cust ins reject, *action undefined*, shift over)

69. (waiting, end of shift, log out, *attempt*: system ins reject, *action undefined*, shift over)

70. (waiting, end of shift, log out, *attempt*: cust loan accept, *action undefined*, shift over)

71. (waiting, end of shift, log out, *attempt*: cust loan reject, *action undefined*, shift over)

72. (waiting, end of shift, log out, *attempt*: cust cancel, *action undefined*, shift over)

73. (waiting, end of shift, log out, *attempt*: end of shift, *action undefined*, shift over)

Note that forcing an "end of shift, log out, shift over" sequence at the end of each test reduces the likelihood that the any error condition created during the test could interfere with subsequent results.

As discussed earlier, these tests are conservative in that each undefined event is tried on its own. During test execution, if testers find that the system ignores undefined events robustly, these tests could be incorporated into other tests and the number of tests reduced.

Now, to generate the switch table to the 1-switch level, I first simplified the state transition diagram with the letter-and-number nomenclature shown. This version is shown in Figure 3–39.

From the diagram, I can generate the 1-switch table shown in Table 3–37. Notice that I have used patterns in the diagram to generate the table. For example, the maximum number of outbound transitions for any state in the diagram is four, so I use four columns on both the 0-switch and 1-switch columns. I started with six 1-switch rows per 0-switch row, because there are six states, though I was able to delete most of those rows as I went along. This leads to a sparse table, but who cares as long as it makes generating this beast easier.

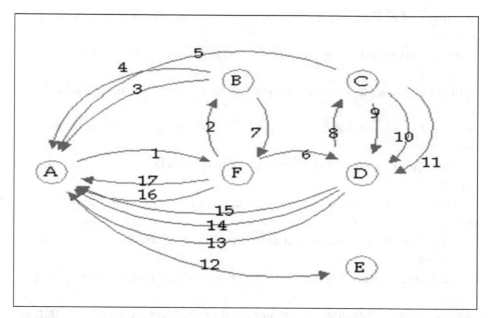

Figure 3–39   *HELLOCARMS state transition diagram for 1-switch table*

Table 3–37   *HELLOCARMS switch table*

0-switch				1-switch			
A1	A12			A1F2	A1F6	A1F16	A1F17
B3	B4	B7		B3A1	B3A12		
				B4A1	B4A12		
				B7F2	B7F6	B7F16	B7F17
C5	C9	C10	C11	C5A1	C5A12		
				C9D8	C9D13	C9D14	C9D15
				C10D8	C10D13	C10D14	C10D15
				C11D8	C11D13	C11D14	C11D15
D8	D13	D14	D15	D8C5	D8C9	D8C10	D8C11
				D13A1	D13A12		
				D14A1	D14A12		
				D15A1	D15A12		
F2	F6	F16	F17	F2B3	F2B4	F2B7	
				F6D8	F6D13	F6D14	F6D15
				F16A1	F16A12		
				F17A1	F17A12		

Now, having generated the table, I can check to see what's already covered by the existing tests. Notice that the row coverage–generated tests don't count, because you don't want to assume that anything that happens after the invalid event is typical.

Here are the existing tests, rewritten using the letter-number nomenclature to make the coverage check easier.

1. (A1 F2 B7 F6 D8 C9 D15)
2. (A1 F2 B7 F6 D8 C10 D15)
3. (A1 F6 D8 C11 D14)
4. (A1 F2 B4)
5. (A1 F16)
6. (A1 F17)
7. (A1 F2 B3)
8. (A1 F6 D13)
9. (A1 F6 D8 C5)
10. (A12)

The coverage analysis is shown in Table 3–38.

Table 3–38   *HELLOCARMS switch table with 0-switch coverage*

0-switch				1-switch			
A1	A12			A1F2	A1F6	A1F16	A1F17
B3	B4	B7		B3A1	B3A12		
				B4A1	B4A12		
				B7F2	B7F6	B7F16	B7F17
C5	C9	C10	C11	C5A1	C5A12		
				C9D8	C9D13	C9D14	C9D15
				C10D8	C10D13	C10D14	C10D15
				C11D8	C11D13	C11D14	C11D15
D8	D13	D14	D15	D8C5	D8C9	D8C10	D8C11
				D13A1	D13A12		
				D14A1	D14A12		
				D15A1	D15A12		
F2	F6	F16	F17	F2B3	F2B4	F2B7	
				F6D8	F6D13	F6D14	F6D15
				F16A1	F16A12		
				F17A1	F17A12		

Now, I generate additional tests to achieve 1-switch coverage. To keep this simple, I've used the letter-number nomenclature, though eventually I'd need to translate back into the logical test case style of a full sequence of events and actions, with starting and ending state.

74. (A1 F2 B3 A1 F16 A1 F2 B3 A12)
75. (A1 F2 B4 A1 F2 B4 A12)
76. (A1 F2 B7 F2 B7 F16 A12)
77. (A1 F2 B7 F2 B7 F17 A12)
78. (A1 F17 A1 F6 D14)
79. (A1 F6 D14)
80. (A1 F6 D8 C5 A1 F6 D8 C5 A12)
81. (A1 F6 D8 C9 D8 C9 D13 A12)
82. (A1 F6 D8 C10 D8 C9 D14 A1 F6 D15 A1 F6 D14 A12)
83. (A1 F6 D8 C10 D8 C10 D14)
84. (A1 F6 D8 C10 D13 A1 F17)
85. (A1 F6 D8 C10 D15 A12)
86. (A1 F6 D8 C11 D8 C11 D14)

Notice that much of the testing involves creating tests that go back into a waiting state and then start a new application without logging out. If I were really focused on test execution efficiency, I could compress some of these tests into the initial test set just by requiring that the first ten tests be run sequentially with no log out between them.

   Notice that the 1-switch tests cover two flows that might be impossible:

- Escalating the application more than once for senior telephone banker approval
- Offering insurance more than once during the same application

You'd need to check with the business analysts and system designers to see if the system should allow this. Full 1-switch coverage is shown in Table 3–39.

Table 3–39   *HELLOCARMS switch table with 0-switch and 1-switch coverage*

0-switch				1-switch			
A1	A12			A1F2	A1F6	A1F16	A1F17
B3	B4	B7		B3A1	B3A12		
				B4A1	B4A12		
				B7F2	B7B6	B7F16	B7F17
C5	C9	C10	C11	C5A1	C5A12		
				C9D8	C9D13	C9D14	C9D15
				C10D8	C10D13	C10D14	C10D15
				C11D8	C11D13	C11D14	C11D15
D8	D13	D14	D15	D8C5	D8C9	D8C10	D8C11
				D13A1	D13A12		
				D14A1	D14A12		
				D15A1	D15A12		
F2	F6	F16	F17	F2B3	F2B4	F2B7	
				F6D8	F6D13	F6D14	F6D15
				F16A1	F16A12		
				F17A1	F17A12		

3.2.7 Combinatorial Testing Techniques

For the last three techniques we've discussed—decision tables, use cases, and state-based testing—there has been a discernable, analyzable way in which factors interact. For decision tables and their graphical cousins, cause-effect graphs, we see the interaction between conditions and system actions. For use cases, we see how certain conditions are handled normally, while others result in exception handling. For state-based tests, events and conditions act on the system, based on its state, resulting in actions and state transitions.

What about situations where the interaction of the factors cannot be so easily determined, or even where there is supposed to be no interaction? For example, if you are testing compatibility of a browser-based application with the various browser types and versions, connection speeds, operating system types and versions and patch levels, and virus and spyware scanning programs, you have four main factors, each with close to a dozen or so options. Your application should run properly, regardless of the configuration, but will it? The only way to know for sure is to test all the possible configurations, but that's impossible here. If you have four factors, each with a dozen options, you have $12 \times 12 \times 12 \times 12$—or 20,736—distinct configurations.

Combinatorial techniques allow us to try to control this combinatorial explosion, when we have unconstrained options. There are three specific techniques we'll look at for selecting a subset of all possible combinations of options, with classification trees being the most flexible and powerful. All-pairs tables and orthogonal arrays require that the options be independent and compatible, but classification trees allow constraints. All three techniques can be used at any test level where combinations of options are an issue, which is usually integration test, system test, and acceptance test, but not component test—at least if your programmers are writing their code properly! All-pairs tables and orthogonal arrays generate only pairs of options across the possible pairs of factors, but classification trees also can create tables with single instances of some options and high-order combinations of other options.

As you can imagine, these techniques are good at finding bugs related to undesired interactions between pairs of options, so you must carefully identify the factors and the options to ensure they are tested. Also, you must accept that high-order interactions will probably not be tested, except by accident. If you have reason to think that particular combinations of options will be problematic, you should use domain analysis or decision tables to identify those combinations.[4]

Conceptually, in pairwise testing we make sure that each option is represented in at least one test configuration, that each possible pair of options is represented in at least one test configuration, and that each option and pair of options is represented about equally as a percentage of the total configurations. Not all possible higher-order combinations, such as triples, quadruples, quintuples, and so forth, will be covered.

What I meant a moment ago by "unconstrained options" was that, for the most part, the options are independent of each other. Any option for any factor can coexist with any other option for any other factor. Configuration testing is a classic example of that. We have different software versions that should all cohabit and interact appropriately on a computer. Any situation where they don't get along is a bug.

Okay, so what's our model for pairwise testing? There are two basic models. One is called an *orthogonal array*. The other is called an *all-pairs table*. Both are tables. The tables, read row-wise, will tell you which particular options to include in a given test configuration. The tables are created either directly (in

---

4. You can find another discussion of combinatorial testing in Tim Koomen, et al.'s book *TMAP Next*.

ISTQB Glossary

Domain analysis: A black-box test design technique that is used to identify efficient and effective test cases when multiple variables can or should be tested together. It builds on and generalizes equivalence partitioning and boundary values analysis. See also boundary value analysis, equivalence partitioning.

Orthogonal array: A two-dimensional array constructed with special mathematical properties, such that choosing any two columns in the array provides every pair combination of each number in the array.

Orthogonal array testing: A systematic way of testing all-pairs combinations of variables using orthogonal arrays. It significantly reduces the number of all combinations of variables to test all pair combinations.

the case of the all-pairs table) or by mapping the test problem to be solved onto an existing table (in the case of the orthogonal array). By their nature, the tables are guaranteed to contain all existing options for every factor at least once and every pair of options across all pairs of factors.

Our coverage criterion for these tables is obvious, given that statement: We need to have each row represented in at least one test. By doing so, we will have tested every option for every factor at least once, and every pair of options across all pairs of factors at least once.

The bug hypothesis is that this level of coverage will suffice. In other words, if there are going to be problems with options, most of those problems will arise either from a single instance of an option or from a given pair of options. The problems that are specific to triples, quadruples, and so forth—the higher-order combinatorial problems—are less likely.

Orthogonal Arrays and All-Pairs Tables

There are two basic approaches to pairwise testing, as I mentioned a moment ago. The first is to use orthogonal arrays. There are plenty of these available on the Internet and in various textbooks. For example, there are online libraries of orthogonal arrays.[5]

Alternatively, you can use a tool to build all-pairs tables. Again, an Internet search will reveal a fair number of these. A clearinghouse for pairwise testing

---

5. At the time of writing, one such library was located at www.york.ac.uk/depts/maths/tables/orthogonal.htm.

tools, both freeware and commercial, can be found online.[6] You can use the tools listed on that site to build classification trees, which I'll explain later in this section.

There is a subtle difference between orthogonal arrays and all-pairs tables. The number of rows will often differ, as will the number of times each pair of options is represented. For compatibility testing, this is usually not important.

For this book, I'm going to demonstrate the use of orthogonal arrays to do pairwise testing. If you decide to use a tool, you'll follow the directions that come with it.

Figure 3–40 shows the simplest possible orthogonal array. There are two factors, factor 1 and factor 2. Each factor has two options, zero and one. As you can see, each option for each factor is represented in the orthogonal array. Further, each pair of options across the two factors is represented in one (and only one) row.

Test	Factor	
	1	2
1	0	0
2	0	1
3	1	0
4	1	1

Figure 3–40   *Simple orthogonal array*

Okay, this not a surprise. There are two options, and there are four rows. Surprise, surprise, two times two is four. So far, nothing very interesting happening with orthogonal arrays.

Figure 3–41 is where the interesting things start to happen. We have a slightly larger orthogonal array. There are three factors. There are two options for each factor. But there are still only four rows.

Test	Factor		
	1	2	3
1	0	0	0
2	0	1	1
3	1	0	1
4	1	1	0

Figure 3–41   *Larger orthogonal array*

---

6. At the time of writing, this site was www.pairwise.org.

How did that happen? Are we missing pairs? Nope, we're not. Notice that there are four pairs for each pair of factors, as before. So, let's enumerate them:

1. For the first pair of factors, factor 1 and factor 2, we have 00, 01, 10, and 11, in rows 1, 2, 3, and 4.
2. For the second pair of factors, factor 1 and factor 3, we have 00, 01, 11, and 10, in rows 1, 2, 3, and 4. All four pairs, just occurring in a different row.
3. For the third pair of factors, factor 2 and factor 3, we have 00, 11, 01, and 10, in rows 1, 2, 3, and 4. All four pairs, again, just occurring in a different row than the previous pairs of factors.
4. Now, if we wanted all the triples, notice, we would have to have eight rows. However, in pairwise testing, I've explicitly renounced any intention of achieving that level of coverage. I'm going to assume that testing every option for every factor, and every pair of options for every pair of factors, will suffice.

Now, the orthogonal array we just looked at isn't very interesting for testing. We can only deal with situations with three factors, which might suffice in some cases, but, more importantly, we can only deal with two options per factor. How can we select an orthogonal array that will fit the testing problem we have?

There are three rules to selecting an orthogonal array.

First, there must be at least as many columns as factors. Now, it's often the case that you'll find an array with too many columns. No problem. If there are too many columns, you can drop the extra columns.

Second, there must be at least enough numbers in the columns to hold the options for each factor. In the previous examples, there were only two numbers, zero and one. If you have three options for a factor, you'd have to have at least three numbers, zero, one, and two. Again, you'll often find an array with too many numbers. Not a problem. Spare numbers that don't map to any option can be replaced by any valid option for that factor, this being referred to as "tester's choice" and usually shown with a tilde "~".

Third, there must be at least as many rows as the product of the two largest numbers of options. For example, if one factor has four options, and another has three, and yet another has two, then you need to have at least four times three or twelve rows. Again, you'll often find an array with too many rows. Here we have something of a problem. If there are too many rows, you cannot drop them if interesting pairs exist in the rows. So, you'll have to scrutinize rows, two at a time, to see if you can combine them using the "tester's choice" options.

Having selected an orthogonal array, you then map your testing problem onto it. Follow the process here:

1. Drop any extra columns that you might have.
2. Map factors to the columns by adding column headings.
3. Select one column at a time, and map the options for that factor onto the numbers. In other words, replace each instance of "0" with the first option for that factor, each instance of "1" with the second option for that factor, and so forth. Using Word or Excel's Find and Replace commands makes this easy. If you finish this process and there are still numbers in the column, re-place those numbers with tildes to indicate tester's choice. Now, you can stop here, but often at this point you'll have more rows than you need. If it takes an hour or more to test each configuration and you aren't looking for ways to fill spare time during test execution, you should continue to step four.
4. Drop any extra rows with no interesting single options or pairs of options. In other words, any row that consists of all tildes can be deleted. Any pair of rows where one row has tildes where another row has options and vice versa, and any option specified in each row is the same, you can merge the two rows.
5. You can run this step now or during test execution. For any spare cells—the ones that still have tildes—you can specify options that will make for easier tests, or to cover popular configurations, or whatever else you like. As I said, it's tester's choice.

This process is entirely mechanical and very easy to do in Excel or Word. You simply import the text file orthogonal array that you downloaded into Excel or Word, and follow these five steps.

By the way, during the mapping process, you'll find out quickly if you made a mistake in your selection of an orthogonal array. One warning sign will be that the mapping process will fail because of insufficient columns or options. Another, somewhat subtler, is that you'll have a large number of rows with all or mostly tildes.

Example: Pairwise Techniques

Okay, enough discussion about this process; let's see an example. Let's return to the example of testing the www.rbcs-us.com Web site. In particular, let's assume we want to do compatibility testing during the functional tests by ensuring that proper combinations of configurations are used.

There are four factors we are interested in, each having two, three, or four options.

The first factor is connection speed. We have two options: relatively low-speed Wi-Fi and high-speed wired.

The second factor is the operating system. We have four options: Mac, Linux, Windows 7, and Windows 8.

The third factor is the security settings. We have four options: native operating system security only, Symantec's product, Trend Micro's product, and McAfee's product.

The fourth factor is the browser. We have three options: Firefox, Internet Explorer, and Chrome.

So, we need an array with four columns, one for each factor. Now, if we could find one, we could use an array with two numbers in one column, three in another column, and four in the other two columns. However, arrays are usually symmetrical in the numbers they have in each column, so we'll probably end up with four numbers per column. Since the two factors with the largest number of options, security settings and operating system, each have four options, we need sixteen rows.

In Figure 3–42 you see the selection and mapping of the orthogonal array. In the middle of Figure 3–42 you see the text file array that I found.

Saving this file to the hard disk, importing it into Excel, adding the column headings, and doing a search-and-replace on each column took less than five minutes. So, the mapping is done.

Since this array is a perfect fit, we can skip step four, the compression of rows.

	Test	Speed	OS	Security	Browser
00000	1	wifi	Mac	OS	Firefox
01111	2	wifi	Linux	Symantec	IE
02222	3	wifi	W7	Trend	Chrome
03333	4	wifi	W8	McAfee	~
10123	5	wired	Mac	Symantec	Chrome
11032	6	wired	Linux	OS	~
12301	7	wired	W7	McAfee	Firefox
13210	8	wired	W8	Trend	IE
20231	9	~	Mac	Trend	~
21320	10	~	Linux	McAfee	Chrome
22013	11	~	W7	OS	IE
23102	12	~	W8	Symantec	Firefox
30312	13	~	Mac	McAfee	IE
31203	14	~	Linux	Trend	Firefox
32130	15	~	W7	Symantec	~
33021	16	~	W8	OS	Chrome

Figure 3–42   *Selection and mapping of the orthogonal array*

Spend a few moments now verifying all the pairs of options across all the pairs of factors. There are six pairs of factors:

1. Connection speed with operating system
2. Connection speed with security settings
3. Connection speed with browser
4. Operating system with security settings
5. Operating system with browser
6. Security settings with browser

During testing, we just have to make sure that we have at least one test configuration during at least one test that corresponds to a row in this array.

Orthogonal Arrays Exercise

Assume that you are planning compatibility testing of the HELLOCARMS system for eventual Internet use. Globobank intends to support PCs running the following:

- Operating systems: Windows 7, Windows 8, or Mac
- Browsers: Internet Explorer (but on Windows PCs only), Firefox, or Chrome

Globobank intends to support connection speeds of both dial-up and broadband.

Figure 3–43, Figure 3–44, and Figure 3–44 show orthogonal arrays you might use.

The exercise consists of three parts:

1. Select the appropriate array.
2. Map the factors (OS, browser, and connection speed) and the options within each factor into the array.
3. Handle rows with spare cells and pairs that represent impossible configuration combinations.

The answers to the three parts are shown on the next pages. You should review the answer to each part (and, if necessary, revise your answer to the next part) before reviewing the answer to the next part.

		Factors	
Test	1	2	3
1	0	0	0
2	0	1	1
3	1	0	1
4	1	1	0

Figure 3–43 *Orthogonal array 1*

		Factors		
Test	1	2	3	4
1	0	0	0	0
2	0	1	1	2
3	0	2	2	1
4	1	0	1	1
5	1	1	2	0
6	1	2	0	2
7	2	0	2	2
8	2	1	0	1
9	2	2	1	0

Figure 3–44 *Orthogonal array 2*

Test			Factors		
	1	2	3	4	5
1	0	0	0	0	0
2	0	1	1	1	1
3	0	2	2	2	2
4	0	3	3	3	3
5	1	0	1	2	3
6	1	1	0	3	2
7	1	2	3	0	1
8	1	3	2	1	0
9	2	0	2	3	1
10	2	1	3	2	0
11	2	2	0	1	3
12	2	3	1	0	2
13	3	0	3	1	2
14	3	1	2	0	3
15	3	2	1	3	0
16	3	3	0	2	1

Figure 3–45   *Orthogonal array 3*

Orthogonal Arrays Debrief

First, we select an appropriate orthogonal array. There are three factors and a maximum of three options per factor. So we need an array with three columns, three numbers per column, and nine rows. That is the array shown in Table 3–40.

Now, we map the factors and options onto the array, which gives us the result shown in Table 3–40.

Table 3–40   *Mapped HELLOCARMS orthogonal array*

Test	Factor		
	OS	Browser	Speed
1	W7	IE	Low
2	W7	Firefox	High
3	W7	Chrome	~
4	W8	IE	High
5	W8	Firefox	~
6	W8	Chrome	Low
7	Mac	IE	~
8	Mac	Firefox	Low
9	Mac	Chrome	High

But we have a problem. The requirements said that we would support Internet Explorer only on Windows systems. Test seven has a combination of Mac with

Internet Explorer. Of course, we are guaranteed that this situation would arise, since we are guaranteed that all pairs of options across all pairs of factors will occur at least once in the table.

Fortunately, due to the tester's choice mapping, the solution is trivial. There are no pairs in that row other than the invalid pair of Mac OS with Internet Explorer browser. So, in this case, we can delete the row, obtaining the final test configuration set shown in Table 3–41.

Table 3–41   *Final HELLOCARMS test configuration*

| | | Factor | |
Test	OS	Browser	Speed
1	W7	IE	Low
2	W7	Firefox	High
3	W7	Chrome	~
4	W8	IE	High
5	W8	Firefox	~
6	W8	Chrome	Low
7	Mac	Firefox	Low
8	Mac	Chrome	High

At this point, there are four points I should make before we wind down this discussion of pairwise techniques.

First, notice that I don't call Table 3–41 an orthogonal array. It isn't, because it no longer has the properties of an orthogonal array once I deleted row 7.

Second, if you did the search-and-replace portion of the mapping differently, you might have found that the row with the invalid Mac/Internet Explorer pair had two other pairs in it. So, in that case, you have to capture those pairs in other rows—using tester's choice or adding a row—before you can delete the row with the invalid pair.

That brings us to the third point: Be very, very cautious about deleting and merging rows. The pairs arise from interactions between pairs of columns. Make sure there are no unique pairs—i.e., pairs of options not covered in some other row—present in a row before you delete it. If you are going to merge two rows, make sure that any specified options—i.e., options that are not tester's choice—in one row correspond either to a tester's choice option in the other row or that the specified options are the same in both rows.

Finally, all-pairs tables can be smaller, so it's worth having a freeware tool handy. However, in many cases, the mapping to an orthogonal array is so quick and easy, and results in so few extra rows, that you might tend to use that technique more.

Classification Trees

The pairwise techniques are handy, and compatibility testing of the kind we looked at in the previous part arises frequently in testing. However, sometimes factors are constrained, in that certain options for one factor won't coexist with certain options for another factor. Other times, we want to test certain factors or certain combinations of factors more heavily than others.

If we are looking at configuration options for a program, for example, some of those options probably do interact.

So, conceptually, classification trees are a way to test constrained combinations of factors. They also allow us to test some factors more heavily than others.

The underlying model is a graphical representation of the factors and the options for each factor, usually prepared using equivalence partitioning. There are also rules for factor and option combination, including the level of combinations to achieve across certain factors (e.g., all triples for three factors, but only pairs for the other factors).

Given the model, you can then derive the tests, usually shown as a table of option combinations across the factors. As a practical matter, this is going to have to be done by a tool.

As with orthogonal arrays and all-pairs tables, the coverage criterion is that you have to have every row represented in a least one test.

Again, as with pairwise testing, the bug hypothesis is that this level of coverage will suffice. The difference is that we can have varying levels of coverage depending on the factors. We are going to hypothesize a higher likelihood of combined option misbehaviors for certain factors, or a higher level of risk based on business need. We can have factors combined in all pairs, all triples, all quadruples, or even higher-order combinations. Of course, the more higher-order combinations we have, the bigger the table and the more the tests.

Example: Classification Trees

Suppose that we are testing the Microsoft Word font menu as shown in Figure 3–46. In particular, we are interested in the following factors and options, because we worry that they might interact improperly:

- Style: regular, italic, bold, bold italic
- Size: smallest (8), typical (12), largest (72)
- Strikethrough: no, yes, double
- Height: normal, subscript, superscript
- Caps: normal, small caps, all caps

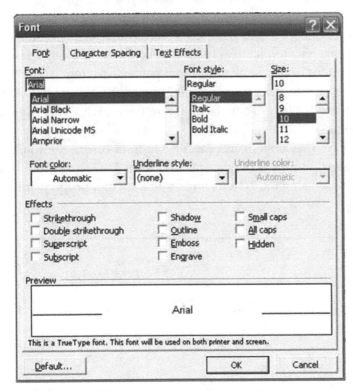

Figure 3–46   *Microsoft Word font menu*

So, we will use the classification tree technique to generate tests to check for interactions. To use this technique, a tool is necessary. Fortunately, at this time, there are free tools available. I'm going to show examples created using a previous version of Testona, but lately I have found myself using the ACTS tool more frequently.[7]

Once you have the tool downloaded and installed, spend a few minutes reading the manual so you can understand how to use it.

---

7. The two sources currently are at www.testona.net and csrc.nist.gov/acts/.

For each testing problem to which you want to apply this technique, you start by identifying some aspect of interest. This is some collection of things you think might interact in some interesting way, so you want to test combinations.

Now, you identify the classifications within that area of interest. These are what I referred to as "factors" in my discussion about pairwise testing. These are the things you think might interact. In some cases, you'll identify sub-classifications for one or more classifications.

Once you are done with that, you use standard equivalence partitioning and boundary value analysis to identify classes for each classification. These correspond to the "options" in my discussion about pairwise testing.

Now, you define the rules for combining the classifications. Do you want pairs of all factors? Triples of some factors? Are there exclusions—e.g., classes that can't combine?

Once you have that done, you generate the tests (using the tool). It will create a table, much like the orthogonal array. Figure 3–47 shows the classification tree that I drew using the Testona tool, to address font property interaction problems.

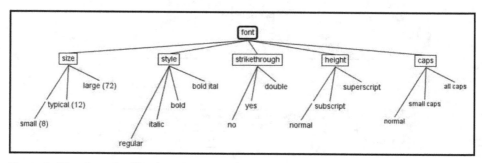

Figure 3–47   *Font classification tree*

You can see that font is the root of the tree. We have size, style, strikethrough, height, and caps as the classifications. Each classification has three or more classes.

Figure 3–48 shows the table produced when I generated tests for all pairs. There are fourteen rows in the table. The first row says we should test a small (8-point) font with regular style, double strikethrough, subscript height, and all caps.

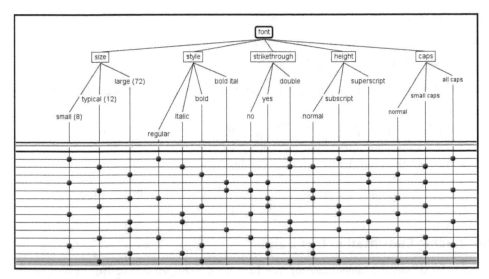

Figure 3–48 *Font classification pairs table*

At this point, we haven't really done anything we couldn't have done with pair-wise testing.

In Figure 3–49, I've shown the table and tree that result when I tell the tool to generate triples of sizes, height, and caps, as well as all pairs across all factors. There are now thirty tests. Study the figure to see some of the combinations covered in the table.

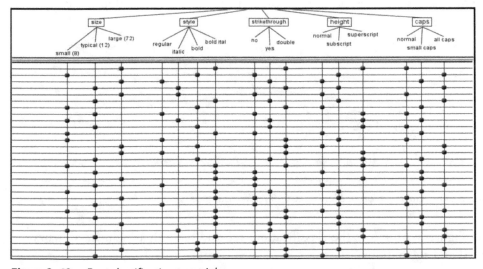

Figure 3–49 *Font classification tree triples*

Life Insurance Classification Tree Exercise

In this exercise, you'll build on your solution to the decision table exercise. The exercise consists of four parts:

1. Create a classification tree for the decision table, showing classifications and classes.
2. Use the tool to generate all pairs for age and body mass index only.
3. Use the tool to generate all pairs possible.
4. Use the tool to generate all triples possible.

As usual, check your answer for each part before proceeding to the next part.

Life Insurance Classification Tree Debrief

Figure 3–50 shows the classification tree I created. Now, your tree might look a little different, but only in terms of formatting. If you don't have a root node with six classifications on it, with four of the classifications having Boolean classes and the BMI and age classifications having the ranges shown, you made some mistake.

One thing you might have done is to include the ranges of BMI and age as sub-classifications, with boundary values as classes underneath them, if you want to force testing of boundary values. However, notice that you can accomplish this by mapping boundary values onto the table, and you typically will have at least two representatives of each option when you're doing pairwise combinations.

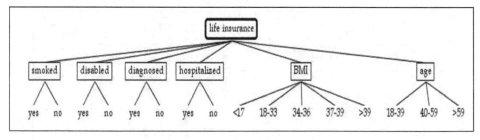

Figure 3–50   *Classification tree for HELLOCARMS life insurance*

Now, Figure 3–51 shows the classification tree and table that includes all pairs of BMI and age options.

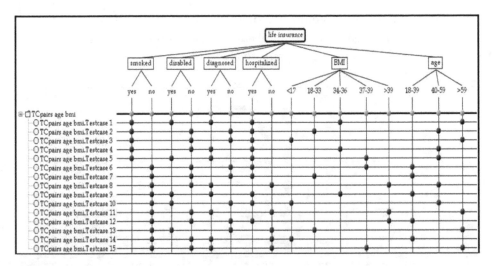

Figure 3–51   *HELLOCARMS classification tree tests (pairs of BMI and age)*

Changing the rule to require all pairs across all factors, I generate the tests shown in Figure 3–52. Notice that this figure also shows the tests generated for pairs of age and BMI, to allow you to compare them.

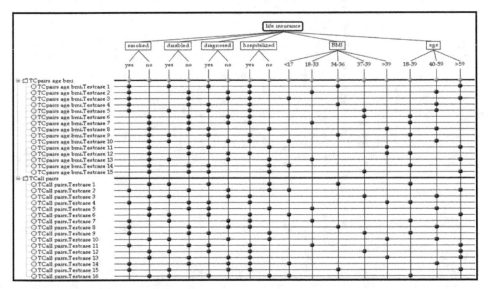

Figure 3–52   *HELLOCARMS classification tree tests (all pairs)*

Finally, changing the rule to require all triples across all factors, I generate the tests shown in Figure 3–53. Notice that this figure also shows the tests generated for pairs of age and BMI and for all pairs, to allow you to compare them.

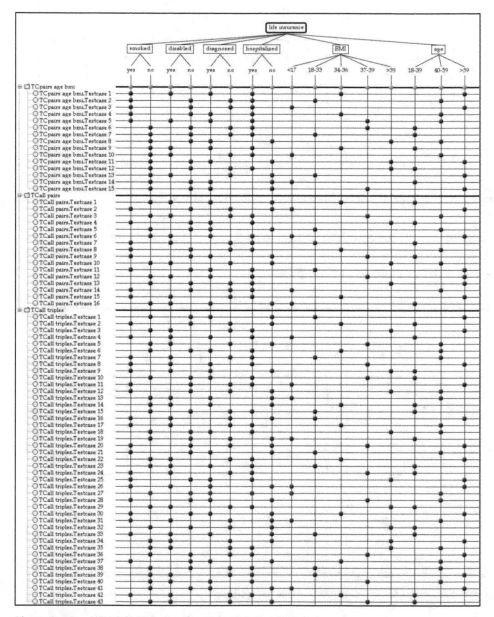

Figure 3–53 *HELLOCARMS classification tree tests (all triples)*

3.2.8   User Story Testing

User stories are how requirements are expressed and documented on Agile projects, and they are the basic building blocks by which the software's feature set grows incrementally in each iteration or sprint. The user story is something like a very concisely expressed use case, focused on what the user wants to accomplish rather than the steps by which the goal is accomplished. The user story and its associated acceptance criteria should provide a testable set of functional and non-functional areas by which you can verify the user story. They are used for all levels of testing in Agile, though acceptance testing may be done via a demonstration.

Depending on the level of testing being performed, drivers and stubs may be necessary. Fortunately, many of the open-source tools associated with Agile development provide harnesses that allow testing of units without any additional development of such drivers or stubs.

The usual rule is that you should have one or more tests for each acceptance criteria. In some cases, these can be automated using techniques such as acceptance test-driven development and behavior-driven development. Such tests can find functional and non-functional defects, problems with error handling, user interface bugs, and problems with integration between the new features and existing ones.[8]

Example: User Story

Let's look at an example of a user story. Suppose you are testing a browser-based application that allows people to pay their bills online. For example, these bills could be for a utility company that offers trash pickup, electricity, water, and natural gas services, each of which are separate accounts. Assume that someone might buy one, two, three, or all four such services, with each service being its own account. Each account is separate, can be managed separately, and can be paid separately.

> **ISTQB Glossary**
>
> **Defect taxonomy:** A system of (hierarchical) categories designed to be a useful aid for reproducibly classifying defects.

---

8. One reference for more information on user stories and testing them is found in Mike Cohn's *User Stories Applied.*

For this application, a business stakeholder suggests the following user story:

> As a customer, I want to be able to open a popup window, within the "enter payment amount" window, that shows the last thirty transactions on my account, with backward and forward arrows that allow me to scroll through my transaction history, so that I can see my transaction history without closing the "enter payment amount" window.

This feature allows customers to compare what they paid in various periods in the past years.

As a tester, you would now work with the business stakeholder and the developer to create sufficiently detailed and testable acceptance criteria. At that point, you can design a set of user story acceptance tests.

Here are the acceptance criteria.

- The window is initially populated with the thirty most recent transactions. If there are no transactions, it should display "no transaction history yet."
- Pressing the backward scroll button will scroll back ten transactions. The forward scroll button will scroll forward ten transactions. Again, these are not statements found in the original user story. Rather, they are elaborations agreed on with the developer and business stakeholder in this process. They can be added to the user story now or can be documented elsewhere.
- Transaction data is retrieved only for the current account. This criterion is implied by the user story, but it's somewhat ambiguous, so this criterion makes it unambiguous.
- Transaction history shows for only one account, even if the user has multiple accounts.
- The transaction history displays in two seconds or less, which is an example of a non-functional acceptance criteria.
- In terms of look and feel, the acceptance criteria say that the back and forward buttons are at the bottom, that the window conforms to the corporate user interface standard, that you can minimize or close the window through standard controls, and that it opens properly in any supported browser.

If you look back at the user story itself while I do so, you might think, "I don't see how these acceptance criteria follow from the user story." Well, they don't. Remember that part of defining the acceptance criteria is to work collaboratively with the business stakeholder and the developer. During this process, you remove ambiguity from the user story by defining the acceptance criteria. All of these criteria address topics that must be defined in order to develop and test the feature.

3.2.9   Domain Analysis

When we use the combinatorial techniques discussed earlier, we are trying to deal with the fact that if we try to test all possible combinations, we'll have an exponentially increasing number of tests. For example, if we have ten input fields on a screen, and each has only two equivalence partitions, if we were to try to test all possible combinations of input equivalence partitions, we would have to run over 1,000 tests, since two times two times two times two times two times two times two times two times two times two equals 1,024, or two to the power of ten.

If there are boundary values for the input fields, we have at least four boundary values to test, so ten such input fields would mean four to the power of ten or 1,048,576.

This is clearly untenable, but notice that testing such combinations would mean that we have no way of predicting the interaction of these fields. With pairwise techniques and classification trees, we admit that we have no way of predicting the interaction, so we simply focus on pairs interacting, or, in the case of classification trees, we might allow more possible interactions among certain inputs or other factors.

But what if we can actually analyze the interaction between these inputs or other factors? That's the basic idea of domain analysis.

In domain analysis, we will identify the way one or more factors interact, and the way in which one or more factors determine the way in which those factors interact. It's a lot like multidimensional equivalence partitioning or multidimensional boundary value analysis, combined with the idea of decision tables where we look at how the interactions of factors determine the actions taken. It's really a brilliant idea, which my colleague and coauthor on the technical test analyst book, Jamie Mitchell, describes as very similar to calculus, which is the mathematical process of analyzing change. As with many brilliant testing ideas, it was developed by Boris Beizer.[9]

A domain is a set of values defined on one dimension or multiple dimensions. I will show you an example of one dimension and an example of multiple

---

9. Beizer describes the technique in *Software Test Techniques*. There's a discussion of it found in my book *Pragmatic Software Testing*. Robert Binder has a very advanced take on it in *Testing Object-Oriented Systems*.

dimensions. These two examples will, I hope, open your eyes to the power of this technique, which is underused—to say the least—in software testing. You can use this technique at any level of testing where we can identify multiple factors that interact, which is usually integration test and system test. The main trick to the technique is identifying the factors, their interaction, and which factors determine the way the interaction works.

The technique involves creating a model, usually a graphical model but sometimes a tabular model, of the way that factors interact. This model identifies the domains. You then must apply some rules—which at first seem strange, partly due to their names, but make sense once you consider the reasons—to select test values. You then create tests that cover those values in each domain. Testing with these values will find functional problems, issues with the boundaries where behavior changes, bugs in terms of how the factors interact, and situations where errors are not handled correctly.

Conceptually, what we are doing with the ON and OFF values, as you'll see, is testing boundary values. The IN and OUT values test typical values. These values are identified by analysis of the inputs, outputs, internal data processing, or other factors that clearly interact to determine system behaviors. These factors can be about any data type you can imagine: decimal numbers, integers, dates, times, sets, or whatever.

Typically, the design of the tests involves first creating a graphical model of the various domains. The models are, less frequently, tabular or mathematical, so we'll focus on graphical models here. Once the model is created, you use the model to identify four types of test values: IN, OUT, ON, and OFF. Once the values are identified, as with boundary values analysis and equivalence partitioning, you'll create tests to cover the values, ideally the minimum number of tests.

What we are looking for here are bugs where the factors interact improperly or interact in some unintended fashion.

Example: Frequent Flyer Program

In Table 3–43 you see a table that describes how a frequent flyer program works. Based on your status level, you may receive additional points for travel, as a way of encouraging you to give the airline more of your business. For any given trip, one of four formulas is selected to calculate points awarded, based on the total distance travelled in the previous or current year, which is the factor that determines the status level.

So, we have three interacting factors: the status level, the distance traveled, and the points awarded. Table 3–42 shows how those three factors interact.

Table 3–42   *Frequent flyer program*

Status Level	None	Silver	Gold	Platinum
Trip Bonus	0%	25%	50%	100%
Distance Traveled	d	d	d	d
Points Awarded	d	1.25*d	1.5*d	2*d

In Figure 3–54 you see a graphical view of the four different possible calculations. If we can assume that what we want to test is the interaction between the three factors, then we can test each calculation—called a *domain* in domain analysis. The testing of the input and output data validation can be handled with another test, so that here we can focus on the business logic that implements the calculation.

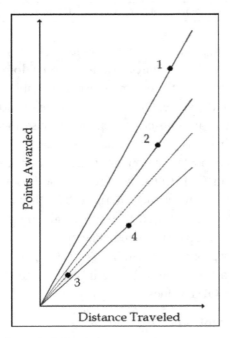

Figure 3–54   *Frequent flyer calculation tests*

When Boris Beizer created the domain analysis technique, he said that, where possible, you should select four types of test values, based on the domains. These are the ON, OFF, IN, and OUT values. The values are defined as shown in Table 3–43.

Table 3–43   *Domain test values*

Name	Description	Frequent Flyer Example
On	A value on a domain boundary that may be inside or outside of the domain	1 (on platinum) 2 (on gold) 3 (on silver) 4 (on none)
Off	A value just off a domain boundary by the smallest recognizable amount and outside of the domain	1 (off gold) 2 (off platinum) 2 (off silver) 3 (off gold) 3 (off none) 4 (off silver)
In	A value inside the domain, not on or off	No such value possible
Out	A value outside the domain, not on or off	No such value possible

An ON value is a value that lies on a domain boundary. It may be inside or outside of the domain itself. An OFF value is a value just off a domain boundary by the smallest recognizable amount. The smallest recognizable amount is determined by the precision of the value. OFF values must be outside of the domain itself. OFF and ON values are chosen to test the precise location where the behavior of the system changes due to a domain boundary.

An IN value is a value inside the domain, which does not meet the criteria to be either an ON or an OFF value. An OUT value is a value outside the domain, which also does not meet the criteria to be either an ON or an OFF value. IN and OUT values are chosen to test typical values for all domains, which might detect unexpected changes in behavior.

For the frequent flyer program shown in Figure 3–54, all four of the values chosen are both ON and OFF values. You're in either one status level or the other. There are no IN or OUT values.

Example: Missile Interception

Let's look at a more complicated example. Figure 3–55 shows a hypothetical example of an anti-missile system, where the two domains have to do with two different ways of calculating the current vertical position (i.e., altitude), labeled as *yc*, depending on how long it took the laser range finding signal to return from the missile. If the return time is less than one millisecond, then the calculation ignores the accelerating effect of gravity on the incoming missile. That's domain one. In domain two, the calculation includes the effect of gravity.

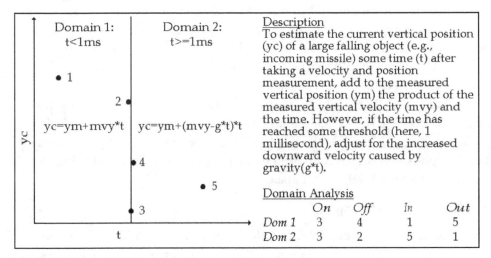

Figure 3–55 *Anti-missile system domain example*

So, we have five interacting factors:

- Elapsed time since the measurement was taken, *t*, which is included in the calculations and is also the variable that determines where the boundary is.
- The measured vertical velocity, *mvy*, which is included in the calculations.
- The gravitational constant, *g*, which is included in the domain 2 calculation.
- The measured vertical position, *ym*, which is included in the calculations.
- The calculated vertical position, *yc*.

Notice that we have drawn the graph based on the time, being the factor that determines the domain boundary, and *yc*, being the calculated factor.

Now, with the model—that is, the graphical representation of the domains—created, we can select the test values. For each domain, we need one test value each that meets the definition for an ON and an OFF value, and, if possible, one value each that meets the definition for an IN and an OUT value.

Reuse of a single value that qualifies as such a value for more than one domain is allowed.

You can see the selected values in Figure 3–55. The point labeled "3" where t is equal to exactly one millisecond, sits on the boundary between domain 1 and domain 2. Notice that the yc value is arbitrary; any possible yc value is acceptable, as long as t is one millisecond. The points labeled "2" and "4" are just off of the boundary by whatever the smallest recognizable difference is; in this case it appears to be about one microsecond, so the t value appears to be .999 milliseconds for "2" and 1.001 milliseconds for "4." Again, the yc values are arbitrarily chosen and could be any value.

The point labeled "1" looks to have a t value of about .25 milliseconds. It's far from the boundary, so it qualifies as an IN value for domain 1 and an OUT value for domain 2. The point labeled "5" seems to have a t value of about 1.8 milliseconds. It's also far from the boundary, so it qualifies as an IN value for domain 2 and an OUT value for domain 1.

When Domain Rules Change

In the missile interceptor example, the calculations within each domain do not change, regardless of the values of any of the factors. However, in some cases, the calculations within a domain might change. Suppose we reevaluate the frequent flyer example, in this case looking not at a single trip, but at the total distance traveled for a year. Since travel in the current year can change your status, a traveler who starts in a lower tier of status can be promoted to a higher tier based on the distance traveled. So, for a traveler who starts with no status, the calculation can change to silver, gold, and even platinum over the course of the year.

What test values must be used? At the very least, you should include values in each segment. If you are particularly concerned about the subdomains within each domain—and subdomains are effectively what each segment represents—you can even identify ON, OFF, IN, and OUT values within the domain with respect to the subdomains. Doing so will increase the number of test values, of course, so you should consider whether the level of risk justifies such testing.

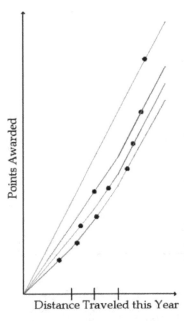

Description

Suppose we look at the total number of points awarded to a frequent-flyer for a whole year. A traveler's status is based on the total distance traveled in the current year or the total distance traveled in the past year. At 25,000, the status increases to silver. At 50,000, the status increases to gold. At 100,000, the status increases to platinum. Any distance traveled after the status changes accrues bonus points based on the new status, both in the current year or the next year.

Additional Domain Tests

Cover values in each rule segment. This adds one new test for travelers starting in the gold domain, two for travelers starting in the silver domain, and three for travelers starting with no status.

Figure 3–56   *Frequent flyer example where domain rules change*

Domain Exercise

In order to allow lending to people with imperfect credit, assume that Globo-bank adopts the following risk fee:

- Applicants with serious derogatory credit events within the last year will be denied.
- Applicants with serious derogatory credit events more than one year old but less than five years old will pay a 1% risk fee on top of their existing loan fees.
- Applicants with serious derogatory credit events five years or more in the past do not pay the risk fee.

Note that, in the event of denial, the 1% risk fee must still be calculated and archived with the loan.

   Use domain analysis to design tests for this feature.

Domain Debrief

The domain analysis shown in Figure 3–57 provides the three domains, the ON, OFF, IN, and OUT points for each domain, and a logical test oracle for each domain. Note that you would need to confirm the precision of date values for the purposes of the boundaries, but it's probably one day.

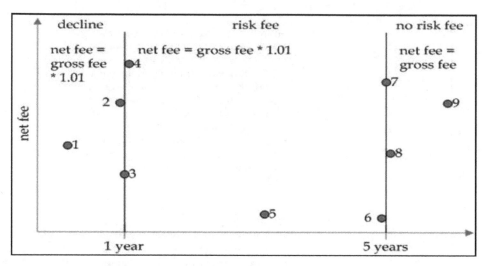

Figure 3–57   *HELLOCARMS domain analysis*

The coverage analysis shown in Table 3–44 shows coverage of the ON, OFF, IN, and OUT points for each domain.

Table 3–44   *Domain coverage analysis*

	on	off	in	out
decline	3	4	1	5
risk fee	3, 7	2, 8	5	1, 9
no risk fee	7	6	9	5

3.2.10 Applying Techniques to Requirements

Let's wind down this section by making sure that you understand how to connect the techniques with the test basis.

Specification-based tests derive from the test basis, often a requirements specification. This is particularly true at the higher levels of testing like system test, system integration test, and acceptance test.

Since requirements specifications mostly focus on behavior, the primary test design techniques are the behavioral (or black-box) techniques we've covered in this section.

Now, seldom do developers, designers, and business analysts give you the models that we described. For example, if you do get a decision table or a use case embedded in the requirements, great, use it. However, you might have to figure out how to create the model yourself.

So, to apply the techniques from this section, here's a simple three-step process:

1. Analyze the requirements specification.
2. Create the model or models corresponding to the test design technique or techniques that you think will apply best.
3. Derive tests from the models as described in this section.

Let's look at an example. Here are two requirements from the Internet appliance project:

* Support popular email attachments: HTML, text, .jpg, .gif, .au, .wav, and URL.
* If an unsupported attachment is received, send an automated reply to the sender indicating which attachments are OK to send.

By discussions with the marketing people and designers, we discovered that the maximum attachment size was 1MB.

Figure 3–58 shows the application of equivalence partitioning and boundary value analysis to those two requirements.

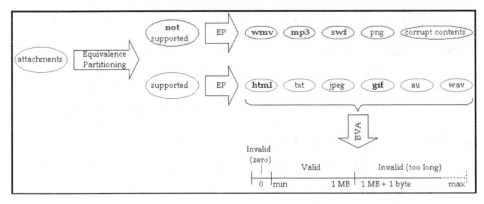

Figure 3–58   *Example: Requirements EP and BVA*

Notice that, for the supported partition, we are going to test six supported file types, with five tests per type based on the boundary value analysis.

For the unsupported partition, we are going to test four unsupported (but typical) file types. We will also test six examples of correct extensions but corrupted contents.

Example: EP and BVA Tests

Figure 3–45 shows the tests derived from this analysis. Study them to satisfy yourself that all the equivalence classes and boundary values were covered.

Table 3–45   *Tests derived from EP and BVA*

#	Test Procedure Step	Expected Result
1.	Send email with minimum-length HTML attachment.	Confirm correct receipt on Internet appliance.
2.	Repeat step 1 with 1MB HTML.	Confirm correct receipt.
3.	Repeat steps 1 and 2 for .txt, .jpg, .gif, .au, and .wav files.	Confirm correct receipt
4.	Send 0 length attachment with HTML extension.	Confirm error message on Internet appliance.
5.	Repeat step 5 for .txt, .jpg, .gif, .au, and .wav files.	Confirm error message on Internet appliance.
6.	Repeat steps 4 and 5 with attachments of exactly 1MB + 1 byte length.	Confirm error message to sender (bounce message).
7.	Repeat step 6 with attachments of maximum outbound send length (usually around 10MB).	Confirm error message to sender (bounce message). Confirm NO corruption of user's inbox.
8.	Send a .wmv file of legal size.	Confirm error message to sender (bounce message).
9.	Repeat step 8 for .mp3, .swf, and .png files.	Confirm error message to sender (bounce message).
10.	Send an HTML file of legal size but with corrupted contents.	Confirm error message on Internet appliance.
11.	Repeat step 10 for .txt, .jpg, .gif, .au, and .wav files.	Confirm error message on Internet appliance.

Requirements-Based Test Exercise

Refer to the HELLOCARMS system requirements document. Consider requirement element 010-020-040.

The exercise consists of two parts:

1. Select appropriate techniques for test design.
2. Apply those techniques to generate tests, achieving the coverage criteria for the techniques.

As always, check your work on the first part before proceeding to the second part.

Requirements-Based Test Debrief

First, remember from exercise 2, where we tested escalation of calls and rejection of invalid property values, that the following rules apply to loans:

- The minimum property value is $25,000.
- The maximum property value is $5,000,000.

Now, we don't need to repeat those tests, but certainly this is interesting input for the fee calculation.

I selected three techniques. First, I use a simple decision table on the fee percentage selection as shown in Table 3–46.

Table 3–46   *HELLOCARMS property type fee*

Conditions	1	2	3	4	5
Property Type	One-family	Rental	Commercial	Condo/coop	Undeveloped
Actions					
Fee Percentage	0	1.5	2.5	3.5	4.5

Next, for the rental and condominium and cooperatives, I apply equivalence partitioning as shown in Table 3–47.

Table 3–47   *Property type equivalence partitions*

#	Partition	Subpartition (if any)
1	One-family	-
2	Rental	Duplex
3	Rental	Apartment
4	Rental	Vacation
5	Commercial	-
6	Condo/coop	Condo
7	Condo/coop	Coop
8	Undeveloped	-

For the fee calculations, I apply boundary value analysis to each of the fee calculations, including where there is no fee, as shown in Table 3–48. You might argue that just calculating a zero fee, a minimum fee, and a maximum fee is enough, but I'd say that this is a high-risk calculation that needs extensive testing.

Table 3–48   *Property fee boundary values*

#	Partition	Boundary Value
1	0	0
2	0	0
3	1.5	375
4	1.5	75,000
5	2.5	625
6	2.5	125,000
7	3.5	875
8	3.5	175,000
9	4.5	1,125
10	4.5	225,000

Based on these three techniques, I generated the test cases shown in Table 3–49. If you refer back to the prior tables in this debrief, you can see that I've achieved 100% coverage of the decision table, the equivalence partitions, and the boundary values.

Table 3–49   *Property type and fee test cases*

						Test case					
Conditions	1	2	3	4	5	6	7	8	9	10	11
Type	1fam	1fam	Rent	Rent	Rent	Com	Com	CC	CC	Und	Und
Subtype	-	-	Dup	Apt	Vaca	-	-	Condo	Coop	-	-
Value	25K	5M	25K	5M	1M	25K	5M	25K	5M	25K	5M
Actions											
Fee %	0	0	1.5	1.5	1.5	2.5	2.5	3.5	3.5	4.5	4.5
Fee Amount	0	0	375	75K	15K	625	125K	875	175K	1,125	225K

Notice that I've done coverage analysis only for the equivalent partitions and boundary values in Figure 3–50 and Table 3–51, because each column in the decision table had at least one partition and at least two boundary values associated with it. Therefore, if I cover the partitions and boundary values, I'm guaranteed to cover the decision table.

Table 3–50   *Equivalence partition coverage*

#	Partition	Subpartition (if any)	Test Case
1	One-family	-	1, 2
2	Rental	Duplex	3
3	Rental	Apartment	4
4	Rental	Vacation	5
5	Commercial	-	6, 7
6	Condo/coop	Condo	8
7	Condo/coop	Coop	9
8	Undeveloped	-	10, 11

Table 3–51   *Boundary value coverage*

#	Partition	Boundary Value	Test Case
1	0	0	1
2	0	0	2
3	1.5	375	3
4	1.5	75,000	4
5	2.5	625	6
6	2.5	125,000	7
7	3.5	875	8
8	3.5	175,000	9
9	4.5	1,125	10
10	4.5	225,000	11

3.3   Defect-Based Techniques

Learning objectives
(K2) Describe the application of defect-based testing techniques and differentiate their use from specification-based techniques.
(K4) Analyze a given defect taxonomy for applicability in a given situation using criteria for a good taxonomy.

Now, we're going to move from systematic techniques for test design into less structured but nonetheless useful techniques. We start with defect-based techniques.

In defect-based techniques, we have a list of the defects we expect to see, or at least want to test for some reason. This list is often called a *taxonomy*, being an organized, hierarchical list. You create tests to cover the defects on the taxonomy. This can be used at any level of testing, but system test is probably the most common. You do need to have a taxonomy that is relevant to your product for these techniques to work, so most of the trick to using these techniques is finding or building a good taxonomy. There are no formal coverage criteria for these techniques; just cover as much of the taxonomy as makes sense, based typically on risk. You will find some subset of whatever types of defects are on the taxonomy, so keep in mind that these techniques should be used to augment, not replace, other techniques.

Conceptually, we are doing defect-based testing any time the type of the defect sought is the basis for the test.

Usually, the underlying model is some list of defects seen in the past. If this list is organized as a hierarchical taxonomy, then the testing is defect taxonomy based.

To derive tests from the defect list or the defect taxonomy, we create tests designed to reveal the presence of the defects in the list.

Now, for defect-based tests, we tend to be more relaxed about the concept of coverage. The general criterion is that we will create a test for each defect type, but it is often the case that the question of whether to create a test at all is risk weighted. In other words, if the likelihood or impact of the defect doesn't justify the effort, don't do it. However, if the likelihood or impact of the defect were high, then you would create not just one test, but perhaps many. This should be starting to sound familiar to you, yes?

The underlying bug hypothesis is that programmers tend to repeatedly make the same mistakes. In other words, a team of programmers will introduce roughly the same types of bugs in roughly the same proportion from one project to the next. This allows us to allocate test design and execution effort based on the likelihood and impact of the bugs.

ISTQB Glossary

Defect taxonomy: A system of (hierarchical) categories designed to be a useful aid for reproducibly classifying defects.

Defect Taxonomies

Let's discuss a bit further what a defect taxonomy is and where to get one. A defect taxonomy is a structured list of defect types, where the structure is via a two-level, three-level, or even four-level hierarchy of categories and subcategories into which specific defect types are placed. The best defect taxonomies are based on actual observation of defects. Hypothetical defect taxonomies can be used, but they are basically educated guesses about what kinds of defects will be seen.

There are defect taxonomies available, both commercially and from open source. If you decide to acquire an external taxonomy, you'll want it to be as close as possible to a specific match for your product in terms of application domain and technology. Alternatively, you can develop your own taxonomy.

If you want to develop your own taxonomy or customize a taxonomy you have acquired, you first need to consider your objectives for using the taxonomy and the level of detail you want. If you have studied existing taxonomies, you'll be in a better position to make these decisions. Start at the highest level of abstraction, and work down to the specific defect types. It's also a good idea to include examples of each defect type, which will be especially useful if those are examples of defects previously observed with this product. Putting this level of detail into your taxonomy takes more effort, but you'll find it's more powerful, and produces more consistent results regardless of who uses it.

Examples: Three Types of Taxonomies

Table 3–52 shows an example of a portion of a taxonomy from the syllabus. The taxonomy is specifically focused on input validation for various types of fields. Only text fields and date fields are shown in this excerpt, but the complete taxonomy would cover all possible types of fields. Notice that some of the tests that you would derive from this taxonomy overlap with tests that would be derived with techniques such as equivalence partitioning and boundary value analysis, while others do not overlap with the other techniques. Of course, you should not introduce redundant tests, so there's no need to run such overlapping tests.

Table 3–52   *Taxonomy excerpt*

Text Field
Valid data is not accepted.
Invalid data is accepted.
Length of input is not verified.
Special characters are not detected.
User error messages are not informative.
User is not able to correct erroneous data.
Rules are not applied.

Date Field
Valid dates are not accepted.
Invalid dates are not rejected.
Date ranges are not verified.
Precision data is not handled correctly (e.g., hh:mm:ss).
User is not able to correct erroneous data.
Rules are not applied (e.g., ending date must be greater than starting date).

Figure 3–59 shows an example of a defect taxonomy focused on root causes. It was reproduced in my book *Managing the Testing Process*, but was derived from Boris Beizer's taxonomy in *Software Testing Techniques*.

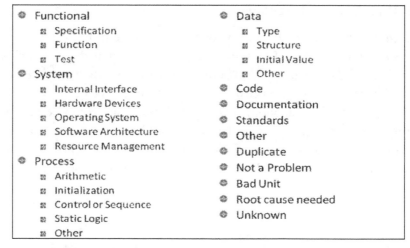

Figure 3–59   *Root-cause-focus taxonomy*

There are eight main categories along with five bookkeeper categories that are useful when classifying bugs in a bug tracking system. Let's go through these in detail.

1. In the category of **functional** defects, there are three subcategories:
    a. **Specification:** The functional specification—perhaps in the requirements document or in some other document—is wrong.
    b. **Function:** The specification is right, but the implementation of it is wrong.
    c. **Test:** Upon close research, we found a problem in test data, test designs, test specifications, or somewhere else.
2. In the category of **system** defects, there are five subcategories:
    a. **Internal Interface:** The internal system communication failed; in other words, there was an integration problem of some sort internal to the test object.
    b. **Hardware Devices:** The hardware that is part of the system or that hosts the system failed.
    c. **Operating System:** The operating system—which presumably is external to the test object—failed.
    d. **Software Architecture:** Some fundamental design assumption proved invalid, such as an assumption that data could be moved from one table to another or across some network in some constant period.
    e. **Resource Management:** The design assumptions were okay, but some implementation of the assumption was wrong; for example, the design of the data tables introduces delays.
3. In the category of **process** defects, there are five subcategories:
    a. **Arithmetic:** The software does math wrong. This doesn't mean just basic math; it can also include sophisticated accounting or numerical analysis functions, including problems that occur due to rounding and precision issues.
    b. **Initialization:** An operation fails on its first use, when there is no data in a list, and so forth.
    c. **Control or Sequence:** An action occurs at the wrong time or for the wrong reason—for instance, seeing screens or fields in the wrong order.
    d. **Static Logic:** Boundaries are misdefined, equivalence classes don't include the right members and exclude the wrong members, and so forth.
    e. **Other:** A control-flow or processing error that doesn't fit in the preceding categories has occurred.

4. In the category of **data** defects, there are four subcategories:
   a. **Type:** The wrong data type—whether a built-in or user-defined data type—was used.
   b. **Structure:** A complex data structure or type is invalid or inappropriately used.
   c. **Initial Value:** A data element's initialized value is incorrect, like a list of quantities to purchase that defaults to zero rather than one.
   d. **Other:** A data-related error occurs that doesn't fit in the preceding buckets.
5. The category of **code** applies to some simple typo, misspelling, stylistic error, or other coding error that results in a failure. Theoretically, these couldn't get past a compiler, but, in these days of scripting on browsers, this stuff does happen.
6. The category of **documentation** applies to situations where the documentation says the system does X on condition Y, but the system does Z—a valid and correct action—instead.
7. The category of **standards** applies to situations where the system fails to meet industry, governmental, or vendor standards or regulations, or follow coding or user interface standards, or adhere to naming conventions, and so forth.
8. **Other:** The root cause is known, but fits none of the preceding categories, which should be rare if this is a useful taxonomy.

The five housekeeping categories are:

1. **Duplicate:** You find that two bug reports describe the same bug.
2. **Not a Problem:** The behavior noted is correct. The report arose from a misunderstanding on the part of the tester about correct behavior. This situation is different than a test failure because this occurs during test execution, and is an issue of interpretation of an actual result.
3. **Bad Unit:** The bug is a real problem, but it arises from a random hardware failure that is unlikely in the production environment.
4. **Root Cause Needed:** Applies when the bug is confirmed as closed by test, but no one in development has supplied a root cause.
5. **Unknown:** No one knows what is broken. Ideally, this applies to a small number of reports, generally when an intermittent bug doesn't appear for quite a while, leading to a conclusion that some other change fixed the bug as a side effect.

Notice that this taxonomy is focused on root cause, at least in the sense of what ultimately proved to be wrong in the code that caused the failure.

You could also have a process root-cause taxonomy that showed at which phase in the development process that bug was introduced. Notice that such a taxonomy would be useless to us for designing tests. Even the root-cause-focused taxonomy can be a bit hard to use for purposes of test design, especially if you don't understand programming.

Table 3–53 shows an example of a bug taxonomy—a rather coarse-grained one—gathered from the Internet appliance case study we've looked at a few times in this book. This one is focused on symptoms. Notice that this makes it easier to think about the tests we might design. However, its coarse-grained nature means that we'll need to have additional information—lists of desired functional areas, usability and user interface standards and requirements, reliability specifications, and the like to use this to design tests.

I've also shown the percentage of bugs we actually found in each category during system test.

Table 3–53   *Symptom-focused taxonomies*

Description	Count	%
Failed functionality	425	46%
Missing functionality	179	19%
Poor usability	106	11%
Build failed	62	7%
Bad system design/architecture	51	5%
Reliability problem	49	5%
Data loss	18	2%
Slow performance	16	2%
Code obsolete	16	2%
Deviation from specification	8	1%
Bad user documentation	2	0%
Total	932	100%

Defects Exercise

Evaluate the UI defect taxonomy shown earlier in the book. Specifically, determine:

- Which items, if any, are applicable for HELLOCARMS?
- Which items, if any, are not applicable for HELLOCARMS?

For each item, explain the evaluation.

Defects Debrief

In Table 3–54, you can find my evaluation for each of the items, including explanations for the evaluation.

Table 3–54   *Defect taxonomy testing*

Field	Apply?	Reason
Text fields		
Valid data is not accepted.	Yes	The need for data validation is universal for any GUI application.
Invalid data is accepted.	Yes	The need for data validation is universal for any GUI application.
Length of input is not verified.	Yes	Buffer overflows are extremely common security vulnerabilities.
Special characters are not detected.	Yes	SQL injection and OS injection attacks are extremely common security vulnerabilities.
User error messages are not informative.	Yes	This being a GUI application, with various levels of skills in its users, good error messages are important.
User is not able to correct erroneous data.	Yes	This being a GUI application, with various levels of skills in its users, people need to be able to correct input mistakes.
Rules are not applied.	Yes	This is a banking application, and various regulations and policies (e.g., escalation of certain loans) should be enforced.
Date fields		
Valid dates are not accepted.	Yes	The need for data validation is universal for any GUI application.
Invalid dates are not rejected.	Yes	The need for data validation is universal for any GUI application.
Date ranges are not verified.	Yes	The need for data validation is universal for any GUI application.
Precision data is not handled correctly.	Yes	Banking applications deal with very precise financial and date-related data that must be checked precisely.
User is not able to correct erroneous data.	Yes	This being a GUI application, with various levels of skills in its users, people need to be able to correct input mistakes.
Rules are not applied.	Yes	This is a banking application, and various regulations and policies (e.g., escalation of certain loans) should be enforced.

3.4   **Experience-Based Techniques**

Learning objectives
(K2) Explain the principles of experience-based techniques and the benefits and drawbacks compared to specification-based and defect-based techniques.
(K3) For a given scenario, specify exploratory tests and explain how the results can be reported.
(K4) For a given project situation, determine which specification-based, defect-based, or experience-based techniques should be applied to achieve specific goals.

Experience-based testing, which takes on many forms, is a type of testing that utilizes the testers' relevant skills, intuition, and experience. Usually these skills, intuition, and experience arise from work as a tester, business analyst, developer, or user of a similar application or one built using similar technologies.

The techniques have various pros and cons, which depend on the particular project, product, and organization considering the techniques. On the pro side, the techniques can find lots of defects relatively cheaply, they do not produce heavy documentation, and they allow test teams to take advantage of the disparate experience of their testers. On the con side, coverage is hard to determine and often weak when the testers are under pressure, the tests are hard to reuse unless they are documented as they are created (which undermines the light-weight documentation benefit), the lack of documentation can be a problem if confidence building or regulatory compliance is necessary, and, of course, the techniques will be weak if the skills of the testers applying them are low.

Experience-based testing techniques, thus, are often used as part of a reactive test strategy. However, they can be—and, in my opinion, should be—used in conjunction with other strategies, such as analytical strategies, to augment the tests produced using those strategies.

Error Guessing

One experience-based technique is called *error guessing*. The tester—who ideally has a programming background—guesses about what mistakes could be made, and thus what defects would be introduced. The tester then creates tests to find failures associated with those defects. This error guessing can also be used during risk analysis to identify and assess risks.

ISTQB Glossary

Error guessing: A test design technique where the experience of the tester is used to anticipate what defects might be present in the component or system under test as a result of errors made, and to design tests specifically to expose them.

Error guessing can be used at any test level, both on its own and as a way of augmenting other techniques. In skilled hands, it can be used to do an informal, real-time smoke test. As with all experience-based techniques, coverage is hard to measure, the power of the technique is entirely based on the testers' ability to predict bugs, and each tester is likely to do it very differently. To measure coverage, you can add a defect taxonomy, but that limits the creativity of the process, which is part of its strength. It's best used as a purely creative adjunct to other test techniques, where it will allow the tester to find many defects that would escape detection by purely structural or behavioral techniques.

Error guessing is a term introduced by Glenford Myers in the first book on software testing, *The Art of Software Testing*.

Conceptually, error guessing involves the tester taking guesses about a mistake that a programmer might make and then developing tests for it. Notice that this is what might be a called a *gray-box test*, since it requires the tester to have some idea about typical programming mistakes, how those mistakes become bugs, how those bugs manifest themselves as failures, and how we can force failures to happen.

Now, if error guessing follows an organized hierarchical taxonomy, like defect-taxonomy-based tests, then the taxonomy is the model. The taxonomy also provides the coverage criterion, if it is used, because we again test to the extent appropriate for the various elements of the taxonomy. Usually, the error guessing follows mostly from tester inspiration.

As you can tell so far, the derivation of tests is based on the tester's intuition and knowledge about how errors (the programmer's or designer's mistakes) become defects that manifest themselves as failures if you poke and prod the system in the right way. Now, error-guessing tests can be part of a set of analytical, predesigned, scripted tests. However, they often aren't, but are added to the scripts (ideally) or used instead of scripts (less ideal) at execution time.

The underlying bug hypothesis is very similar to that of defect-taxonomy-based tests. Here, though, we not only count on the programmer to make the same mistakes, but we also count on the tester to have seen bugs like the ones in this system before, and to remember how to find them.

Checklist Testing

Another form of experience-based testing is checklist testing. In checklist testing, we have a list of test conditions that we want to cover, and that list is relatively stable from one release to the next. The test conditions on the checklist can come from relevant standards, the test team's collective experience, past failures that were observed, best practices, or whatever. The checklists should be kept up to date as needs evolve, but they do tend to change rather slowly.

These checklists can be used at any test level, provided we have testers who are experienced enough to translate the test conditions into test cases. They are a good way of providing such testers with guidance for conducting a quick but thorough regression test or smoke test. The tests do tend to have limited reproducibility, and you can miss things due to the very abstract nature of the checklist, but, given the right tester and the right checklist, they can be very useful. Such tests can find a wide variety of bugs, depending on the defects.

With checklist testing, we now get into an area that is often very much like quality risk analysis in its structure.

Conceptually, the tester takes a high-level list of items to be noted, checked, or remembered. What is important for the system to do? What is important for it not to do?

The checklist is the model for testing, and the checklist is usually organized around a theme. The theme can be quality characteristics, user interface standards, key operations, or any other theme you'd like to pick.

To derive tests from a checklist, either during test execution time or during test design, you create one test to evaluate the system per the test conditions on the checklist.

Now, we can specify a coverage criterion, which is that there be at least one test per checklist item. However, the checklist items are often very high level.

By very high level, I don't mean high-level test. You might remember we looked at those when we talked about use case testing. A high-level or logical test gives rules about how to generate the specific inputs and expected results but doesn't necessarily give the exact values, as a low-level or concrete test would.

A test checklist is even higher level than that. It will give you a list of areas to test, characteristics to evaluate, general rules for determining test pass or failure, and the like. So, you can develop and execute one set of tests, while another competent tester might cover the same checklist differently. Notice that this is not true for many of the specification-based techniques we covered, where there was one right answer.

ISTQB Glossary

Checklist-based testing: An experience-based test design technique whereby the experienced tester uses a high-level list of items to be noted, checked, or remembered, or a set of rules or criteria against which a product has to be verified.

The underlying bug hypothesis in checklist testing is that bugs in the areas of the checklist are either likely, important, or both.

Notice again that much of this harkens back to risk-based testing. But notice that, in some cases, the checklist is predetermined, rather than developed by an analysis of the system. As such, checklist testing is often the dominant technique when the testing follows a methodical test strategy. When testing follows an analytical test strategy, the list of test conditions is not a static checklist, but rather is generated at the beginning of the project, and periodically refreshed during the project, through some sort of analysis, such as quality risk analysis.

Example: Usability Checklist

Figure 3–60 shows an example of a checklist, this one for usability of a system. It's drawn from Jakob Nielsen's book *Usability Engineering*.

- Simple and natural dialog
- Speak the user's language
- Minimize user memory load
- Consistency
- Feedback
- Clearly marked exits
- Shortcuts
- Good error messages
- Prevent errors
- Help and documentation

Figure 3–60 *Usability checklist*

Simple and natural dialog means that the exact right content and amount of information is provided to the user when needed and where needed (screen-wise). The graphics and colors on the screen should reinforce and direct user attention toward—not conflict with or distract the user from—the message. The amount of information should be what is needed, and no more, and certainly not extraneous details that don't matter.

Speaking the user's language means not talking down to the user, but also not using terms, jargon, acronyms, and so on that the user won't understand.

Minimize user memory load means not forcing the user to keep too many details in her head from one screen to the next, giving useful prompts and visual cues about what to do next or how to get help, and so forth.

Consistency means that screens look and feel the same, hot keys remain constant, color schemes are similar (e.g., red means bad and green means good throughout), and so forth.

Providing feedback means keeping the user informed about what has happened, especially when there is processing time going by or when something has failed.

Clearly marked exits mean that it's obvious how to get out of the screen, mode, or dialog you're in and back to a place you were before—including out of the system.

Shortcuts allow experts to bypass the handholding the new users need.

Good error messages are intuitive and helpful. They avoid codes, they are precise about the problem, and they are polite and soothing.

Preventing errors means that we minimize opportunities for users to make mistakes. This, of course, improves testability, because it reduces the number of invalid tests we have to try.

And, even though it's used less often than most support people would like, we should provide help and documentation.

Okay, so how do we use this checklist for testing? Well, imagine going through the screens on the system, methodically, checking off each of these main areas on each screen and for each transition between screens. If you see problems, you report a bug against this heuristic for the screen or screen transition where you saw the problem. Notice the subjectivity involved in the evaluation of test pass or fail results.

Exploratory Testing

Exploratory testing is yet another experience-based technique. As the name suggests, we simultaneously learn, plan, design, and run our tests, as well as reporting our results frequently. As we learn, the focus of our tests change. Very little documentation is typically produced. It is used during system test and sometimes acceptance test, ideally as a way to augment other test techniques or in severely under-documented situations.

Because exploratory testing is unpredictable by its very nature, it can be hard to manage. Scheduling can be handled by incorporating exploratory testing into periods of pre-designed testing, because otherwise it becomes very hard to schedule. Coverage and reproducibility are an issue, unless documentation is created during test execution, which then reduces coverage. At a high level, coverage can be measured by test charters, but that will be coarse grained at the test condition level. Exploratory testing can be very good at finding bugs in particular scenarios, especially ones that arise in validating unusual workflows that span multiple functional areas.

Exploratory testing, like checklist testing, often follows some basic guidelines, like a checklist, and often relies on tester judgment and experience to evaluate the test results. However, exploratory testing is inherently more reactive and more dynamic, in that most of the action with exploratory testing has to happen during test execution.

Conceptually, exploratory testing is happening when a tester is simultaneously learning the system, designing tests, and executing tests. The results of one test, largely, determine what we test next.

Now, that is not to say that this is random or driven entirely by impulse or instinct. Notice that we could use Nielsen's list of usability heuristics not only as a preplanned checklist, but also as a heuristic to guide us to important or problematic software areas. The best kinds of exploratory testing usually do have some type of model, either written or mental.

According to this model, we derive tests by thinking how best to explore some area of testing interest. In some cases, to keep focus and provide some amount of structure, the test areas to be covered are constrained by a test charter.

As with checklist testing, we can specify a coverage criterion, which is that there be at least one test per charter (if we have them). However, the charters, like checklist items, are often very high level.

The underlying bug hypothesis is that the system will reveal buggy areas during test execution that would be hidden during test basis analysis. In other words, you can only learn so much about how a system behaves and misbehaves by reading about it. This is, of course, true. It also suggests an important point, which is that exploratory testing, and indeed experience-based tests in general, make a good blend with scripted tests, because they offset each other's weak spots.

Exploratory Test Charters

The inability to say what was tested during exploratory testing, to any degree of accuracy, has long been seen as its Achilles heel. The whole confidence-building objective of testing is undermined if we can't say what we've tested and how much we've tested it, as well as being able to say what we haven't yet tested. Notice that analytical test strategies do a good job of this, at least when traceability is present.

One way people have come up with to reduce this problem with exploratory testing is to use test charters. A test charter specifies the tasks, objectives, and deliverables, but in very few words. The charters can be developed well in advance—even, in fact, based on analysis of risks as we have done for some clients—or they can be developed just immediately before test execution starts and then continually adjusted based on the test results.

Right before test execution starts for a given period of testing, exploratory testing sessions are planned around the charters. To whatever level of documentation and formality is required, these charters document the consensus between test analyst and test manager about the following:

- What the test session is to achieve
- Where the test session will focus
- What is in and out of scope for the session
- What resources should be used, including how long it should last

Now, given how lightweight the charters are—as you'll see in a moment—you might expect that the tester would get more information. And, indeed, the charters can be augmented with defect taxonomies, checklists, quality risk analyses, requirements specification, user manuals, and whatever else might be of use. However, these augmentations are to be used as reference during test execution, rather than as objects of analysis—i.e., as a test basis—prior to the test execution starting.

Example: Exploratory Testing

In Figure 3–61 we see an example of how this works. This is an actual exploratory testing session log from a project we did for a client. We were in charge of running an acceptance test for the development organization on behalf of the customers. If that sounds like a weird arrangement, by the way, yes, it was.

Exploratory Testing Session Log

Tester _Name_____   Date _When_____

Time on-task _1:45_____   Charter completed? _yes_____

Charter

Test the security of the login page, see if it's possible to log in without a password.

Bugs reported

937 – Log in form vulnerable to SQL injection
939 – System identifies a valid username when the password is wrong

Issues that need followup

* Lockout feature on three unsuccessful login attempts doesn't seem to work

---

Figure 3–61   *Example: Exploratory testing*

At the top of the log, we have captured the tester's name and when the test was run. It also includes a log of how much time was spent and whether the tester believes that the charter was completely explored—remember, this is subjective, as with the checklists.

Below the heading information, you see the charter. Now, it's not unusual to have a test called "test login security," or even a sentence like this in the description of a test or listed as a condition in a test. However, understand that *this is all there is*. There are no further details specified in the test for the tester. You see how we are relying very heavily on the tester's knowledge and experience?

Under the charter section are two sections that indicate results. The first lists the bugs that were found. The numbers correspond to numbers in a bug tracking system. The second lists issues that need follow-up. These can be—as they are here—things that might be bugs but that we didn't have time to finish researching. Or, it could indicate situations where testing was incomplete due to blockages. In that case, of course, we'd expect that the charter would not be complete.

Applying the Best Technique

So, what is true about applying these defect- and experience-based techniques?

You probably noticed a distinctly lower level of formality than the specification-based techniques. In addition, the coverage criteria are informal and usually subjective.

So, testers must apply knowledge of defects and other experiences to utilize these techniques. Since many of them are defect focused, they are a good way to detect defects.

The extent to which they are dynamic and detection focused rather than analytical and prevention focused varies. They can be quick tests integrated into—or dominating—the test execution period. In these tests, the tester has no formally pre-planned activities to perform. They can involve pre-planned sessions with charters but no detail beyond that. They can involve the creation of scripted test procedures.

They are useful in almost all projects, but are particularly valuable under the following circumstances:

- There are no specifications available.
- There is poor documentation of the system under test.
- You are forced to cope with a situation where insufficient time was allowed for the test process earlier in the lifecycle—specifically, insufficient time to plan, analyze, design, and implement.
- Testers have experience with the application domain, with the underlying technology, and, perhaps most importantly, with testing.
- We can analyze operational failures and incorporate that information into our taxonomies, error guesses, checklists, explorations, and attacks.

I particularly like to use defect- and experience-based techniques in conjunction with behavior-based and structure-based techniques. Each of the techniques covered in the Advanced syllabus—both for test analysts and technical test analysts, have their strengths and weakness. So, using defect- and experience-based tests fills the gaps in test coverage that result from systematic weaknesses in these more structured techniques.

Example: Selecting and Mixing Techniques

In the Internet appliance project, we used a mixture of dynamic, chartered, exploratory testing and analytical, risk-based, scripted testing. Some key details of how that worked are shown in Table 3–55. The test manager and the three test engineers, who together had over 20 years total experience, did the exploratory testing. Test technicians did the scripted testing. Some of them had no testing experience, and others had just a little.

Table 3–55   *Example: Selecting and mixing techniques*

Staff	7 Technicians	3 Engineers + 1 Mngr.
Experience	< 10 years total	> 20 years total
Test type	Precise scripts	Chartered exploratory
Test hrs/day	42	6
Bugs found	928 (78%)	261 (22%)
Bug effectiveness	22	44
Scripts run	850	0
Inputs submitted	~5,000–10,000	~1,000
Results verified	~4,000–8,000	~1,000

During test execution, the technicians each spent about six hours per day running tests. The rest of the time, three to four hours per day, was spent reading email, attending meetings, updating bug reports, doing confirmation testing, and the like.

The engineers and managers, being heavily engaged in other tasks, could spend only one to two hours per day doing exploratory testing. Due to their heavy experience, you can see that, even so, the experienced testers were star bug finders.

However, when we start looking at coverage, we can see the picture change. The technicians ran about 850 test scripts over the three months of system test. That covered a lot of ground, well-documented ground yielding well-documented results that we could show to management. The exploratory testing didn't really leave any clear documentation behind. We weren't using the session-log approach that I showed earlier, in part because we were relying on the technicians to gather the coverage evidence with the scripts.

Now, how about sheer volume of input? I can't say for sure, but I'd estimate that the manual scripted tests resulted in somewhere between 5,000 and

10,000 inputs of various kinds—strings, dates, radio buttons, and so on—while the exploratory testing was probably at best a fifth of that. Similarly, scripted tests probably resulted in many more explicit checks of results. Now, hour-for-hour the exploratory testing was probably just as effective, but it would have been less effective if we'd had to gather the session logs, as that would have slowed us down.

So, which was better? Ah, it wasn't that kind of experiment. It wasn't an experiment at all; it was a proven way of mixing two strategies, each with different strengths.

The exploratory testing was very effective at finding bugs on an hour-per-hour basis, and we found a number of bugs that wouldn't have been found by the scripts. The reusable test scripts gave us good regression risk mitigation, good risk mitigation, and good confidence building. Overall, a successful blended approach.

Selecting Techniques Exercise

Consider the following test techniques that we've covered in this book:

- Equivalence partitioning
- Boundary value analysis
- Decision tables
- Use case tests
- State-based tests
- Pairwise tests
- Classification trees
- Defect-taxonomy tests
- Error-guessing tests
- Checklist-based tests
- Exploratory tests
- Software attacks

Without redundancy to previous exercises or examples, identify uses for the techniques on the HELLOCARMS project. List specification element numbers and descriptions of the application as appropriate.

Selecting Techniques Debrief

Table 3–56 shows a listing of where I would apply the different techniques covered in this book to the HELLOCARMS project.

Table 3–56   *Applying all the techniques to HELLOCARMS*

Test Technique	Requirements Section or Element/Description
Equivalence partitioning	010-010-040 Armed with the list of the valid inputs for each field, check every input field to ensure they can reject invalid values.
Boundary value analysis	010-010-040 Extend the testing of input validation using boundary value analysis.
Decision tables	010-020-010, 010-020-020, 010-020-030 Develop a decision table based on the credit policies (presumably in another document), and then design tests from that decision table.
Use case tests	010-010-050 Develop a use case that describes how the payoff features work, then design tests from that use case.
State-based tests	010-010-060 Develop a state-transition diagram for the application (rather than the telephone banker as was done in a previous exercise). Test the application's state-based behaviors, including the ability to interrupt and return to the interview.
Pairwise tests	010-010-220 Test pairwise combinations of existing products from Globobank with potential customers, as well as pairwise combinations of products from other banks with Globobank home equity products.
Classification trees	010-030-040 Develop a classification tree for the various attributes of the loan/line-of-credit payoff feature. Design tests to cover that classification tree, emphasizing combinations where various boundaries are reached (e.g., entire loan used to pay off one or more existing loans, just enough loans paid off to allow new loan to be made, and so on).
Defect-taxonomy tests	010-040 Create a defect taxonomy for every security-related failure observed at Globobank for similar applications, augmented by information on security-related failures at other banks for similar applications. Design tests to check for these defects.
Error-guessing tests	Entire system Obtain a list of known and/or past interfacing problems between LoDoPS, GLADS, and other applications that will interoperate with HELLOCARMS. Design tests to provoke those problems, where possible.
Checklist-based tests	010-010-020 Identify every screen, flow between screens, and script. Ensure each was tested.
Exploratory tests	010-010-170 Use a mix of PC configurations, security settings, connection speeds, customer personas, and existing customer relationships to test applications over the Internet.
Software attacks	000 Introduction Attacks, especially security attacks, on the structure of the system.

Exploratory Testing Exercise

Consider the use of exploratory testing you identified in the previous exercise or some other use of the technique on the HELLOCARMS project.

The exercise consists of four parts:

1. Identify a list of test charters for testing this area.
2. Document your assumption about the testers who will use the charters.
3. Assign a priority to each charter and explain why.
4. Explain how you would report results.

As always, check your work on the preceding part before proceeding to the next part.

Exploratory Testing Debrief

In the selecting techniques exercise I selected requirements element 010-010-170, which has to do with allowing applications over the Internet. I wrote that I would "use a mix of PC configurations, security settings, connection speeds, customer personas, and existing customer relationships to test applications over the Internet."

Let's see what that might look like.

First, I would use pairwise techniques to generate a set of target PC configurations, including browser brand and version, operating system, and connection speeds. Since we've already discussed how to do that, I won't rehash it here. I will mention, though, that I would build these configurations prior to test execution, storing drive images for a quick restore during testing.

Next, I would create a list of customer personas. *Personas* refers to the habits that a customer exhibits and experience that a customer has.

Nervous customer: Uses Back button a lot, revises entries, has long think time
Novice Internet user: Makes a lot of data input mistakes, has long think time
Power user: Types quickly, makes few mistakes, uses copy and paste from other PC applications (e.g., account numbers), has very short think time
Impatient customer: Types quickly, makes many mistakes, has very short think time, hits Next button multiple times

Now, I would create a list of existing customer banking relationship types.

- Limited accounts, none with Globobank
- Limited accounts, some with Globobank
- Limited accounts, all with Globobank
- Extensive accounts, none with Globobank
- Extensive accounts, some with Globobank
- Extensive accounts, all with Globobank

Notice that these two lists allow a lot of tester latitude and discretion. Notice also that, for the existing customer banking relationships, as with the PC configurations, it would again make a lot of sense for the tester to create this customer data before test execution started.

Finally, I would create a list of test charters, as shown in Table 3–57.

Table 3–57   *Test charters for HELLOCARMS exploratory testing*

General rules for test charters:
• For each of the following charters, restore your test PC to a previously untested PC configuration prior to starting the charter. Make sure each configuration is tested at least once.
• For each of the following charters, select a persona. Make sure each persona is tested at least once.
• For each of the following charters, select an existing customer banking relationship type. Make sure each customer banking relationship type is tested at least once.
• Allocate 30–45 minutes for each application; thus each charter is 30–120 minutes long.
Charters:
1. Test successful applications with both limited and extensive banking relationships, where customer declines insurance.
2. Test a successful application where customer accepts insurance.
3. Test a successful application where the system declines insurance.
4. Test a successful application where property value escalates application.
5. Test a successful application where loan amount escalates application.
6. Test an unsuccessful application due to credit history.
7. Test an unsuccessful application due to insufficient income.
8. Test an unsuccessful application due to excessive debt.
9. Test an unsuccessful application due to insufficient equity.
10. Test cancellation of an application from all possible screens (120 minutes).
11. Test a fraudulent application, where material information provided by customer does not match decisioning mainframe's data.
12. Test a fraudulent application, where material information provided by customer does not match LoDoPS data.

Yes, these charters might revisit some areas covered by our other, specification-based tests. However, because the testers will be taking side trips that wouldn't be in the scripts, the coverage of the scenarios will be broader.

Now, what is my assumption about the testers who will use these charters? Obviously, they have to be experienced testers, because the test specification provided is very limited and provides a lot of discretion. They also have to understand the application well, as I am not giving them any instructions on how to carry out the charters. They also understand PC technology at least well enough to restore a PC configuration from a drive image, though it would be possible to give unambiguous directions to someone on how to do that.

In terms of the priority to each charter, I have listed them above in priority order. Notice that I start with the simplest case, a successful application with no insurance, and then add complexity from there. My objective is to use the exploratory tests during the scripted tests, in parallel. As the test coverage under the scripts gets greater and greater, so also does the complexity of the exploratory scenarios.

As for results reporting, I would have each charter tracked as a test case in my test management system. For bug reports, though, it would be very important that the tester perform adequate isolation to determine if the configuration, the persona, the banking relationship, or the functionality itself was behind the failure.

3.5 Sample Exam Questions

1. Which of the following is a typical defect that equivalence partitioning would identify?

   A. Improper handling of sequences of events

   B. Improper handling of combinations of conditions

   C. Improper handling of large and small values

   D. Improper handling of classes of inputs

2. Which of the following is a typical defect that boundary value analysis would identify?

A. Improper handling of sequences of events

B. Improper handling of combinations of conditions

C. Improper handling of large and small values

D. Improper handling of classes of inputs

3 Which of the following is a typical defect that decision table testing would identify?

A. Improper handling of sequences of events

B. Improper handling of combinations of conditions

C. Improper handling of large and small values

D. Improper handling of classes of inputs

4. Which of the following is a typical defect that state-based testing would identify?

A. Improper handling of sequences of events

B. Improper handling of combinations of conditions

C. Improper handling of configuration combinations

D. Improper handling of classes of inputs

5. Which of the following is a typical defect that classification tree testing would identify?

A. Improper handling of sequences of events

B. Improper handling of typical workflows

C. Improper handling of configuration combinations

D. Improper handling of classes of inputs

6. Which of the following is a typical defect that use case testing would identify?

    A. Improper handling of large and small values

    B. Improper handling of configuration combinations

    C. Improper handling of classes of inputs

    D. Improper handling of typical workflows

7. Which of the following is a typical defect that pairwise testing would identify?

    A. Improper handling of sequences of events

    B. Improper handling of typical workflows

    C. Improper handling of configuration combinations

    D. Improper handling of classes of inputs

8. Assume you are a test analyst working on a banking project to upgrade an existing automated teller machine system to allow customers to obtain cash advances from supported credit cards. The system should allow cash advances of at least 500 dollars for all supported credit cards. The correct list of supported credit cards is American Express, Visa, Japan Credit Bank, Eurocard, and MasterCard.

    Assume that, in the following list of valid input tests, the first item in the parenthesized triple represents the credit card, the second item represents the amount to withdraw, and the third item represents the expected result. Which of the following selections gives a set of tests that covers the equivalence partitions for credit cards and shows the correct expected result?

    A. (American Express, $20, succeed); (Visa, $100, succeed); (Japan Credit Bank, $500, succeed); (Eurocard, $200, succeed); (MasterCard, $400, succeed)

    B. (American Express, $20, succeed); (Visa, $600, fail); (Japan Credit Bank, $500, fail); (Eurocard, $200, succeed); (MasterCard, $400, succeed)

    C. (American Express, $20, succeed); (Japan Credit Bank, $500, succeed); (Eurocard, $200, succeed); (MasterCard, $400, succeed)

D. (American Express, $20, succeed); (Visa, $600, succeed); (Japan Credit Bank, $500, succeed); (Eurocard, $200, succeed); (MasterCard, $400, succeed)

9. Assume you are a test analyst working on a banking project to upgrade an existing automated teller machine system to allow customers to obtain cash advances from supported credit cards. The system should allow cash advances from 20 dollars to 500 dollars, inclusively, for all supported credit cards. The correct list of supported credit cards is American Express, Visa, Japan Credit Bank, Eurocard, and MasterCard. The user interface starts with a default amount of 100 dollars for advances, and the ATM keypad is used to increase or decrease that amount in 20-dollar increments.

   Assume that, in the following list of tests, the first item in the parenthesized triple represents the credit card, the second item represents the amount to withdraw, and the third item represents the expected result. Which of the following selections gives a set of tests that covers the boundary values for cash advances and shows the correct expected result?

   A. (American Express, $20, succeed); (Visa, $500, succeed); (Japan Credit Bank, $520, fail); (Eurocard, $0, fail)

   B. (American Express, $20, succeed); (Visa, $600, fail); (Japan Credit Bank, $500, fail); (Eurocard, $200, succeed); (MasterCard, $400, succeed)

   C. (American Express, $20, succeed); (Japan Credit Bank, $500, succeed); (Eurocard, $520, succeed); (MasterCard, $400, succeed)

   D. (American Express, $20, succeed); (Visa, $600, fail); (Japan Credit Bank, $500, succeed); (Eurocard, $200, succeed); (MasterCard, $400, succeed)

10. Assume you are a test analyst working on a banking project to upgrade an existing automated teller machine system to allow customers to obtain cash advances from supported credit cards. The system should allow cash advances from 20 dollars to 500 dollars, inclusively, for all supported credit cards. The correct list of supported credit cards is American Express, Visa, Japan Credit Bank, Eurocard, and MasterCard. The user interface starts with a default amount of 100 dollars for advances, and the ATM keypad is used to increase or decrease that amount in 20-dollar increments.

   Consider the decision table shown in Table 3–58 that describes the handling of these transactions.

Table 3-58 *Cash advance decision table*

Conditions	1	2	3	4	5
Supported card	N	Y	Y	Y	Y
User authenticated	-	N	Y	Y	Y
Allowed advance amount	-	-	N	Y	Y
Within available balance	-	-	-	N	Y
Actions					
Reject card	Y	Y	N	N	N
Prompt for new amount	N	N	Y	Y	N
Dispense cash	N	N	N	N	Y

Assume that you want to design a set of tests where the following coverage is achieved:

- Decision table coverage
- Boundary values for allowed and disallowed advance amounts
- Successful advance for each supported card

Design a set of tests that achieves this level of coverage with the minimum possible number of tests. Assume each test consists of a single combination of conditions to create and a single combination of actions to check. How many tests do you need?

A. 4

B. 5

C. 6

D. 10

11. Assume you are a test analyst working on a project to create a programmable thermostat for home use to control central heating, ventilation, and air conditioning (HVAC) systems. You want to test the ability of the thermostat to properly interact with the central HVAC unit.

At any given moment, the HVAC unit is in either an *off* state (the initial state) or an *on* state. The thermostat can send the HVAC unit either a *start* event or a *stop* event. If the unit is in an *on* state and it receives a *stop* event, it will always deactivate and display an "idle" message.

If the unit is in an *off* state and it receives a *start* event, it will activate and display an "active" message if all conditions are normal. However, if the unit is in an *off* state and it receives a *start* event, it might fail to activate under one of three conditions:

- No power to the HVAC unit, the compressor, or other component
- A failure of the HVAC unit, the compressor, or other component
- To prevent damage to the HVAC unit, the compressor, or other component

If it fails to activate, it displays an error code associated with the condition that caused the failure to activate.

Analyze these requirements to draw a state transition diagram for this thermostat. Use a separate state transition to show each failure-to-activate event/condition pair.

Which of the following statements is true?

A. There are two states and three transitions.

B. There are two states and five transitions.

C. There are five states and three transitions.

D. There are five states and two transitions.

12. Continue with the scenario in the previous question.

Use the state transition diagram you created to generate tests that achieve state and transition coverage (i.e., 0-switch coverage) subject to the following additional rules for these tests:

A test *must* begin with the HVAC unit in the initial state.

A test *must* complete when the HVAC unit returns to the *off* state from the *on* state.

All tests *can only* complete with the HVAC unit in the *off* state.

Design the minimum number of tests possible.

How many tests did you design?

A. 1

B. 2

C. 4

D. 8

13. Assume you are a test analyst working on a project to create a programmable thermostat for home use to control central heating, ventilation, and air conditioning (HVAC) systems. In addition to the normal HVAC control functions, the thermostat also has the ability to download data to a browser-based application that runs on PCs for further analysis.

    You are planning for compatibility testing of the application and this feature. You identify the following factors and, for each factor, the following options:

    Supported PC/thermostat connections: USB and Bluetooth

    Supported operating systems: Windows 7, Windows 8, Windows 10, Mac, Linux

    Supported browsers: Internet Explorer, Firefox, Chrome

    Assume that you plan to use a classification tree to design the tests. You want to cover all possible pairs of operating systems with PC/thermostat connections because you are concerned about possible data transfer issues, but you only care that every browser be tested at least once.
    What is the minimum number of configurations you'll need to test?

    A. 5

    B. 10

    C. 15

    D. 30

14. Continue with the scenario in the previous question.
    Assume instead that you plan to use an orthogonal array to design the tests. You want to cover all possible pairs of options across all three possible pairs of factors.

    What is the minimum number of configurations you'll need to test?

    A. 5

    B. 10

    C. 15

    D. 30

15. Continue with the scenario in the previous question.

Assume that Figure 3–62 describes an informal use case for the data transfer feature.

Thermostat data download: Normal workflow

1.   User connects PC to thermostat using either USB cable or Bluetooth module

2.   User points browser to analysis site (specified in manual)

3.   User clicks on Download Thermostat Data button

4.   Browser displays "Download Complete" message

Exceptions:

- PC-to-thermostat connection fails; browser displays error message "Could not connect to thermostat" after step 3.

- User cannot connect to analysis site; browser displays appropriate error message depending on the nature of the problem.

- Data download fails before completion; browser displays error message "Download failed, please try again" after step three.

Figure 3–62   *Informal data transfer use case*

Which of the following statements (or some similar statement) would be found in a test designed to cover one of the exception workflows in this use case?

A. Click Download Thermostat Data button, wait for the "Download Complete" message, and then proceed to the Analysis workflow to verify the data.

B. Click Download Thermostat Data button and immediately disconnect the USB cable or Bluetooth module.

C. Click Download Thermostat Data button, wait for the "Download Complete" message, and then disconnect the USB cable or Bluetooth module.

D. Click Download Thermostat Data button, wait for the "Download Complete" message, and then close the browser.

16. Which of the following statements captures a key difference between specification-based and defect-based test design techniques?

    A. Specification-based techniques derive tests from the structure of the system, while defect-based techniques derive tests from what is known about defects.

    B. Defect-based techniques derive tests from the structure of the system, while specification-based techniques derive tests from the behavior of the system.

    C. Defect-based techniques derive tests from the structure of the system, while specification-based techniques derive tests from an analysis of the test basis.

    D. Defect-based techniques derive tests from what is known about defects, while specification-based techniques derive tests from an analysis of the test basis.

17. Which of the following is an example of the use of a defect taxonomy for test design?

    A. Using frequency of defect occurrence as an input into quality risk analysis

    B. Selecting test inputs that are likely to reveal a failure associated with a particular defect, if present

    C. Updating the defect taxonomy after test execution to reflect the latest findings

    D. Sending the defect taxonomy, along with frequency of defect occurrence, to development for process improvements

18. Which of the following is an important principle for use of experience-based test techniques?

    A. Tester skill is a critical factor in assignment of test execution tasks.

    B. Tester skills are less important than ensuring 100% tester utilization.

    C. Testers should always focus on defect-preventing activities.

    D. Testers should be evaluated based on the number of defects they find.

19. Assume you are a test analyst working on a project to create a programmable thermostat for home use to control central heating, ventilation, and air conditioning (HVAC) systems. In addition to the normal HVAC control functions, the thermostat also has the ability to download data to a browser-based application that runs on PCs for further analysis.

Consider the following exploratory test charter:

Load various thermostat data sets to the application and evaluate the standard reports the application can produce.

Which of the following statements is true and consistent with the approach to exploratory testing described in the Advanced Test Analyst syllabus?

A. All actions associated with executing this charter should occur during test execution, after receipt of the initial test object.

B. All of the thermostat data sets should be created prior to test execution, while all other actions associated with executing this charter should occur during test execution.

C. Most of the thermostat data sets could be created prior to test execution, provided those data sets could be modified during test execution based on test results.

D. All data, inputs, and expected results for this test charter should be specified in a concrete test before the start of test execution.

20. Consider the following software fault attack proposed by Whittaker's technique:

Force all possible incoming errors from the software/OS interfaces to the application.

Which of the following is the kind of failure you are looking for when testing using this attack?

A. Application crashes when unsupported characters are pasted into an input field using the Windows Clipboard

B. Application splash screen has incorrect spelling of company name

C. Application fails to display financial numbers in currency format on reports

D. Application miscalculates total monthly balance due on credit cards

21. Assume you are a test analyst working on a banking project to upgrade an existing automated teller machine system to allow customers to obtain cash advances from supported credit cards.

    When the user first inserts a valid credit card type, the system considers the user to be in the *unauthenticated* state. Prior to requesting a cash advance, though, the user must enter the *authenticated* state. The user authenticates by entering the proper PIN.

    When authenticating the user, the system should allow the user to enter their PIN up to three times before failing the authentication and rejecting the card. On the first and second try, the system should prompt the user to reenter the PIN.

    Suppose you are concerned that, depending on the exact number of invalid PINs entered, the system might behave improperly. Which of the following test design techniques is specifically targeted at such failures?

    A. Equivalence partitioning extended by boundary value analysis

    B. Pairwise testing with orthogonal arrays

    C. State-based testing using N-1 switch coverage

    D. Classification tree testing using two-factor authentication

22. If we say that a set of tests has achieved 100% structural decision coverage on a particular module in a program, what does that mean?

    A. That all bugs present in that module were necessarily revealed by those tests.

    B. That every control flow branch had been executed at least once by those tests.

    C. That every dataflow in that module was exercised at least once by those tests.

    D. That every path through that module was exercised at least once by those tests.

4 Testing Software Quality Characteristics

"[Quality is] fitness for use. Features [that] are decisive as to product performance and as to product satisfaction .... The word 'quality' also refers to freedom from deficiencies...[that] result in complaints, claims, returns, rework and other damage. Those collectively are forms of product dissatisfaction."

Joseph M. Juran, in *Planning for Quality*

The fourth chapter of the Advanced Test Analyst syllabus is concerned with tests of software characteristics. In this chapter, the Advanced Test Analyst syllabus expands on a concept introduced in the Foundation syllabus, that of ISO 9126 software quality characteristics, to explain testing as it relates to these various attributes of functional and non-functional software quality. There are two sections.

1. Introduction
2. Quality Characteristics for Business Domain Testing

Let's look at each section and how it relates to test analysis.

4.1 Introduction

Learning objectives
Recall of content only.

In the previous chapter, we looked at a variety of test design techniques in different categories. Each technique has its strengths and weaknesses, its proper and improper application. In this chapter, we'll talk about how to take advantage of the strengths of various techniques to evaluate the quality of the software we are testing.

As a way of structuring the conversation about quality characteristics, we use the ISO 9126 standard. This standard is gradually being replaced by the ISO 25000 standard, but the changes won't affect the way we use the standard to illustrate testing of specific quality characteristics. We also use the standard as a way to divide the testing of software quality characteristics across technical test analysts and test analysts. As this is a book for test analysts, we'll focus on the characteristics of functionality and usability. That includes testing of compliance to any relevant functionality or usability standards.

As we work through this chapter, keep in mind that testing for software quality is not just a matter of using the right techniques. You also have to consider when to use the techniques and how to incorporate them into the lifecycle. The lifecycle often influences the type of documentation supplied for the software and when the software will be available for testing. Some of the techniques benefit from or even require tool support. And, of course, the expertise of the testers is another important consideration.

Division of Quality Characteristics

In Table 4–1 you see the division of the ISO 9126 quality characteristics across test analysts and technical test analysts. As you can see, with the exception of security, test analysts are responsible for testing all functional sub-characteristics. Test analysts are responsible for testing all sub-characteristics related to usability, including one that is not listed explicitly in the standard, accessibility.

ISTQB Glossary

Attractiveness: The capability of the software product to be attractive to the user.

Learnability: The capability of the software product to enable the user to learn its application.

Operability: The capability of the software product to enable the user to operate and control it.

Understandability: The capability of the software product to enable the user to understand whether the software is suitable and how it can be used for particular tasks and conditions of use.

Table 4–1   *Division of quality characteristics*

Characteristic	Sub-characteristics	TA	TTA
Functionality	Accuracy, suitability, interoperability, compliance	X	
	Security		X
Reliability	Maturity (robustness), fault tolerance, recoverability, compliance		X
Usability	Understandability, learnability, operability, attractiveness, compliance	X	
Efficiency	Performance (time behavior), resource utilization, compliance		X
Maintainability	Analyzability, changeability, stability, testability, compliance		X
Portability	Adaptability, installability, coexistence, replaceability, compliance		X

4.2   Quality Characteristics for Business Domain Testing

Learning objectives

(K2) Explain by example what testing techniques are appropriate to test accuracy, suitability, interoperability, and compliance characteristics.

(K2) For the accuracy, suitability, and interoperability characteristics, define the typical defects to be targeted.

(K2) For the accuracy, suitability, and interoperability characteristics, define when the characteristic should be tested in the lifecycle.

(K4) For a given project context, outline the approaches that would be suitable to verify and validate both the implementation of the usability requirements and the fulfillment of the user's expectations.

Functional testing focuses on what the system does, rather than how it does it. Non-functional testing is focused on how the system does what it does. Both functional and non-functional testing are black-box tests, being focused on behavior. White-box tests are focused on how the system works internally—i.e., on its structure.

Functional tests can have, as their test basis, the functional requirements. These include both the requirements that are written down in a specification document and those that are implicit. The domain expertise of the tester can also be part of the test basis.

Functional tests will vary by test level or phase. A functional integration test will focus on the functionality of a collection of interfacing modules, usually in

> **ISTQB Glossary**
>
> **Usability testing:** Testing to determine the extent to which the software product is understood, easy to learn, easy to operate, and attractive to the users under specified conditions.

terms of the partial or complete user workflows, use cases, operations, or features these modules provide. A functional system test will focus on the functionality of the application as a whole, complete user workflows, use cases, operations, and features. A functional system integration test will focus on end-to-end functionality that spans the entire set of integrated systems.

The test analyst can employ various test techniques during functional testing at any level. All of the techniques discussed in Chapter 3 will be useful.

We should keep in mind that test analyst is a role, not a title, job description, or position. In other words, some people play the role of test analyst exclusively, but others play that role as part of another job. So, when dedicated, professional testers do functional testing, they are test analysts both in position and in role. However, when domain experts do the analysis, design, implementation, or execution of functional tests, they are working as test analysts. When developers do the analysis, design, implementation, or execution of functional tests, they are working as test analysts.

For test analysts in the ISTQB Advanced syllabus, we consider functional and usability testing as concerned with the following quality attributes:

- Accuracy
- Suitability
- Interoperability
- Usability
- Accessibility

Let's look more closely at each of these areas in the rest of this section.

Accuracy Testing

Functional accuracy testing is concerned with adherence to specified or implied functional requirements. In other words, does the system give the right answer and produce the right effects? Accuracy, in this case, also refers to the right degree of precision in the results.

> **ISTQB Glossary**
>
> **Accuracy testing:** The process of testing to determine the accuracy of a software product.

Functional accuracy testing can include tests of computational accuracy. Indeed, for any application that is used for math, statistics, accounting, science, engineering, or other similar math-intensive functionality, testing of computational accuracy is critical. We want to make sure that all data and situations are handled correctly. Accuracy testing is important at all stages in the lifecycle and in all test levels. To test accuracy properly, you must have a reliable and precise test oracle, which can include specifications, legacy systems, competitors' systems, and more.

Functional accuracy testing can require the use of many of the test techniques in Chapter 3.

Example: Accuracy Testing

Let's revisit the test designs we did for Quicken's stock buy/add screen, specifically the number of shares, the price per share, and commission fields. We applied equivalence partitioning and boundary value analysis to these fields and identified thirteen specific input values for each field.

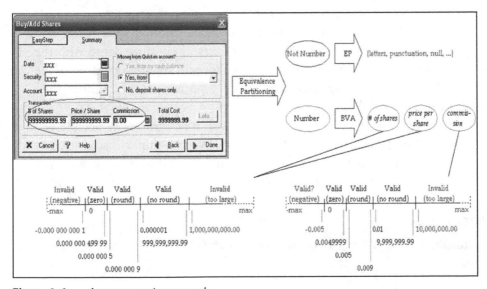

Figure 4–1   *Accuracy testing example*

In this case, as shown in Figure 4–1, we would also want to add testing of the total cost field. This is a calculated output field. It is calculated by using the three input fields. As we can see in Figure 4–1, there is something not right with the calculation. The combination of the maximum number of shares and the maximum price per share is not giving us the right result in the total cost field. Or perhaps the number is right, internally, but is overflowing the display space. Either way, I'd report this as a bug.

Suitability Testing

Functional suitability testing is focused on the appropriateness of a set of functions, relative to its intended, specific tasks. In other words, given the problem we need to solve, can the system solve it?

Notice that there is an element of validation to this focus. We are intent on demonstrating the value of the system in some specific situation. You should remember from the Foundation syllabus the shorthand way of thinking about validation: "Are we building the right system?"

This is in contrast to verification, which is about following the right process, having traceability between functions and requirements and between tests and requirements, and using that traceability to show that the requirements are met. The shorthand way of thinking about verification is: "Are we building the system right?"

Suitability testing starts, at the earliest, during integration testing, as you need to have enough of the system present for the system to actually solve a real-world problem. Suitability testing usually continues through system test and into acceptance test. For example, in Agile projects, the feature demo with the product owner, the tester, and the developer is a form of suitability testing. If the user's needs are not met, regardless of whether requirements are fulfilled, then the software is not suitable.

Based on what we're trying to accomplish here, it's clear that we need to test in ways that strongly resemble actual workflows. We can employ use cases, test scenarios, and exploratory testing. Other techniques tend to be a bit too fine-grained or distracted by bug hunting to serve the purpose. Indeed, you have to

> **ISTQB Glossary**
>
> **Suitability testing:** The process of testing to determine the suitability of a software product.

be careful with exploratory testing to make sure that the charters reflect the need to explore real-world usage of the product.

Example: Suitability Testing

Let's revisit the informal e-commerce purchase use case shown in Figure 4–2. Basically, this use case says that we should be able to put items in a shopping cart, initiate a checkout, enter the information the system needs to process the purchase, and confirm the purchase before it's done.

The use case also says that the system needs to reject attempts to check out with an empty cart, to reject invalid inputs in the purchase information, and to recognize an abandoned cart when it sees one.

E-commerce purchase: Normal workflow
1. Customer places one or more Items in shopping cart
2. Customer selects checkout
3. System gathers address, payment, and shipping information from Customer
4. System displays all information for User confirmation
5. User confirms order to System for delivery

Exceptions
- Customer attempts to check out with empty shopping cart; System gives error message
- Customer provides invalid address, payment, or shipping information; System gives error messages as appropriate
- Customer abandons transaction before or during checkout; System logs Customer out after 10 minutes of inactivity

---

Figure 4–2   *Suitability testing example: use case*

In Table 4–3 we test the suitability of the system's functionality to handle the typical workflow. We had an implied requirement to accept all four major credit cards, so we tested those. We also had an implied requirement to support both US and international customers, so we tested those.

Table 4–2   *Suitability tests (typical)*

#	Test Step	Expected Result
1	Place one item in cart.	Item in cart
2	Click "Check out."	Checkout screen
3	Input valid US address, valid payment using American Express, and valid shipping method information.	Screens display correctly; valid inputs accepted
4	Verify order information.	Shown as entered
5	Confirm order.	Order in system
6	Repeat steps 1–5, but place two items in cart, pay with Visa, and ship internationally.	As shown in steps 1–5
7	Repeat steps 1–5, but place the maximum number of items in cart and pay with MasterCard.	As shown in steps 1–5
8	Repeat steps 1–5, but pay with Discover.	As shown in steps 1–5

In Table 4–3 we test the suitability of the system's functionality under exceptional conditions. We check the empty cart. We check the inputs of invalid information on all screens, including the ability of the system to stop us from proceeding unless a form is correctly filled. Finally, we test the abandonment of a cart from all possible screens. We have clear traceability from the tests back to the use cases.

Table 4–3   *Suitability tests (exception)*

#	Test Step	Expected Result
1	Do not place any items in cart.	Cart empty
2	Click "Check out."	Error message
3	Place item in cart; click "Check out;" enter invalid address, then invalid payment, then invalid shipping information.	Error messages; can't proceed to next screen until resolved
4	Verify order information.	Shown as entered
5	Confirm order.	Order in system
6	Repeat steps 1–3, but stop activity and abandon transaction after placing item in cart.	User logged out exactly ten minutes after last activity
7	Repeats steps 1–3, but stop activity and abandon transaction on each screen.	As shown in 6
8	Repeat steps 1–4; do not confirm order.	As shown in 6

Interoperability Testing

Functional interoperability involves testing the ability of systems or components to exchange information and use that information, in all intended environments: Environments refers to hardware, of course, but also software, middleware, connectivity infrastructure, database systems, and operating systems. This would include not only elements of the environment that the system must interoperate directly with, but also those with which it interoperates indirectly.

As you might imagine, there's a major test configuration element involved with understanding the test environments needed. The environments are then tested with selected major functions. If you suspect that particular functions might interact in particular ways with particular test environments, be sure to test those. If not, then we can test arbitrary combinations of functions with environments.

Interoperability is, of course, about systems interacting with each other. Good interoperability implies ease of integration with other systems with few, if any, major changes.

Design features can raise important considerations for testing software interoperability. Examples include the following:

- The system use of industrywide data or communications standards, such as XML
- The ability of the system to provide standard, flexible, and robust interfaces
- The ability of the system to automatically detect and adapt to various interfaces, communication speeds, protocols, and the like

Since these are design issues, you may need to consult design specifications as well as requirements specifications.

As a test analyst, you can expect to do a lot of interoperability testing when you are developing or integrating commercial off-the-shelf (COTS) software and tools. That's also true if you are developing systems of systems from off-the-shelf or custom-developed applications. Interoperability is important during component integration testing, system testing, and system integration testing.

For testing of functional interoperability, especially end-to-end functionality, you can employ use cases and test scenarios. To determine the environments, you can use equivalence partitioning when you can understand the possible interactions between one or more environments and one or more functions. When interactions are not clear, you can use pairwise testing and classification trees to generate somewhat more arbitrary configurations. Decision

> **ISTQB Glossary**
>
> **Interoperability testing:** The process of testing to determine the interoperability of a software product.

tables can be useful to identify conditions that interact, and state transition diagrams may apply with stateful interfaces.

Let's look at an example.

Example: Testing Interoperability

Suppose we combine the use case example that we just revisited with the pairwise example shown earlier. We can use the orthogonal array as our environment mix and spread the tests across it.

Looking at the use case, we see four typical tests:

The first is American Express, to purchase one item, for shipping in the US. Let's call that test A.

The second is Visa, to purchase two items, for shipping internationally. Let's call that test B.

Table 4–4   *Pairwise testing of interoperability*

1	wifi	Mac	OS	Firefox	A
2	wifi	Linux	Symantec	IE	B
3	wifi	W7	Trend	Chrome	C
4	wifi	W8	McAfee	~	D
5	wired	Mac	Symantec	Chrome	D
6	wired	Linux	OS	~	C
7	wired	W7	McAfee	Firefox	B
8	wired	W8	Trend	IE	A
9	~	Mac	Trend	~	B
10	~	Linux	McAfee	Chrome	A
11	~	W7	OS	IE	D
12	~	W8	Symantec	Firefox	C
13	~	Mac	McAfee	IE	C
14	~	Linux	Trend	Firefox	D
15	~	W7	Symantec	~	A
16	~	W8	OS	Chrome	B

The third is MasterCard, to purchase as many items as the cart will hold, for shipping in the US. Let's call that test C.

The fourth is Discover, to purchase one item, for shipping in the US. Let's call that test D.

In Table 4–4 you can see the combination of tests with the environments. To execute the test, you first obtain the correct configuration, and then you run the test derived earlier from the use case.

The technique would be similar for the negative tests. Remember that we don't want to mix negative and positive tests, especially here, because we're testing for the ability of the e-commerce system to complete an entire function—a purchase—on various supported environment configurations.

Usability Testing

Usability testing, naturally enough, focuses on the users. This is why many notable usability experts and usability test experts have a background in psychology, rather than being primarily technologists or domain experts. Knowledge of sociology, user interface standards, and ergonomics is also helpful. Finally, an understanding of national standards related to accessibility can be important for applications subject to such standards.

Users can vary in terms of their skills, abilities, and disabilities. Something an old technology hand such as me finds easy to understand can be mystifying to my business partner, whose background is in psychology. Being a former Unix programmer and system administrator, I find command lines, short commands, and Internet infrastructure simple, while my business partner finds even the simpler Windows interfaces complicated sometimes. The same software can be used by different users with different abilities, and sometimes with certain disabilities, which can make accessibility testing important. Usability testing can identify situations where some or all users may find it difficult to use the system effectively, efficiently, and in a way they find satisfactory.

Children tend to be remarkably clever in using technology. When my oldest daughter was about three years old, I put an old laptop with a CD drive into her room. I put some CDs in there, too, including an encyclopedia. Later that night, my wife was spooked to hear a man's voice coming from my daughter's room. We discovered that she had figured out how to enable a setting on the encyclopedia that reads each entry aloud.

These kinds of settings and features—text to speech and speech to text—can be very useful to the disabled, especially those who have limited hand mobility or who are sight impaired. The deaf or those with cognitive disabilities might need different types of assistive technologies.

Ultimately, a usable piece of software is one that is suitable for the users. So, usability testing measures whether the users are effective, efficient, and satisfied with the software. Effectiveness implies that the software enables the users to achieve their goals accurately and completely under expected usage conditions. Efficiency implies that these goals can be achieved in some realistic, reasonable period. Satisfaction, in this context, is really the antonym of frustration; in other words, a satisfied user who has effectively and efficiently reached her goals with the system feels that the software was about as helpful as it could have been.

What attributes lead to a satisfied, effective, efficient user? One is understandability, the simplicity or difficulty of figuring out what the software does and why you might need to use it. Another is learnability, the simplicity or difficulty of figuring out how to make the software do what it does. Yet another is operability, the degree of simplicity or difficulty inherent in carrying out certain distinct tasks within the software's feature set. Finally, there is attractiveness, which is the extent to which the software is visibly pleasing, friendly, and inviting to the user.

If we are performing usability testing, like most other testing, we can have as goals both the detection and removal of defects and the demonstration of conformance or nonconformance to requirements. In usability testing, the detection and removal of defects is sometimes referred to as *formative evaluation*, while the testing of requirements is sometimes referred to as *summative evaluation*.

In usability testing, we want to observe the effect of the actual system on real people, actual end users. (This is not to say that testers are not real people, but rather that we are not really the people who use the software.) To do so, we need to observe users interacting with the system under realistic conditions, possibly with video cameras, mock offices, and review panels.

Usability testing is sometimes seen as its own test level, but it can also be integrated into functional system testing. However, since usability testing has a different focus than standard functional testing, you can improve the consistency of the detection and reporting of usability bugs with usability guidelines. These guidelines should apply in all stages of the lifecycle, to encourage developers to build usable products in the first place.

Usability testing is a form of validation, of course, since we are focused on the users' needs and perspectives. Such testing should be done in a way that mimics, as much as possible, the real usage of the system. Some specialized usability testing labs have video cameras and two-way mirrors that provide for observation of the usability testers as they work. Tests are done in environments set up to look like the real usage environment, such as a mock office. Tests can be done by review panels, each reviewer having a particular perspective, or by actual users.

When actual users are doing usability testing, they might use test scripts, use cases, or user stories, or simply work from their understanding of how they'll use the system. We often want to observe them. How is the system affecting them? Do they look happy, productive, focused on their work? Or unhappy, frustrated, and stymied by the software?

If you are doing usability tests, as a test analyst you might not have a complete understanding of the users' perspectives and needs. So, usability guidelines and specifications should be available to help fill those gaps.

There are three main techniques for usability testing.

The first is called inspection, evaluation, or review. This involves considering the specification and designs from a usability point of view. Like all such reviews, it's an effective and efficient way to find bugs sooner rather than later. You can use actual users when you have things like screenshots and mock-ups.

A form of review, a heuristic evaluation, provides for a systematic inspection of a user interface design for usability. It allows us to find usability problems in the design, then resolve them, and then reevaluate. That process continues until we are happy with the design from a usability point of view. Often, a small set of evaluators is selected to evaluate the interface, often by referring to known and recognized usability principles.

The second form of usability testing is validation of the actual implementation. This can involve running usability test scenarios. Unlike functional test scenarios that look at the inputs, outputs, and results, the usability test scenarios look at usability attributes, such as speed of learning or operability. Usability test scenarios will often go beyond a typical functional test scenario, in that they include pre- and posttest interviews with the users performing the tests. In the pretest interviews, the testers receive instructions and guidelines for running the sessions. The guidelines include a description of how to run the test, time allowed for tests and even test steps, how to take notes and log results, and the interview and survey methods that will be used.

There also are syntax tests that evaluate the interface, what it allows, and what it disallows. And there are semantic tests that evaluate the meaningfulness of messages and outputs. As you might guess, some of the black-box techniques we've looked at, including use cases, can be helpful here.

> **ISTQB Glossary**
>
> **Heuristic evaluation:** A usability review technique that targets usability problems in the user interface or user interface design. With this technique, the reviewers examine the interface and judge its compliance with recognized usability principles (the "heuristics").
>
> **SUMI:** A questionnaire-based usability test technique for measuring software quality from the end user's point of view.
>
> **WAMMI:** A questionnaire-based usability test technique for measuring website software quality from the end user's point of view.

A final form of usability tests is surveys and questionnaires. These can be used to gather observations of the users' behavior during interaction with the system in a usability test lab. There are standard and publicly available surveys like SUMI (Software Usability Measurement Inventory) and WAMMI (Website Analysis and Measurement Inventory). Using a public standard allows you to benchmark against other organizations and software. Also, SUMI provides usability metrics, which can measure usability for completion or acceptance criteria.

Example: Usability Testing

In Figure 4–3 you see some introductory information from a document that described the usability test scenarios for the Internet appliance project I've referred to from time to time.

Notice that we define the goals of the test in the first paragraph.

The next paragraph describes the structure of the test set. It consists of four major scenarios. We have weighting on those scenarios, which corresponds to how important the test designer feels they are. There are then some simple instructions on how to use the checklist.

In Figure 4–4 you see one of the specified steps of the test scenarios. As you might guess, this is from the packaging and hardware scenario.

This step is designed to check whether the user has any practical way to see if everything that is supposed to be in the box actually is.

Execution of the tests is simple. Just check the appropriate boxes, and then tally the score once all the scenarios are done.

Each item in this checklist pertains to a [usability characteristic] or quality of [the system under test] that influences how effective a very novice user will be in unpacking, assembling, powering on, and configuring software on a [it]. This [checklist] is intended to predict an end-user's experience with [the system].

This [checklist] consists of four major sections:

· Packaging and hardware (100 points)

· Software installation and configuration (100 points)

· Internet connection and online registration (50 points)

· Software discovery and usage (50 points)

For each section, complete the checklist by choosing the most appropriate answer to each question. To score the section, add up the points corresponding to the selected answers, and record the scores in the summary table at the end of the section.

Figure 4–3   *An overview of the usability checklist*

(pts)	Is there a complete inventory of parts to enable the customer to determine if anything is missing? (e.g., outer box labels, packing slip, or setup "roadmap")
5	☐ The inventory list is complete and includes pictures with enough detail to precisely identify parts
3	☐ The inventory list is complete, but is text only
2	☐ The inventory list is incomplete
0	☐ No inventory list

Figure 4–4   *An excerpt from the usability checklist*

Accessibility Testing

Accessibility testing is a special form of usability testing that is focused on people who have particular needs or restrictions that affect how they use technology. There are various standards and regulations that can be useful in designing usability tests and in detecting relevant defects. Of course, if you are required to comply, these standards and regulations aren't just useful; they're mandatory.

Accessibility must be designed into the system. Trying to retrofit a user interface to be accessible after it is built is unlikely to work.

Since accessibility is basically a special form of usability testing, like usability testing, it should be considered a validation test. Also like usability testing, it can only occur once enough of the system is available to perform actual tasks, which generally means that it happens during component integration testing, system testing, and user acceptance testing.

Example: Accessibility Testing

Here you see a brief excerpt from the US Section 508 standard:

> When electronic forms are used, the form shall allow people using assistive technology to access the information, field elements, and functionality required for completion and submission of the form, including all directions and cues.

To test to this standard, we'd need to use equivalence partitioning to identify and test each assistive technology, such as text-to-speech programs. We would also need to test that we can access and use all the fields and functions in each form.

HELLOCARMS Usability Exercise

While at first only Globobank employees will use the HELLOCARMS system, eventually a number of different types of users will do so. It's important that the system be usable by each type of user.

This exercise consists of two parts:

1. Identify at least three user groups that will use the HELLOCARMS system.
2. For each user group, outline the usability tests needed for each of the following attributes: understandability, learnability, operability, and attractiveness.

As always, check your work on the preceding part before proceeding to the next part.

HELLOCARMS Usability Debrief

The user groups include the following:

- Telephone bankers and senior telephone bankers
- Customers (via the Internet)
- Branch bank employees at retail banking centers

There are a few others groups identified in the HELLOCARMS system requirements document as well.

So, the next part of the exercise involves you giving two or three bullet items of what you'd want to test to cover the four sub-characteristics of usability.

First, let's make sure we have the same definitions for each sub-characteristic, from ISO 9126:

Understandability: The capability of the software product to enable the user to understand whether the software is suitable and how it can be used for particular tasks and conditions of use.

Learnability: The capability of the software product to enable the user to learn its application.

Operability: The capability of the software product to enable the user to operate and control it.

Attractiveness: The capability of the software product to be attractive to the user.

Here's what I came up with for each user group

For telephone bankers and senior telephone bankers:

- For learnability, I would have actual bankers first go through a draft of the user's guide and perhaps user training (though I would hope we wouldn't need a training for this application). I would then survey them on whether they found various features learnable. After the actual tests were run (next bullet), I would survey them again on how well the user guide taught them the system.
- For understandability and operability, I would have actual bankers participate in an alpha test (overlapping the system integration test) and would ask them to run use-case-based tests, and then survey them on their experience.
- Finally, after the test were over, I would ask the users to review screen shots and rate the color scheme, graphics, and text in terms of attractiveness.

For customers:

- I would repeat the tests I outlined for telephone bankers, but with the change that I would not use training or user's guides in the learnability scenario. Rather, I would integrate that into the use of the product and ask them to use online help as needed to learn the application as they use it. I would then survey them just once, after the tests, to see how they felt about the learnability.

For branch bank employees:

▓ I would repeat the tests for the telephone banker, but with two changes:
1. There would be no training or user's guides, as I would expect them to be too busy for that.
2. I would run the alpha test once, then wait two weeks, then run it again.
3. I would then survey the bankers on how hard they found it to run the application after not using it for a while.

4.3 Sample Exam Questions

1. Assume you are a test analyst working on a project to create a programmable thermostat for home use to control central heating, ventilation, and air conditioning (HVAC) systems. In addition to the normal HVAC control functions, the thermostat has the ability to download data to a browser-based application that runs on PCs for further analysis. The application can export that data in the following formats: comma-separated variable (CSV), Excel (XLS), and tab-separated text (TXT). The application can encrypt the data using AES 128-bit, AES 256-bit, and public key encryption.

   Which of the following tests would address the interoperability of this application?

   A. Encrypting data using a public key and checking that the appropriate private key can decrypt it

   B. Evaluating the ability of typical users to download and analyze data from this application

   C. Logging thermostat operation statistics on a paper log at regular intervals during operation and checking the exported data against the log

   D. Exporting data in Excel format and loading it in OpenOffice's spreadsheet application

2. Continue with the scenario in the previous question.

   Which of the following tests would address the accessibility of this application?

   A. Encrypting data using a public key and checking that the appropriate private key can decrypt it

   B. Using a text-to-speech application to read the data from the application's screen

   C. Evaluating the ability of typical users to download and analyze data from this application

   D. Exporting data in Excel format and loading it in OpenOffice's spreadsheet application

3. Continue with the scenario in the previous question.

   Which of the following tests would address the usability of this application?

   A. Encrypting data using a public key and checking that the appropriate private key can decrypt it

   B. Using a text-to-speech application to read the data from the application's screen

   C. Evaluating the ability of typical users to download and analyze data from this application

   D. Exporting data in Excel format and loading it in OpenOffice's spreadsheet application

5 Reviews

"When I use a word," Humpty Dumpty said, in a rather scornful tone, "it means just what I choose it to mean, neither more nor less."

"The question is," said Alice, "whether you can make words mean so many different things."

"The question is," said Humpty Dumpty, "which is to be master—that's all."

Alice was too much puzzled to say anything; so after a minute Humpty Dumpty began again. "They've a temper, some of them—particularly verbs: they're the proudest—adjectives you can do anything with, but not verbs—however, I can manage the whole lot of them! Impenetrability! That's what I say!"

"Would you tell me, please," said Alice, "what that means?"

Alice has a not-so-enlightening requirements clarification session with Humpty Dumpty, prior to Humpty's unpleasant lesson about gravity.

From *Through the Looking Glass,* by Lewis Carroll

The fifth chapter of the Advanced Test Analyst syllabus is concerned with reviews. As you will recall from the Foundation syllabus, reviews are a form of static testing where people, rather than tools, analyze the project or one of the project's work products, such as a requirements specification. The primary goal is typically to find defects in that work product before it serves as a basis for further project activity, though other goals can also apply. The Advanced Test Analyst syllabus covers checklists and strategies for effective and successful reviews. Chapter 5 of the Advanced Test Analyst syllabus has two sections.

1. Introduction
2. Using Checklists in Reviews

Let's look at each section and how it relates to test analysis.

5.1   Introduction

Learning objectives
(K2) Explain why review preparation is important for the test analyst.

According to a study by David Rico for the US Department of Defense, reviews are the single most efficient way to improve software quality, saving $32 on average for every dollar invested. Anything this valuable deserves careful planning, active participation, and diligent follow-up to ensure that every potential benefit is extracted. As explained in the Foundation syllabus, a tester has a unique, failure-focused, risk-aware, test-conscious perspective on work products such as requirements specifications, design and architecture documents, user stories, use cases, and even, if able to understand it, code.

Reviews are not like a party, where success simply involves people showing up and being sociable. Reviews are complex social activities, and all the participants must be trained in how to collaborate successfully for the maximum benefit. Training alone is not enough, as ongoing commitment and management support are required to keep up the momentum.

What we have seen with clients is that the preparation time and effort is as important as the review meeting itself. When people don't invest the time to prepare for the review, the results are usually no better than a copy edit, where cosmetic, spelling, and grammar errors are found, but the important problems are missed. Careful study of the work product to be reviewed, including checking cross-referenced and relevant documents for inconsistencies, is important. During preparation, you should also ask yourself what is not there that should be. That's often harder than noticing what is there that is wrong.

One significant dysfunction in reviews occurs when the author feels criticized personally. The author will usually react by getting defensive and rejecting the input. This reduces the effectiveness of the review, reduces team morale, and demotivates authors from submitting their work products for review. Instead, all review participants should see their role as collaborating with the author to help improve the work product, a team effort to achieve the best possible result.

If there is a problem in the work product, you should point that problem out in a way that does not insult or demean. For example, the same defect in a requirement can be brought up by saying, "I'm sorry, but I'm not clear how I'm supposed to test this; can we maybe clarify that?" Or you could say, "What a completely ambiguous and untestable requirement!" It's important to bring up issues with testability, of course. However, do so in a way that is positive, encouraging, and supportive, as that will be much more successful than a critical attack on the document, which can't help but cause hurt feelings and resistance.

Review Effectiveness Example

Capers Jones, in his studies of thousands of projects across hundreds of clients, has found some interesting data on reviews, their applications, and the defect removal effectiveness of various types of reviews.[1] Notice in Table 5–1 the significant variation between the least effective, the average, and the most effective reviews. What we have seen with clients is that failure to prepare is a major reason for reviews to be ineffective.

Table 5–1   *Comparative Review Effectiveness Based on Work Product*

Work Product under Review	Least	Average	Most
Requirements	20%	30%	50%
High-level design	30%	40%	60%
Functional design	30%	45%	65%
Detailed design	35%	55%	75%
Code	35%	60%	85%

A major influence on the effectiveness of reviews is the extent to which the participants prepare. To ensure defect removal at the "most effective" end of the scale, be sure to allow adequate time for all preparation activities.

---

1. Specifically, for the table shown in this section, I relied primarily on Jones's book *Software Assessments, Benchmarks, and Best Practices,* but similar figures can be found in his other works. I particularly like *The Economics of Software Quality.*

5.2 Using Checklists in Reviews

Learning objectives
(K4) Analyze a use case or user interface, and identify problems according to checklist information provided in the syllabus.
(K4) Analyze a requirements specification or user story, and identify problems according to checklist information provided in the syllabus.

Checklists are very useful tools for reviews. Not only do they help us remember what kinds of problems to look for, they also lessen the chances of personal conflict. After all, if it's on the checklist, pointing out a problem can't be an attack, right?

The best checklists include both generic sections and focused sections. For example, we can generically say that documents should have unique names, be version controlled, and have a modification history. For a requirements specification, we can have rules about ambiguity, completeness, and so forth. For state diagrams, we can have rules about notation and naming conventions.

Checklists might even have sections that are specific to the participants. Programmers, architects, and testers all have a different perspective on documents.

Requirements Checklist

For a requirements checklist, you should include the following items:

- Testability: How hard will it be to test this requirement? For example, if a marketing person wants a system to have Six Sigma availability—possibly because they heard someone talking about how cool Six Sigma is—you'll want to explain the kind of investment required to test for, not to mention achieve, 99.9997% uptime.
- Acceptance criteria: What would it mean for this requirement to be fulfilled? This is related to the testability item, but is more focused on the question of whether we have a reliable, precise test oracle. Without a test oracle, a requirement can't be considered testable.
- Use cases: Do we have examples of how this requirement will be used by some customer, user, or other stakeholder to achieve some goal or useful result? The inability to identify a use case for a requirement can indicate

goldplating, the inclusion of some feature someone thinks is cool but which is not needed.

- Unique identifiers: For purposes of horizontal traceability—e.g., traceability of requirements to their associated tests—each requirement document, and each individual requirement, should be uniquely numbered.

- Traceability: When there are multiple levels of requirements, which is a common situation for large systems and systems of systems, it's important to have horizontal traceability as well as vertical traceability. Vertical traceability refers to the ability to trace from business requirements to functional requirements, from functional requirements to system requirements, and from system requirements to specific use cases.

- Versioning: As with all documents, requirements should have version numbers and a change history.

Both horizontal and vertical traceability are important not only to check for incompleteness of implementation and testing, but also to ensure proper updates for dependent requirements and tests when requirements change.

Of the requirements checklist items, your main focus as a tester will be on testability, horizontal traceability, and acceptance criteria, as these are your particular areas of interest and expertise. However, you should also consider the other items too; don't just assume other review participants will check for those.

Use Case Checklist

When reviewing use cases, you should check the following items:

- Main path: Is this clearly defined? Are there missing or assumed steps, actions, inputs, or outputs along the way? Is it unique, or is there more than one main path? Is there a single actor or multiple actors? Multiple main paths could indicate a compound use case that should be split, the inability of stakeholders to agree on what is typical usage of the system, or a situation where the use case serves two or more actors.

- Alternative paths: Are all strange, unusual, and atypical events, situations, interrupts, and exceptions accounted for? For those situations and exceptions that are errors, such as leaving a required field blank or entering a negative value in a field that must be greater than zero, do you have clearly defined error handling and recovery?

Messages: Are the user interface messages that will be seen along the main and alternative paths defined, either in the use case itself or in a referenced document?

For each path—the main path and all the alternative paths—you should ask the questions about testability and acceptance criteria mentioned earlier.

User Interface Checklist

A user interface checklist should include the following items:

- Is each field clearly defined, both for input and output fields, and is the function of each button, command, and menu defined?
- For any invalid input that could occur or invalid action that could be taken, do we have clear error messages defined, along with clearly defined recovery paths? When a user makes an error in one field, is correct data in other fields preserved, or is it nonsensically cleared, forcing the user to enter everything again?
- Do we have a complete set of user prompts defined, and are they consistent? For example, if an action is unavailable on a menu, is it always grayed out, or is it sometimes not shown or sometimes shown but fails to activate without explanation?
- Is the tab order of the fields defined and logical?
- Can users use keyboard alternatives such as hot keys, Altkey sequences, and tabbing, and enter keys instead of mouse actions where that makes sense?
- Are shortcuts defined for common actions?
- Where are there dependencies between fields, and are those clearly indicated and logical?
- Is the screen layout well defined, consistent, meaningful, and matching to the requirements, use cases, and any corporate user interface standards such as color schemes, trademarks, etc.? Is each screen attractive and appropriate to the usage situation?
- If some actions will take a noticeable amount of time, does the interface give a processing indicator?
- Is ease of use promoted by conformance, on each screen and between screens, to minimum mouse click requirements?
- Is the navigation flow within each screen and between screens logical? When accomplishing a task, will the user find the workflow within each screen and between screens understandable, intuitive, and logical?

Will it be easy for the typical user to learn each screen and the sequencing of screens?

Is context-aware help available, and perhaps even wizards to speed common tasks that may be complex or multistep? Are fields given extra explanation via automatic hover text?

If sound effects are used, are the sound effects appropriate and configurable? Can they be turned off when necessary and replaced by visual cues such as screen flashing, warning signals, and the like?

If the screens have been translated, is each screen, prompt, field, and message properly localized, including awareness of cultural norms, language usage, taboo words and symbols, and the like?

The best practice is usually to have a single user interface checklist that applies to all of an organization's software, although—in the case where applications differ greatly in purpose, presentation layer, or user community—that might not be possible.

User Story Checklist

On Agile projects, the usual way of capturing a requirement is what is called a user story. A typical user story has the form of, "As an *x*, I want the system to do *y*, so that I can accomplish *z*." For example, "As a customer, I want the system to provide a transaction history screen, so that I can review my previous invoices."

User stories are generally finer grained, smaller than use cases. However, a use case might be composed from multiple user stories. A collection of logically related and sometimes interdependent user stories is also referred to as an epic.

A user story checklist should include the following items:

Is the user story appropriate for the iteration? For example, if the user story is related to some other feature that won't be introduced until a later iteration, does it make sense to include it now, or should it wait? Is the story prioritized, and is the user story appropriate for this iteration given its priority?

As with requirements, do we have clearly defined acceptance criteria, sufficient to serve as a test oracle, and is the entire user story testable?

Is the intended functionality clearly defined, or is there confusion about what the user should be able to do?

Are there dependencies between stories? If those dependencies are unnecessary, can they be removed? If the dependencies are necessary, are dependencies being properly dealt with?

- Is the story a single functional item, or is it a compound item? User stories can suffer from a similar problem as use cases in this regard.
- If a user story includes user interface elements—and often they will—you should use a user interface checklist such as the one mentioned above.

Another commonly used checklist for user stories is INVEST:

- The user stories selected within a particular *iteration* should be independent.
- User stories should be *negotiable*.
- Each user story should be *valuable*.
- Each user story should be defined so you can *estimate* the work required to build and test it.
- Each user story should be of a *size* that it will fit within the iteration.
- Of course, each user story should be *testable*.

These checklists should be used to review user stories during story grooming and iteration planning.

Tailoring Checklists

The checklists given in this section are just examples. You should plan to tailor those checklists for your needs. Organizational tailoring would include ensuring that the user interface checklist includes corporate look-and-feel standards. If you are following an Agile lifecycle, you should select and customize the user story checklist. Each type of document has its own peculiar and particular needs for reviews, so you should have a separate review checklist for project plans, test plans, user stories, requirements, design and architecture documents, code, and so forth.

The checklists are a great way to ensure that you don't forget to look for certain problems, and they can serve as a way to start discussions. However, you should not consider yourself constrained by the checklist. You should also be ready to use two or more checklists, such as the user interface checklist and the use case checklist when the use case has user interface elements. You can and should use standard checklists, such as the ones from Karl Wiegers that I'll be showing you later in this section. However, you should be ready to develop your own extensions to these checklists.

Examples: Wiegers's Review Checklists

In his book *Software Requirements*, Karl Wiegers included a couple useful check-lists, one for reviewing requirements, and one for reviewing use cases.[2] I've adapted them both here. As you go through a requirements specification or a use case, you can keep these questions in mind and scrutinize the document accordingly. Let's go through the requirements checklist first.

In the area of document organization and completeness, the checklist asks the following questions:

- Are internal cross-references correct? If we reference another document or a section within this document, is that reference valid? It's a simple mistake to make and very confusing when it is made.
- Is the level of detail consistent and appropriate? It's very easy for business analysts and marketing people to bounce from laconic to loquacious in their documents.
- Do the requirements provide an adequate basis for design? This is an especially big problem when non-functional requirements are omitted.
- Is the priority of each requirement included? If not, then making trade-offs and deciding order of implementation will be difficult.
- Are all external interfaces defined?
- Is there any missing information? If so, is it clearly marked as TBD (to be determined)?
- Is the expected behavior documented? Many times, people will say, "Oh, that's obvious." Is it really?

In the area of correctness, the checklist asks the following questions:

- Do requirements conflict or duplicate? Assessing this means that you have to read the document twice through, usually.
- Is each requirement clear, concise, and unambiguous?
- Is each requirement verifiable? Could you design a test to show this requirement was met or not met? In fact, a good idea with a mature requirements specification is to try to do just that.
- Is each requirement in scope? Scope creep is an easy thing to happen on a project, and it will come back to haunt the test team if it does happen,

---

2. In addition to Wiegers's book *Software Requirements*, another classic on the topic of reviews is Gilb and Graham's *Software Inspection*.

because you'll have more to test than you planned on and less time to test it in than you planned on.

- Is each requirement free from content and grammar errors? It can make it hard to see other more subtle and important mistakes when you're dealing with bad grammar.
- Can the requirements be implemented within constraints? This is a hard one for a tester to answer, but reflect on your experience.
- Are error messages unique and meaningful?

In the area of quality attributes, the checklist asks the following questions:

- Are all performance objectives properly specified?
- Are all security and safety considerations properly specified?
- Are other pertinent quality attribute goals explicitly documented and quantified, with acceptable trade-offs specified? Really, rather than this generic statement, I would explicitly mention additional quality characteristics, using a standard such as ISO 25000 and my own list of two dozen typical quality risk categories. It's just too common to have non-functional requirements left out.

In the area of traceability, the checklist asks the following questions:

- Is each requirement uniquely and correctly identified? You won't be able to trace tests if requirements aren't identified. Also, make sure that the granularity of the requirements is such that it will be possible to have traceability from tests to requirements. In other words, if the requirement covers too much, then you might need two, ten, twenty tests to test it. What happens when a test fails?
- If you are reviewing a detailed requirement, is each software functional requirement traced to a higher-level requirement?

Finally, the checklist provides some special issues to consider.

- Have we stayed in the proper realm of requirements, not design? In other words, are all requirements actually requirements and not design or implementation solutions?
- Are the time-critical functions identified and their timing criteria specified?
- Have internationalization issues been adequately addressed?

By following this checklist, you should be able to identify a number of defects in requirements. Of course, when reviewing a requirements specification, if you find something strange, you should not dismiss it from consideration simply because you can't figure out how this relates to Wiegers' checklist. A checklist is a mental aid, not a substitute for thought.

Let's turn our attention to Wiegers' use case checklist. It asks the following questions about the use case under review:

- Is the use case a stand-alone, discrete task, or might we have combined two tasks?
- Is the goal of the use case clear? What are we trying to do here?
- Is it clear which actor(s) benefit from the use case? What is the benefit?
- Is the use case written as an abstraction rather than as a specific scenario? In other words, it should be like a logical test, not a concrete test.
- Is the use case free of design and implementation details?
- Are all anticipated exceptions documented? If not, then things could happen that would be undefined, at least in their handling. That's a recipe for unexpected behavior, at least, or program crashes.
- Is every actor and step in the use case pertinent to the task? Again, might we be mixing tasks in a single use case?
- Is each workflow defined in the use case feasible? Can this actually happen? Remember to consider the exceptions, too.
- Is each workflow defined in the use case verifiable? Can you test this workflow?

You might find it interesting to compare and contrast Wiegers's checklists with the ones provided in the Advanced Test Analyst syllabus.

HELLOCARMS Requirements Review Exercise

In this exercise, you apply Wiegers' requirements review checklist and use case review checklist to the HELLOCARMS system requirements document.

This exercise consists of three steps:

1. Prepare: Use the syllabus and Wiegers' checklists to review the HELLO-CARMS system requirements document (through section 010 only), documenting the problems you find.
2. Hold a review meeting: If you are reading this book with others, work in a small group to perform a walkthrough, creating a single list of problems.
3. Compare: Refer to the debrief below, and compare your results to mine.

Obviously, this exercise is more interesting if you can include step two.

HELLOCARMS Requirements Review Debrief

Senior RBCS associate Jose Mata reviewed the HELLOCARMS system requirements document using Wiegers' checklist and provided the following feedback.

- Are internal cross-references correct? If we reference another document or within this document, is that reference valid?
  - ✓ No. Section 010-010-040 states: "Field validation details are described in a separate document," but that document is not identified anywhere in the requirements document.
- Is the level of detail consistent and appropriate?
  - ✓ No. As an example, see section 010-010-180: "Provide features and screens that support the operations of the Globobank's retail branches." That is too vague to be actionable.
  - ✓ Section 010-010-170 states: "Support the submission of applications via the Internet, which includes the capability of untrained users to properly enter applications." This is a huge, and vague, requirement.
  - ✓ Sections 010-010-180 through 010-010-240 start with: "Support the marketing, sales, and processing of…" which is so vague that important functionality can be missed.
- Do the requirements provide an adequate basis for design?
  - ✓ No. Section 010-010-070 states, "Ask each applicant whether there is an existing relationship with Globobank—e.g., any checking or savings accounts," but the list is not complete, and it should be.
  - ✓ Section 010-010-080 states, "Maintain application status from initiation through to rejection, decline, or acceptance…" but we don't know if these states are a subset or if they are comprehensive.
  - ✓ Section 010-010-150 states: "Provide inbound and outbound telemarketing support for all States, Provinces, and Countries in which Globobank operates," but the list is not defined.
  - ✓ Section 010-010-160 states: "Support brokers and other business partners by providing limited partner-specific screens, logos, interfaces, and branding," yet screens, or areas of the interface, are not identified.
  - ✓ Section 010-010-250 states: "Support flexible pricing schemes including introductory pricing, short term pricing, and others," but the "and others" needs to be defined.
- Is the priority of each requirement included?
  - ✓ Yes.

▨ Are all external interfaces defined?

   ✓ No. We don't know how complete the information is. Data structures are hinted at, but not defined. The implied interfaces are with:

- LoDoPS: 010-010-050, 010-010-100, 010-020-050, 010-030-040, 010-030-060, 010-030-070, 010-030-080, 010-030-120, 010-030-103, 010-030-140, 010-030-150
- GLADS: 010-010-070
- Scoring mainframe: 010-020-020, 010-030-020
- GloboRainBQW: 010-030-010

▨ Is there any missing information? If so, is it clearly marked as TBD (to be determined)?

   ✓ Yes.

▨ Is the expected behavior documented?

   ✓ No. For example, section 010-010-080 states: "Maintain application status from initiation through to rejection…" but how and where the status is maintained is not stated.

▨ Is each requirement clear, concise, and unambiguous?

   ✓ No. For example, section 010-010-070 states: "Ask each applicant whether there is an existing relationship with Globobank," but it is unclear how the applicant is asked.

   ✓ Sections 010-010-100, 010-030-040, and 010-030-070 state: "Allow user to indicate on a separate screen which, if any, are existing debts that the customer will retire …" but it's not clear what the screen is supposed to be separate from.

   ✓ Section 010-040-010 states: "Support agreed upon security requirements (encryption, firewalls, etc.)," which is vague.

   ✓ Section 010-040-060 states: "Support fraud detection for processing of all financial applications." This is vague, which is especially bad for a priority one requirement.

▨ Is each requirement verifiable? Could you design a test to show this requirement was met or not met?

   ✓ No. Section 010-010-150 states: "Provide inbound and outbound telemarketing support for…" which is vague and thus not verifiable.

   ✓ Sections 010-010-180 through 010-010-240 start with: "Support the marketing, sales, and processing of…" and the marketing part is not verifiable.

   ✓ Section 010-010-250 states: "Support flexible pricing schemes including introductory pricing, short term pricing, and others," and the "and others" part is not verifiable.

✓ Section 010-030-150 states: "Support computer-telephony integration to provide customized marketing and sales support for inbound telemarketing campaigns and branded business partners," which is vague and this not verifiable.

Is each requirement in scope?

✓ No. For example, section 010-010-170 states: "Support the submission of applications via the Internet, which includes the capability of untrained users to properly enter applications." This is beyond the scope of section 003, since allowing Internet-based customers is slated for subsequent releases.

✓ Section 010-040-030 states: "Allow outsourced telemarketers to see the credit tier but disallow them from seeing the actual credit score of applicants." This is beyond the scope of section 003.

✓ Section 010-040-050 states: "Allow Internet users to browse potential loans without requiring such users to divulge …" This is beyond the scope of section 003.

Is each requirement free from content and grammar errors?

✓ Yes.

Can the requirements be implemented within constraints?

✓ Possibly not. Section 010-040-060 states: "Support fraud detection for processing of all financial applications." This might not be able to be implemented. Specific checks would need to be defined.

Are all security and safety considerations properly specified?

✓ No. Specific types of users, and their permissions, are not defined. Username and password strength are not addressed. Encryption of specific data is not addressed. Maintenance and purging requirements are not addressed. Server physical security requirements are not addressed.

Is each requirement uniquely and correctly identified? Is the granularity of the requirements such that it will be possible to have traceability from tests to requirements?

✓ No. For example, sections 010-010-180 through 010-010-240 start with: "Support the marketing, sales, and processing of …" The granularity of these requirements is too large.

✓ Section 010-010-250 states: "Support flexible pricing schemes including introductory pricing, short term pricing, and others." This and several other compound requirements would be clearer if they were separately numbered requirements. It may be somewhat repetitious, but the requirements would be clearer, and there would be more balance in scoping development and test efforts.

Have we stayed in the proper realm of requirements, not design? In other words, are all requirements actually requirements, not design or implementation solutions?

✓ No. Sections 010-010-100, 010-030-040, and 010-030-070 state: "Allow user to indicate on a separate screen which, if any, are existing debts that the customer will retire …" Specifying a separate screen appears to be a design detail.

5.3 Sample Exam Questions

1. Which of the following types of reviews is generally the most effective at finding the greatest percentage of defects present in the object being reviewed?

    A. Informal

    B. Walk-through

    C. Peer review

    D. Inspection

2. A design specification contains the following statement:

    A 100 MBPS or better network connection using TCP/IP provides the interface between the database server and the application server.

    Suppose that the system under test will need to transfer data blocks of up to 10 gigabytes in size in less than a minute.

    Which of the following statements best describes the likely consequences of this situation?

    A. The system will suffer from usability problems.

    B. The system will suffer from performance problems.

    C. The system will suffer from maintainability problems.

    D. This situation does not indicate any likely problems.

3. Assume you are a test analyst working on a banking project to upgrade an existing automated teller machine system to allow customers to obtain cash advances from supported credit cards. The requirements specification contains the following paragraph:

The system shall allow cash advances of at least 500 dollars for all supported credit cards. The correct list of supported credit cards is American Express, Visa, Japan Credit Bank, Eurocard, and MasterCard.

Which of the following statements is true?

A. The paragraph is ambiguous in terms of supported cards.

B. The paragraph indicates potential performance problems.

C. The paragraph is unclear in terms of advance limits.

D. The paragraph indicates potential usability problems.

4. Which of the following review types involves a determination of compliance or noncompliance?

A. Audit

B. Walk-through

C. Inspection

D. Management review

6 Defect Management

"Faster/random." —The Zen-like and uninformative complete text of a
bug report, observed by the author and some of his associates on one
particular project.

The sixth chapter of the Advanced Test Analyst syllabus is concerned with defect
management. This topic was introduced in the Foundation syllabus. A defect
can exist in any work product, including requirements specifications, user stories, code, technical documentation, or tests. The Advanced Test Analyst syllabus expands on the discussion of defects in the Foundation syllabus, especially
in terms of the type of information we can gather with defect reports. Chapter 6
of the Advanced Test Analyst syllabus has five sections.

1. Introduction
2. When Can a Defect Be Detected?
3. Defect Report Fields
4. Defect Classification
5. Root Cause Analysis

Let's look at each section and how it relates to test analysis.

6.1 Introduction

Learning objectives
Recall of content only.

During test execution, test analysts will evaluate system behavior. As test analysts run their tests, they compare the actual results of the test with the expected
results, looking for situations where the results are unexpected. Such anomalies
can indicate a failure, which is when the system misbehaves due to a defect. In

some cases, though, the anomalies are due to a false positive, which is when the unexpected result is due to a problem with the test, the test data, the test environment, the tester's opinions about correct behavior, and so forth.

Part of defect management is trying to avoid reporting false positives, as such reports lead to frustration and inefficiency. In the real world, some small percentage, say 2%–3%, of defect reports will be false positives, and it's preferable to have a small number of false positives than an equal number of test escapes, which is what will happen if testers are pressured to eliminate all false positives. Nevertheless, the goal should be to only report actual failures whenever possible.

6.2   When Can a Defect Be Detected?

Learning objectives
(K2) Explain how phase containment can reduce costs.

As was discussed in the Foundation syllabus, you shouldn't wait until the end of a project or an iteration to detect and remove defects. Instead, defect detection and removal should be integrated into the lifecycle, regardless of which lifecycle we are following. Static tests (such as static code analysis, requirements reviews, and user story grooming) detect and remove defects directly, while dynamic tests (such as structural, functional, and non-functional unit tests, integration tests, and system tests) detect failures and the symptoms of defects, which then require debugging. For this reason, static testing is usually the cheaper and faster way to remove defects. Also, static testing can typically be done prior to dynamic testing, and it's always preferable to remove bugs earlier than later.

Phase Containment

The holy grail of early defect detection and removal is referred to as *phase containment*. With perfect phase containment, each and every defect is removed in the same phase in which it was introduced. Every requirements problem is found and fixed through a requirements review or user story review. Every coding mistake is found and fixed in a code review or through static analysis. Such a quality Xanadu will never be attained, but you should strive for it.

To measure where you are on phase containment, your bug tracking system must capture the phase of introduction, detection, and removal for all defects. Root cause analysis is used to establish the phase of introduction for each defect.

> **ISTQB Glossary**
>
> **Defect taxonomy:** A system of (hierarchical) categories designed to be a useful aid for reproducibly classifying defects.
>
> **Phase containment:** The percentage of defects that are removed in the same phase of the software lifecycle in which they were introduced.
>
> **Root cause analysis:** An analysis technique aimed at identifying the root causes of defects. By directing corrective measures at root causes, it is hoped that the likelihood of defect recurrence will be minimized.

Any defect found during dynamic testing has escaped from some previous phase, and we should look at why and how it escaped. By determining the process breakdown that leads to the largest number of escapes—remember that the Pareto principle will apply—you can work collaboratively with the developers, product owners, business analysts, and other technical and business stakeholders to improve phase containment and thus minimize the overall cost of quality.

Example: Phase Containment

In Figure 6–1 you see the lifecycle model used for software releases by one of our clients, a major bank. Projects proceed independently of each other, following either Scrum or V-model development, according to the choice of the project manager. Regardless of lifecycle, all requirements and design documents are subjected to a formal review. The independent test team provides a moderator for the review, who is also responsible for tracking defect metrics.

During each project, the programmers create their code and unit tests. Component integration testing, when needed, is collaborative between the programmers and the testers embedded within the development team. Those same embedded testers perform system testing.

If the results of the system testing indicate that the quality of a project's deliverables is ready when the time arrives for entry into the next system integration test period, that project will be accepted as part of that release. You can see that projects 1, 2, and 3 made the May release, while projects 4 and 5 had to wait until the window opened for the July release.

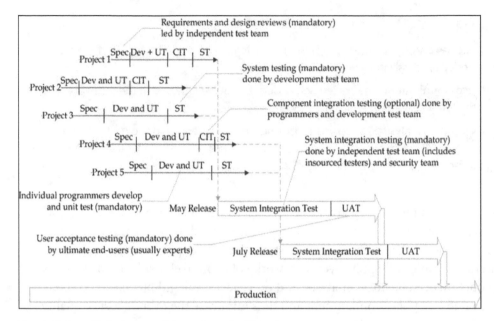

Figure 6–1   *Defect removal throughout the lifecycle*

An independent test team, often assisted by contractors and the bank's security team, handles the system integration test. After system integration testing is complete, user acceptance testing is done by the bank's expert users.

This process does an excellent job of containing defects. Very few defects escape into system integration testing. Of those few that do, the test team finds between 99% and 99.5% of those defects.

6.3   Defect Report Fields

Learning objectives
(K2) Explain the information that may be needed when documenting a non-functional defect.

Ideally, every defect report is actionable, meaning some concrete decision of what to do next can be taken from the report itself or in aggregate across a collection of reports. As with any technical document, good data is essential for the report to be actionable. Good data is complete, which means that nothing relevant is missing, so that the readers have the information they need to take the right action. Good data is also concise, which means that it includes nothing irrelevant that might distract, confuse, or mislead the reader, leading to taking a wrong action or failing to take a necessary action. All data that is present is completely accurate, with no factual inaccuracies or lack of clarity in presentation that again might distract, confuse, or mislead the reader, resulting in wrong actions or lack of necessary actions. Further, the bug report should not be an act of advocacy; rather, it is an objective presentation of facts that will allow the readers to reach their own conclusions about the actions necessary.

Defect tracking systems typically capture three kinds of data in the fields associated with a defect report. One kind of data is classifications, such as severity or root cause, which is generally selected from a pull-down menu or drop-down list. Another kind of data is narrative fields, such as the steps to reproduce, which is free-form text, usually of some limited but sufficient size. Finally, the other kind of data is attachments, such as screenshots or videos.

In order for these fields to be used properly, they must of course be defined properly. Careful study and thought is necessary when setting up a bug tracking tool. However, just because the tool is set up right doesn't mean people will automatically know how to use it. Training is absolutely essential; otherwise testers and developers will enter data that appears valid but is, in fact, mostly noise.

What Data Is Needed?

As with any other technical document, the specific information necessary can vary from one defect report to the next. Different types of defects can have different needs. Some defect management tools can guide and check the entry of data depending on the defect type, though most of our clients don't have such sophisticated abilities built into their defect tools.

Regardless of whether a defect report describes a functional or non-functional failure, we need to make sure that we have documented how we made the failure occur. This includes the steps to reproduce the failure, the data used during the test, the test environment, and state of the system at the beginning of the test. The expected and the actual results should be included, and the anomaly should be clear.

When describing non-functional defects, you'll probably need to include additional information. For performance defects, a detailed description of the load profiles used for testing is important. The same is true for reliability tests, and you'll also want to include core dumps and screenshots of the reliability failure that occurred. Usability defect reports would need to refer to the relevant corporate standards for appearance and usability.

In some cases, the anomaly being reported will be clearly wrong, as the expected results are documented in a specification, an acceptance criteria, a legacy application, or a previous version. However, if the expected results are based on your opinion about what constitutes reasonable behavior, then you'll need to justify that in the report. Simply asserting that a problem exists, without being ready to convince the readers, will likely result in your report being canceled.

Keep in mind that a defect report is written in part to provide the developer with the information needed to fix the underlying bug. However, accurate classification information is necessary to support trend and bug cluster identification. Process improvements made without data will be suboptimal.

An Example of Hidden Insights

Here's an example of why you need to scrutinize actual and expected results very carefully. We were doing some performance testing of some servers, including an email server using the IMAP service. We compared the test results against the results of a simulation, done using a tool called Hyperformix. The simulation predicted 45% IMAP server utilization with 25,000 users and 75% server utilization at 40,000 users, which was considered the top end for our server architecture. When we ran our tests with 25,000 simulated users, we looked at various resources, including CPU resources. As you can see in Table 6–1, for the IMAP1 server the CPU was 41% idle, and for the IMAP2 server the CPU was 45% idle. So, the test results appeared to support the simulation results.

Table 6–1   *CPU utilization during performance testing*

Server	CPU Idle
MTA1	68%
MTA2	79%
Maildb1	67%
Maildb2	89%
IMAP1	59%
IMAP2	55%

However, we did a detailed analysis of performance, too, as you can see in Table 6–2. When we took a closer look at specific IMAP transaction types, we found that there were some problems. The select transactions were slightly over, a little under 20% slower. The banner transactions were over five times slower, and the fetch transactions, which were supposed to take an eighth of a second, were instead taking almost six seconds. Clearly, there were problems here!

Table 6–2   *A detailed analysis of performance*

Transaction	Frequency	Simulation (ms)	Observed (ms)
Connect	1 per connect	0.74	0.77
Banner	1 per connect	2.57	13.19
Authorize	1 per connect	19.68	19.08
Select	1 per connect	139.87	163.91
Fetch	1 per connect	125.44	5,885.04

In order for this detailed comparison to work, you must design yours tests and your simulation models so that the results are comparable.

6.4   Defect Classification

Learning objectives
(K4) Identify, gather, and record classification information for a given defect.

Much of the power of defect reports for project management and process improvement arises from the use of proper defect classification at multiple stages of the defect lifecycle. With proper classifications, we can group defects, as when we identify defect clusters. We can calculate the defect detection effectiveness of testing by comparing the number of bugs found during testing to those found after release. We can assess the effectiveness and efficiency of the overall development process by looking at what percentage of the bugs get fixed prior to release or in each iteration, and how long it takes to fix the bugs. To enjoy these benefits, proper defect classification is essential.

Classifying Defects

When a bug is first identified, most bug tracking systems can be configured to require certain classification fields to be populated by the person who found the bug, often a test analyst. These classifications should include the following:

- What project activity was underway when the bug was found, such as a review, static analysis, unit testing, or system testing.

- The phase in which the defect was introduced, as in requirements or code, though admittedly this will often be an educated guess at this time.
- The phase in which the defect was detected, which of course is a known fact.
- The suspected root cause, such as an off-by-one bug in a condition, data corruption, or the like, which again is an educated guess.
- Whether the failure can be made to manifest itself, via the same set of steps, repeatedly; otherwise, the failure is intermittent and the frequency of occurrence should be noted.
- The symptom that the system displaces when the failure occurs.
- The severity of the problem, which is often a five-point scale based on the impact of the bug on the system itself.
- The priority of the problem, which is also often a five-point scale, this time based on the impact of the bug on the customers, users, and the business.

Each one of these classifications should be a separate pull-down list in the system. All users of the bug tracking system must be trained in how to select the right value for each classification; otherwise, the data will appear meaningful but close inspection will reveal it is mostly random.

Once reported, the defect will often be handed off to a developer for investigation and possible resolution. Once the investigation is complete, the developer should identify the actual root cause, the source of the problem (being the work product in which the defect actually was found), and what type of problem it was. The developer may also adjust some initial classifications, such as the phase of introduction, though it should not be possible for the developer to override the tester's selections in most cases.

Once the developer has fixed the defect, they should note the resolution action taken, as well as any corrective action that would prevent this problem from occurring in the future.

Additional classifications that might occur are the safety impact, the schedule impact, the cost, the project risk, and the quality impact. However, I usually encourage clients to use a small, essential set of classifications, to avoid creating too much work for people during defect management.

Classification Uses

How might we use these classifications? The possibilities are endless, and I often rely on good defect classification data—when I can get it—during client assessments. I find answers to questions like, "What percentage of defect reports were canceled as false positives?" "How long on average did it take for defects of different severities to get resolved?" and "Where are the defect clusters?"

While some classification fields are in common use across many organizations, some of the fields tend to be customized. For example, the phase of introduction, detection, and removal fields should reflect the actual lifecycles in use in the organization, and the project activity field should reflect the activities that actually happen on your projects.

As I mentioned above, the users of the bug tracking system must be trained in its proper use. Any tester reporting a given bug should select exactly the same classifications, and any developer fixing a given bug should also select exactly the same classifications. Anything less means that the bug report information is noise.

As I also mentioned earlier, try to avoid creating too much work by gathering too many classifications. If it's not clear how you will use a particular classification, don't capture it.

In addition, the tool you pick to manage your bugs can make it easier or harder to gather these classifications. So, you should consider that during tool selection.

Example: Classification

Figure 6–2 shows an example of using classification information to learn something interesting about a project. This Pareto chart analyzes the number and percentage of bugs associated with each major subsystem—system, really—in a large, complex project. This project, called the NOP project, tied together ten systems via a wide area network, a local area network, and the phone system to implement a large distributed entertainment application.

As you can see in the graph in Figure 6–2, the interactive voice response (or IVR) application is responsible for about half of the bugs. The customer service application (or CSA) adds about 30% more. The rest of the applications are relatively solid. The content management (or CM) application is less than 10% of the bugs. The interactive voice response server's telephony and OS/hardware layers each are around 5%, with the remaining applications and infrastructure accounting for the other 4%.

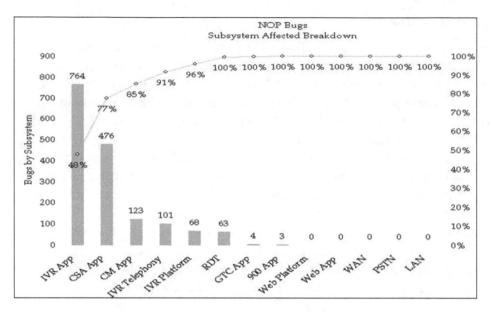

Figure 6–2   *Defect clustering made visible through classification*

HELLOCARMS Defect Exercise

Assume that a select group of telephone bankers will participate in HELLO-CARMS testing as a Beta test. The bankers will enter live applications from customers, but they will also capture the information and enter it into the current system afterwards to ensure no HELLOCARMS defects affect the customers.

The bankers are not trained testers and are unwilling to spend time learning testing fundamentals. So, to avoid having the bankers enter poorly written incident reports and introduce noise into the incident report metrics, management has decided that, when a banker finds a problem, he or she will send an email to a test analyst to enter the report.

You receive the following email from a banker describing a problem:

I was entering a home equity loan application for a customer with good credit. She owns a high-value house, though the loan amount is not very large.

At the proper screen, HELLOCARMS popped up the Escalate to Senior Telephone Banker message. However, I clicked "continue," and it allowed me to proceed, even though no senior telephone banker authorization code had been entered.

From that point forward in this customer's application, everything behaved normally.

I had another customer with a similar application—high-value house, medium-sized loan amount—call in later that day. Again, it would let me proceed without entering the authorization code.

The exercise consists of two parts:

1. What initial classification fields are available from this email?
2. What steps would you take to clarify this report?

HELLOCARMS Defect Debrief

First, I evaluated each of the pertinent initial classifications to see if this email contained the information, or if other information that I would have already is available. My analysis is shown in Table 6–3.

Table 6–3   *Defect report classification information*

Classification	Available?
Project activity	We should know this for all such beta tests.
Phase of introduction	Not available, though I know it was not introduced in the requirements (since the requirements specify the escalation), so I might guess that it was introduced during programming.
Phase of detection	We should know this for all such beta tests, too.
Suspected cause	Not available, though I could try to guess based on a pull-down menu, particularly is I guess this is a programming error.
Repeatability	Available, but more isolation and replication of this issue is needed.
Symptom	Available.
Severity	Available.
Priority	Not available, but again we can assume this is a high priority, since the system allows us to bypass a key risk management feature.

Below, I have annotated the report with some steps I'd take to clarify it before putting it into the system. The original information is shown in italics, while my clarification steps are shown in regular font.

I was entering a home equity loan application for a customer with good credit.

I would want to find out her exact data, including income, debts, assets, credit score, and so on.

She owns a high-value house, though the loan amount is not very large.

I would want to find out the exact value of the house and the loan amount.

I would test various combinations of values and loan amounts to see if I could find a pattern.

At the proper screen, HELLOCARMS popped up the Escalate to Senior Telephone Banker message. However, I clicked "continue," and it allowed me to proceed, even though no senior telephone bank authorization code had been entered.

I would want to find out if the banker entered anything at all into that field.

I would test leaving it empty, inputting blanks, input valid characters that were not valid authorization codes, and some other checks to see whether it is ignoring the field completely.

From that point forward in this customer's application, everything behaved normally.

I would test to see whether such applications are transferred to LoDoPS or are silently discarded. If they are transferred to LoDoPS, does LoDoPS proceed or does it catch the fact that this step was missed?

I had another customer with a similar application—high-value house, medium-sized loan amount—call in later that day. Again, it would let me proceed without entering the authorization code.

Here also I would want to find out the exact details on this applicant, the property value, and the loan amount.

6.5   Root Cause Analysis

Learning objectives
(K2) Explain the purpose of root cause analysis.

Root cause analysis—logically enough—determines the underlying mistake that led to the introduction of a defect. The point of doing so is not idle curiosity, and it should never ever be for reasons of assigning blame or punishment, but rather to look for patterns in mistakes that point out opportunities for process improvements. For example, if executive management insisted on a 25% reduction in defects within the next year, how would you do that? Well, suppose you knew that 50% of the code mistakes relate to branch and loop control conditions, memory management, and inadequate comments in the code. By training programmers in these areas, the number of code mistakes can easily be reduced by 25% in a matter of a year or so.

Root cause analysis is done by the person fixing the defect. This is typically a developer, at least when the defect is in the code. However, if the defect is in the requirements specification, a business analyst might do it. A defect in a user story might be resolved by the product owner.

When reporting a defect, as mentioned before, the tester should make an educated guess about the root cause, and the defect management tool should capture that in a suspected root cause field. When the bug fix comes back for a confirmation test, the test analyst should compare their suspected root cause against the actual root cause. If the two values are the same, then the developer has confirmed the tester's suspicions. If the suspected and actual root causes are different, then the test analyst should understand why, and check to be sure that the developer's assigned value is correct. Since the determination of the root cause is typically done at the same time as the determination of the phase of defect introduction, only if the actual root cause is assigned correctly will the phase of defect introduction be correct.

Some typical root cause classifications include the following:

- Unclear requirement: A requirement or user story was subject to multiple interpretations.
- Missing requirement: A necessary requirement or user story is not present.
- Wrong requirement: A requirement or user story is present, but is incorrectly defined.

Incorrect design implementation: The system's design is correct, but the programmer's implementation of it is wrong.

Incorrect interface implementation: A system user interface or application programming interface is designed properly, but the programmer's implementation of it is wrong.

Code logic error: Due to a simple omission, misunderstanding of the programming language constructs, or a momentary loss of concentration, the programmer created code that runs but gives a wrong answer, such as making the wrong decision at a decision point like a branch or loop.

Calculation error: The programmer has set up a calculation so that it delivers the wrong result, such as through the use of the wrong operator, the selection of the wrong variable, or by neglecting rounding and precision limits of the variable used.

Hardware error: The software is correct, but the hardware is failing, whether consistently or intermittently. Personally, I'm always skeptical when a programmer says that a failure is a hardware problem.

Interface error: An interface is defined and implemented correctly, but the interface is being used improperly.

Invalid data: Some permanent data, such as data stored in a table in a database, is incorrect.

By consistently gathering root cause data for defects, we can determine the most important underlying mistakes. This allows us to use training to reduce the number of defects introduced. We can also look for situations where requirements defects are not detected until dynamic testing, since that means that defects escape from reviews, which is an opportunity to improve phase containment.

Throughout the lifecycle, defects are introduced. Defects can also be detected and removed throughout the lifecycle. With perfect phase containment, the escape rate from each phase is zero. However, to further reduce cost of failure, root cause analysis can be used to reduce the rate of defect introduction in each phase.

As shown in Figure 6–3, in typical industry practice, high numbers of defects are introduced early in the lifecycle and then removed (at a much higher cost) later in the lifecycle. Best practices focus on early defect removal, with later test phases focusing on building confidence and reducing risk. Root cause analysis information should be used to determine and remove the reasons for defect introduction in the first place.

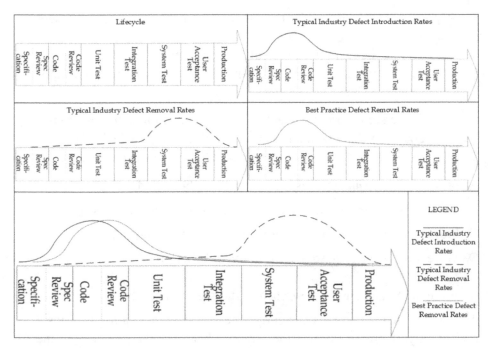

Figure 6–3   *Comparison of typical and best practices in defect removal*

6.6   Sample Exam Questions

1. Assume you are a test analyst working on a banking project to upgrade an existing automated teller machine system to allow customers to obtain cash advances from supported credit cards. The requirements specification contains the following paragraph:

   > The system shall allow cash advances of at least 500 dollars for all supported credit cards. The correct list of supported credit cards is American Express, Visa, Japan Credit Bank, Eurocard, and MasterCard.

   You are reviewing a defect report written by one of your peers. The *steps to reproduce* section of the report contains the following statement:

   1. Inserted an American Express card into the ATM.
   2. Properly authenticated a test account with $1,000 available cash advance balance.
   3. Attempted to withdraw $20 from the account.
   4. Received an error message, "Amount requested exceeds available funds."

5. Reproduced this failure with two other accounts that also had sufficient available credit to cover a $20 withdrawal.
6. Verified that the ATM itself had sufficient cash to service the request.
7. Could not reproduce the problem with Visa, Japan Credit Bank, Euro-card, or MasterCard.

Assume the defect report is currently in a *new* state, indicating it needs a review. Relying on the information given in this scenario, which of the following statements best describes what should happen next to this report?

A. Move it to an *invalid* state as it does not describe a valid defect.

B. Move it to a *defer* state as it does not describe an important defect.

C. Move it to an *open* state for prioritization by project stakeholders.

D. Move it to a *build* state so that the tester will check the fix.

2. Continue with the scenario described in the previous question.

Assume the defect report is currently in a *new* state, indicating it needs a review. Relying on the information given in this scenario, for which of the following fields do you have **insufficient information** to classify the report?

A. Suspected Cause

B. Actual Cause

C. Repeatability

D. Symptom

7 Test Tools

"Rex, I found the control codes I can use to make the tape library cycle back to the first tape for the automated burn-in test."

"Really? Did the vendor tell you?"

"No, Rex, I experimented with various control codes until I found which ones would make the first tape load."

"Did you tell me you didn't think you could figure it out?"

"Yes, I did tell you that, but I figured it out."

"Greg, the next time you tell me you can't do something, I really, really won't believe you now. Have you told the vendor yet?"

"No. I was planning to call them."

"Sure, go ahead and call them, but tell them they have to pay us for it."

A discussion between the author and a senior test automation engineer after the engineer solved a particularly tough test automation problem.

The seventh chapter of the Advanced Test Analyst syllabus is concerned with test tools and automation. While the Foundation syllabus covers this topic as well, the Advanced Test Analyst syllabus goes beyond the Foundation material to provide a solid conceptual background for test tools and automation. In addition, the Advanced Test Analyst syllabus elaborates on the categorization of tools introduced in the Foundation syllabus. Chapter 7 of the Advanced Test Analyst syllabus has two sections.

1. Introduction
2. Test Tools and Automation

Let's look at each section and how it relates to test analysis.

7.1   Introduction

Learning objectives
Recall of content only.

As discussed in the Foundation syllabus, testers and test teams can use test tools to improve their efficiency, accuracy, and coverage. Regression tests can be run many times, economically. Code coverage can be measured accurately across millions of lines of code. Quality attributes that would be impossible to cover manually, such as performance and reliability, can be tested.

7.2   Test Tools and Automation

Learning objectives
(K2) Explain the benefits of using test data preparation tools, test design tools, and test execution tools.
(K2) Explain the test analyst's role in keyword-driven automation.
(K2) Explain the steps for troubleshooting an automated test execution failure.

In spite of the promise of test tools, many test tool projects fail, often due to improper selection or use of the tool. Tools must be carefully selected and managed. There is a wide range of options with tools—some are very sophisticated and powerful, some simple and easy. Some are narrowly focused, some more general. Some are very good, and some are very lousy. The price tag tells you very little about the quality, applicability, or sophistication of the tool. You should always consider all your options, commercial, freeware, and open source, when selecting tools, and be sure to check recent information, as the tool market changes amazingly fast.

After poor selection, misuse of the tool is a leading cause of tool project failure. This is usually due to a lack of skills. So, as a test analyst, you must know how to use the relevant tools effectively. Let's start this section by looking at various tool types and some important considerations for each type.

> **ISTQB Glossary**
>
> **Test data preparation tool:** A type of test tool that enables data to be selected from existingdatabases or created, generated, manipulated, and edited for use in testing.
>
> **Test design tool:** A tool that supports the test design activity by generating test inputs from a specification that may be held in a CASE tool repository—e.g., requirements management tool, from specified test conditions held in the tool itself, or from code.

Test Design and Data Tools

Test design and data tools are sometimes used by test analysts to create and manage tests and test data. Some of the more audacious test design tools claim that they can create tests directly from requirements, though usually that requires the requirements to be formatted in a particular way, which is often not practical. Some of the less audacious but more practical tools, such as those we saw in Chapter 3, can help create tests from a structured description of the test problem to be solved. I'm thinking in particular of the National Institute of Standards and Technology tool Advanced Combinatorial Testing System (ACTS) for combinatorial testing. There are also tools that can help support quality risk analysis, which can be thought of as a form of test design tool. Any tool that supports the analysis process will give the tester insights into the coverage, confidence, and quality risks that they should plan to mitigate.

Test data tools are particularly useful. Realistic test data is often a challenge for our clients. For maintenance testing of systems that manage large volumes of complex data, they can anonymize the production data so that it can be safely, securely used for testing. For new systems, data generation tools can be used to create large volumes of data according to the database structure or a description of the data.

Automated Test Execution Tools

Usually, when a tester is talking about test tools, they're talking about tools that automate test execution. These range from tools like JUnit at the unit test level, to Cucumber at the feature verification test level in Agile projects, to Selenium at the system test level.

Any automated test execution tool is going to do at least two things:

- Submit inputs and other events to the item under test.
- Capture the item's responses, including possibly screen outputs, response times, or resource utilization.

In many cases, the tool will also compare the actual result against an expected result and log the outcome of that comparison.

For most RBCS clients, the typical objective for functional test automation is to save money. The money saved comes from the reduced cost of executing the tests, which must be significant enough to more than repay the cost of the tool acquisition, the cost of developing the automated tests, and the cost of maintaining the automated tests. It is this last item, the cost of maintenance, that is often the downfall of automated test efforts. Skilled technical test analysts should know how to build maintainable test frameworks that avoid such problems.

Some clients are also interested in running more tests during a shorter period. This can be helpful to identify and remove problems earlier. In Agile lifecycles, with their short iterations, fast automated testing is really the only practical way to deal with the increased regression risk associated with changes to the code.

Automated testing can be useful when you want to run the same tests in multiple environments. For example, I once managed the testing of a multi-operating system, multi-database query tool. We had a set of about 1,500 tests—which were mostly predefined queries—that we ported to over a dozen supported database/OS combinations. Since the queries were the same on each configuration, we expected the same results.

Though perhaps not as often spoken, another benefit of automated testing is to take advantage of the pesticide paradox by running exactly the same tests, exactly the same way, every time. Human regression testing tends to be error-prone, since people get bored or distracted and can't be relied upon to do things exactly the same way multiple times.

Finally, automation allows test teams to run tests they can't run manually, such as performance and reliability testing, as mentioned earlier.

Test tools, when used properly, allow test teams to increase coverage and reduce costs.

ISTQB Glossary

Test execution tool: A type of test tool that is able to execute other software using an automated test script—e.g., capture/playback.

Example: Test Architecture

In Figure 7–1 you see an example of an integrated test system architecture. This is an automated test system for an insurance company. The system under test— or, more properly, the system of systems under test—is shown in the middle of Figure 7–1.

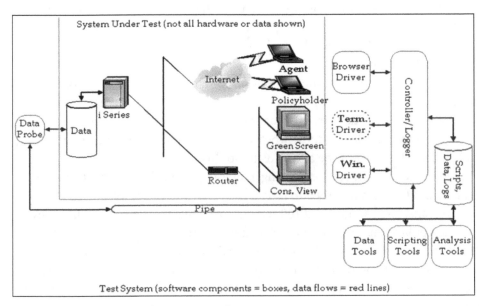

Figure 7–1 *An integrated test system architecture*

On the front end are three main interface types: browsers, legacy Unix-based green-screen applications, and a newer Windows-based consolidated view. The front-end applications communicate through the insurance company's network infrastructure, and through the Internet, to the iSeries server at the backend. (The IBM iSeries servers, once called AS/400 servers, have since been rebranded System i servers.) The iSeries, as you might imagine for a well-established regional insurance company, manages a very large repository of customers, policies, claims histories, accounts payable and receivable, and the like.

On the right side of Figure 7–1, you see the main elements of the test automation system. For each of the three interface types, we need a driver that will allow us to submit inputs and observe responses. The terminal driver is shown in a dotted line because there was some question initially about whether that would be needed. The controller/logger piece uses the drivers to make tests happen, based on a repository of scripts, and it logs results of the tests. The test data and scripts are created using tools as well, and the test log analysis is performed with a tool.

Notice that all of these elements on the right side of Figure 7–1 could be present in a single, integrated tool. However, this is a test system design figure, so we leave out the question of implementation details now. It is a good practice to design what you need first and then find tools that can support it, rather than letting the tools dictate how you design your tests. Trust me on this one; I have the scars to prove it! If you let the tools drive the testing, you can end up not testing important things.

This brings us to the left side and bottom of Figure 7–1. In many complex applications, the action on the screens is just a small piece of what goes on. What really matters is data transformations, data storage, data deletion, and other data operations. So, to know whether a test passed or failed, we need to check the data. The data probe allows us to do this.

The pipe is a construct for passing requests to the data probe from the controller, and for the data probe to return the results. For example, if starting a particular transaction should add 100 records to a table, then the controller uses one of the applications to start the transaction—through a Windows interface via the Windows driver, say—and then has the data probe watch for 100 records being added. See, it could be that the screen messages report success, but only 90 records are added. So, we need a way to catch those kinds of bugs, and this design does that for us.

In all likelihood, the tool or tools used to implement the right side of Figure 7–1 would be one or two commercial or freeware tools, integrated together. The data probe and pipe would probably be custom developed.

Applying Automated Test Execution Tools

As I mentioned before, the return on investment for automation is usually calculated in terms of saved effort to run the regression tests. To maximize the ROI, you want to make sure that the maintenance cost is low and predictable. You also want to make sure that the tests need to be rerun very frequently, as the benefit accrues each time the tests are executed.

We have a number of clients in Agile environments who have made some of their automated functional tests into a smoke test of key features, built into their continuous integration frameworks. The maintenance costs are sometimes a bit higher for these smoke tests, but the fact that the tests are run at least once a day, and in some cases every few hours, pays for that extra costs.

Ideally, there are automated regression tests at every level of testing, from unit test to component integration test to system test to system integration test. At each level of testing, different tools will be used, and different-sized tests will be built, so be smart and don't try to create metrics that add together test case counts for these different tests.

The creation of automated test scripts—as distinct from the tests themselves—should be done by skilled, experienced technical test analysts. From what I've seen in over thirty years in software engineering and testing, at least five years of experience is necessary to become a true expert at test automation, and so it is risky when any significant test automation project is led by someone with less experience.

These test scripts are basically programs, much like the applications being tested. They submit inputs and other events to one or more of the interfaces provided by the item under test and capture the outputs and other results. As mentioned above, they typically include a comparator to check to see whether the actual and expected results match, with the outcome of that comparison captured in a test log. When the scripts work with a graphical user interface, maintenance is particularly tricky, and this is where the years of experience become so essential.

As a test analyst, you can use some of the automated test frameworks to create test cases without extensive automation experience or even an internal understanding of how the scripts work. However, you should be cautious about investing a lot of time or energy into building tests for a testing framework constructed by a technical team where nobody has five years or more of test automation experience. From what I've seen, such frameworks will usually fail.

Let's discuss further the way that maintainable frameworks that interface with GUIs work. Usually, the scripts are highly modularized, with one script for each screen. That way, if one screen changes, only one script must be changed.

Keyword-driven design is often used for such test automation frameworks. The keywords are similar to use case names, in that they describe some business process that a user will carry out to achieve some goal. The process consists of a number of steps. Keywords are based on use cases, business process models, decision tables, and other descriptions of how users get work done with the system. The creation of the keywords via models can be supported by tools, though almost always I see it done manually, with no tools other than graphical ones such as Visio.

As a test analyst, you use the keywords, together with specific input data, to write concrete tests. You are insulated from the complexities of the tool's pro-

> **ISTQB Glossary**
>
> **Keyword-driven testing:** A scripting technique that uses data files to contain not only test data and expected results, but also keywords related to the application being tested. The keywords are interpreted by special supporting scripts that are called by the control script for the test.

gramming language by a front-end script, which handles translating the keyword into a sequence of screen interactions, marshaling all the other scripts and getting them the input data you provided. The resulting frameworks are easy for test analysts to use and relatively easy to maintain.

Keyword-Driven Automation

In keyword-driven automation, as mentioned, you'll construct tests from a keyword, following by input data and expected results. Depending on the granularity of the keywords, you might use a sequence of keywords to implement a single test.

The keywords should be defined by domain experts, working with the technical test analysts who are building the framework. The technical test analyst then creates scripts to implement the keywords. Ideally, this happens in parallel with the implementation of the feature to be tested, which allows the automated test to be used as soon as the feature is delivered. In some cases, a separate test automation team is necessary to achieve this type of result, as having the test automators embedded within the project team—especially if that project team is using Agile methods—often does not leave enough time or focus.

As a test analyst, you'll then bring your domain knowledge to the construction of the tests. The tests are maintainable, because any change to a single screen affects only the script that interfaces with that screen and the tests that contain keywords that result in traversing that screen. Since the tests consist only of keywords, data, and expected results, they are not tightly coupled to the way the program works.

The tests are stored in a spreadsheet or an XML file, typically. In some cases, the test framework will provide a tester-friendly test-building script, too, which manages the construction of the tests and handles creating and maintaining the underlying repository, be it XML, a spreadsheet, or a database. The tester can then launch the tests, using the test execution front-end script. The front-end script navigates the various other scripts, based on the keywords and the data provided, and it logs the comparisons.

After the tests are run, you'll need to analyze the mismatches between actual and expected results. Since the tool does not have any way of applying judgment to the test results, unlike a live tester, the false positive rate will tend to be higher, so you should anticipate spending time manually repeating some of the automated tests to see if a false positive has occurred. If you can't repeat the mismatch that way, you might need to get one of the test automators involved to help debug the script. The main thing is not to simply shrug and say, "Well, gee, must have been a glitch, because everything works fine when I run the test manually."

As one of the reviewers of this material explained, keywords can be used for expected results, too. This involves the creation of what is called a *smart comparator*. This is a comparator that can see patterns in the test results, rather than looking only at the specific results. Building such a smart comparator typically involves collaboration between test analysts and test automators, but it can save you time on the analysis of false positives, making the automated tests more efficient.[1]

A Comment on Keyword-Driven Testing from Jamie Mitchell

It is important to understand that the value of keywords predominantly comes from the fact that they are abstract rather than concrete. To me this is essential. I invented keywords back in the middle '90s, long before anyone had published anything on their use. Because I was having so many problems with maintenance, I analyzed the difference between manual tests and automated scripts. After all, manual tests are very stable, rarely ever needing maintenance even when major changes occurred to the system under test. Automated tests are the very definition of brittle, breaking all the time. My key realization was that a line in a manual test case is an abstraction, an idea. It is only useful when a human mind can make it concrete by supplying context, meaningfulness, and action to it. Assume a manual script with a line that says:

"Open file""C:\xxxxxx""File opens"

---

1. Two useful references for keyword-driven and data-driven test automation are Bath and McKay's earlier-referenced *The Software Test Engineer's Handbook* and Hans Buwalda's *Integrated Test Design and Automation*. Regarding the latter book, while Buwalda sometimes gets the credit for inventing keyword-driven automation, take note of the sidebar from Jamie Mitchell and also the keyword-driven test system for ERMA that I'm about to discuss. My colleagues and I built the ERMA test system before Buwalda's book was published.

This could be run against any version of Microsoft Word, from version 1 in DOS to the very latest version today. The applications we test have functionality, which tends to remain very stable because the users of the software need to do the same tasks, even when the system is revised. Because manual tests are very stable, we can build huge libraries of test cases that can be used for years with very little maintenance.

That was the driving idea behind what I invented back in the '90s and remains true to this day. The true value of keywords is to allow us to create libraries of very stable tests that are abstract, with no concrete elements at all. Those are the assets an organization needs. The implementation of the "pseudo-human" that would add the context, meaningfulness, and action is then just programming, as you mention here.

Example: Keyword-Driven Test System

In Figure 7–3 you see the architecture of a keyword-driven test system my associates and I built. It tested a network security utility called ERMA. ERMA used distributed agents, running on various servers across the network, to add, delete, and modify user accounts. Each of these potential account actions corresponded to a keyword, which was its own script written in a scripting language called Tcl and pronounced *tickle*. The keyword scripts communicated to the standard API of the ERMA system and its agents via a communication script, which meant that if the API changed, we needed to update only that communication script. A parser script was used to decode the test input files, at the direction of the master script that coordinated all the other scripts. The master script also used a logger script to capture the comparison results.

The only thing the test analysts had to build were the test cases, the input data, and the expected results. To make their lives even easier, we built a test management script that would allow the testers to interact with a GUI tool to build, maintain, and modify the test cases, inputs, and results.

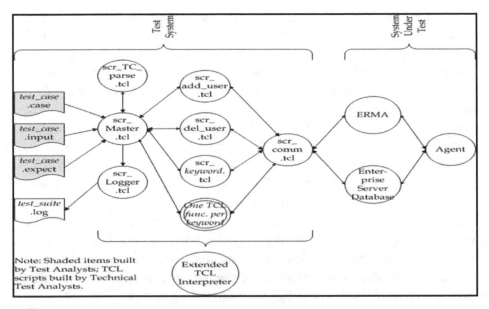

Figure 7–2   *Keyword-driven test system for a security utility*

Improving Automation Success

To improve your odds to automation success, here are some important considerations. First, avoid automating tests that are fundamentally human-centric
tests, such as those that require human judgment to interpret the results or
human interaction to keep the test running. You want to focus on tests that can
run unattended for long periods or that need to be run very often.

If human judgment is limited and occasional, though, this rule can be bent,
if not broken. As a reviewer of this material, Jamie Mitchell, explained, "I built
automated tests for Amex that often needed human intervention. We had a lab
with thirty to forty workstations. The automation ran across all the workstations. When a step occurred which needed human intervention, a timed dialog
box would pop up and start beeping once a second. A human babysat all of the
running workstations. When one would start beeping, they would go to the
machine. The dialog box had detailed instructions for the human. That person
would do whatever, and the script would then start again. The dialogs were
timed such that if no one came within a preset time, the test would automatically continue, fail that test, and move on to the next one. It worked very well,
thank you."

In addition, don't just take an existing mass of manual tests and decide to automate them as they are currently written. Instead, think about how to restructure the tests to cover the same areas but to do so in a more efficient fashion. Manual tests are often written to be relatively short and self-contained, while automated regression tests sometimes can be written to cover more functionality and to do so in greater depth.

That said, there's a caveat to writing large automated regression tests. As Jamie Mitchell explained in his review, "The granularity of automated tests must also consider the possibility that they may fail for other causes than actual SUT failure. I have yet to see an automated framework that does not have spurious failures for whatever reasons—the network failed, the system bogged down and took too long for an action, etc. The longer you make the tests, the more likely you may have a spurious failure causing you to lose more testing. If you have a good framework, having relatively short automated tests does not cause you harm." So, consider the overall reliability of the test environment and various causes of false positives before you decide on the size of the tests.

As mentioned earlier, make sure that the right people are involved in developing the test scripts. If these people are inexperienced, then you should proceed with caution before building too many tests.

Automated tests can have not only false positives, but also false negatives. So, you should plan to audit the tests by selecting a small number of tests to run manually. If the results of this audit don't reveal any false negatives, then you can do the audits rarely. If you do see false negatives, not only should the tests be fixed, but you'll also want to establish a more regular process of auditing the tests.

Finally, you should consider the benefits and the risks of automation. Yes, automation can help you achieve the benefits of fast, cheap, predictable test execution cycles, allowing you to quickly run regression and confirmation tests. It can save you time and money. It can allow you to run tests that are impossible manually. And, in organizations that are meritocratic in their assignment of status, a tester with lots of automated tests can be seen as an alpha geek.

It's also possible for smart keyword-driven automated testing to move the benefit of test automation into the initial testing of a new feature. Those who work in Agile projects may have seen techniques like acceptance test-driven development and behavior-driven development used to provide automated testing of features when first delivered. This can be done using more traditional tools, as well. As Jamie Mitchell wrote when reviewing this material, "If the automators are working from early builds and cooperating with the developers, it is possible to have automation push back into functional testing. I have worked on two different projects where some automation was available by the second day of system test, even for new features. It still had to be backed by humans, but it did add value."

However, there are risks. As I said, maintainability can be a real issue, especially when automating at the graphical user interface, when that GUI is changing, and when inexperienced, insufficiently skilled people are building the scripts. Automating poorly written manual tests generally gives poor regression risk mitigation but at a high cost. During the process of creating the automated regression tests, people are focused, naturally enough, on regression tests, which don't tend to find lots of defects, so the team's overall defect detection effectiveness can fall. Oddly, sometimes people forget the pesticide paradox, and they build their business case for automated regression testing on finding lots of bugs, which of course won't happen unless you are testing an unmaintainable system that is just one big bug cluster. Finally, there's automation for its own sake, where tests are automated because they can be automated, rather than due to some meaningful regression risk mitigation benefit.

Every year, millions of dollars of tool acquisition investments and thousands of person-hours of test automation work are lost due to avoidable automation failures. People use automated tools improperly often without sufficient skills. They expect magical time and money savings from the tools, often immediately, without understanding the need for long-term investment. Or worse yet, management has unrealistic expectations of what the tools will accomplish, often due to exaggerated sales pitches, and management pressures the individual contributors to achieve the impossible.

Teams that intend to create an automated regression test suite need to approach it just as they would developing any other software package. It should be carefully managed. If you know exactly what you need to build and will have time to build it, then you can follow a sequential lifecycle. If you know what you need to build but need to start delivering value immediately, follow an Agile lifecycle. If you are not sure what you need to build or how to build it, follow a spiral lifecycle. Whatever the lifecycle, understand the effort and skills required.

I have seen plenty of test automation teams created, understaffed, underskilled, and under-resourced, shoved off into a corner somewhere, given no guidance, and told to automate all the regression tests. Fail, fail, fail, every time.

I have also seen successful test automation teams. They not only are carefully managed, but also have the technical skills and experience to design and build a maintainable test automation framework. As the scripts are built, they are subjected to the same kind of configuration management that is used for successful software development. As the scripts are built, the scripts are, like any software, carefully reviewed and tested. The overall performance and usability of the framework is designed in from the start, so that large numbers of tests can be run quickly and easily by testers. As I mentioned in my example earlier, you can make the tests easier to run by putting interfaces in place to marshal the management and execution of the scripts.

Fixing a Broken Automation Project

In Figure 7–3 you see how we helped to fix a failed automation project. The first thing we did was encourage the client to stop the current project and fire the incompetent testing service provider that had wasted three years and endless amounts of the client's money to automate less than half the regression tests for only one out of 100 applications that needed testing.

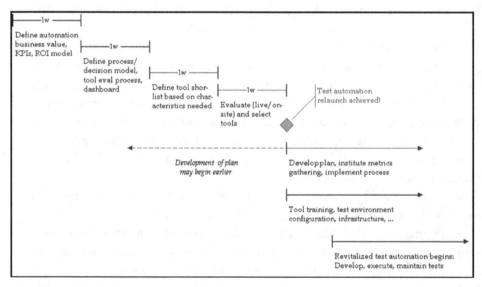

Figure 7–3   *Getting a test automation project back on track*

We started with the basics: What are we trying to achieve? How do we measure performance of the effort, and what constitutes success? How do we measure return on investment? These are the strategic questions that had never been asked by the incumbent automation team, which of course was one reason they had failed: there was no definition of success.

Next, we moved to tactical issues. How should the automation process work? Which lifecycle should we follow? How do we decide which tests to automate? How should we report test results? What are the requirements for the test tool, and how do we evaluate the tools?

With those questions answered, we were able to select three tool vendors who met all our critical requirements. Each of those vendors was invited to do an on-site demonstration of their tool, over the course of a day, with our requirement that they convince us they had a scalable, maintainable solution.

Only once these prerequisites were met did we start our test automation project. It included planning, training, setting up an environment, and developing the tests.

7.3 Sample Exam Questions

1. Which of the following is an example of something that can be used as an automated test oracle?

   A. A legacy system

   B. Manual calculation of results

   C. A requirements specification

   D. A comparator

2. Assume you are a test analyst working on a banking project to upgrade an existing automated teller machine system to allow customers to obtain cash advances from supported credit cards.

   When the user first inserts a valid credit card type, the system considers the user to be in the *unauthenticated* state. Prior to requesting a cash advance, though, the user must enter the *authenticated* state. The user authenticates by entering the proper personal identification number (PIN).

   The system should be able to support up to 1,000 authentication transactions in process at one time. It should be able to complete authentication of a user within two seconds.

Which of the following test tool types is most likely to be useful for this testing?

A. Static analysis tools

B. Performance test tools

C. Dynamic analysis tools

D. Web test tools

3. Assume a project is following a sequential lifecycle model. Which of the following gives an example of applying a static analysis tool at the earliest possible point in the project?

A. Grammatical analysis of a requirements specification

B. Performance simulation of the network and database design

C. Security risk analysis of the application code and database design

D. Automated unit testing with J-unit test frameworks

8 Preparing for the Exam

"Not everyone who doesn't study for the exam will fail. But everyone who does fail didn't study enough."

A frequent warning from the author when teaching ISTQB courses

The eighth chapter of this book is concerned with topics that you need to know in order to prepare for the ISTQB Advanced Test Analyst exam. The chapter starts with a discussion of the ISTQB Advanced Test Analyst learning objectives, which are the basis of the exams.

Chapter 8 of this book has two sections:

1. Learning Objectives
2. ISTQB Advanced Exams

If you are not interested in taking the ISTQB Advanced Test Analyst exam, this chapter might not be pertinent for you.

8.1 Learning Objectives

National boards and exam boards develop the Advanced exams based on learning objectives. A learning objective states what you should be able to do prior to taking an Advanced exam. Each Advanced exam has its own set of learning objectives and its own text. There are no shared learning objectives or text across the three separate Advanced syllabi, so don't bother to read or study the other two Advanced syllabi if you're studying for the Advanced Test Analyst exam. I listed the learning objectives for the Advanced Test Analyst exam at the beginning of each section in each chapter.

The learning objectives are at four levels of increasing difficulty. Question writers will structure exam questions so that you must have achieved these learning objectives to determine the correct answers for the questions. The exams will cover the more basic levels of remembrance and understanding implicitly as part of the more sophisticated levels of application and analysis. For example, to answer a question about how to create a test plan, you will have to remember and understand the contents of such a document. So, unlike Foundation exams, where simple remembrance and understanding often suffice to determine the correct answer, an Advanced exam requires you to apply or analyze the facts that you remember and understand in order to determine the correct answers.

Let's take a closer look at the four levels of learning objectives you will encounter on the Advanced exams. The tags K1, K2, K3, and K4 are used to indicate these four levels, so remember those tags as you review the Advanced Test Analyst syllabus.

Level 1: Remember (K1)

At this lowest level of learning, you will be expected to recognize, remember, and recall a term or concept. Watch for keywords such as *remember, recall, recognize,* and *know.* Again, this level of learning is likely to be implicit within a higher-level question.

For example, you should be able to recognize the definition of *failure* as

- "nondelivery of service to an end user or any other stakeholder," and
- "actual deviation of the component or system from its expected delivery, service or result."

This means that you should be able to remember the ISTQB glossary definitions of terms used in the ISTQB Advanced Test Analyst syllabus. Expect this level of learning to be required for questions focused on higher levels of learning like K3 and K4.

Level 2: Understand (K2)

At this second level of learning, you will be expected to be able to select the reasons or explanations for statements related to the topic and summarize, differentiate, classify, and give examples. This learning objective applies to facts, so you should be able to compare the meanings of terms. You should also be able to understand testing concepts. In addition, you should be able to understand test procedure, such as explaining the sequence of tasks. Watch for keywords such as *summarize, classify, compare, map, contrast, exemplify, interpret, translate, represent, infer, conclude,* and *categorize.*

For example, you should be able to explain the reason tests should be designed as early as possible

- to find defects when they are cheaper to remove and
- to find the most important defects first.

You should also be able to explain the similarities and differences between integration and system testing:

- Similarities: Testing more than one component and testing non-functional aspects.
- Differences: Integration testing concentrates on interfaces and interactions, while system testing concentrates on whole-system aspects, such as end-to-end processing.

This means that you should be able to understand the ISTQB glossary terms used in the ISTQB Advanced Test Analyst syllabus. Expect this level of learning to be required for questions focused on higher levels of learning like K3 and K4.

Level 3: Apply (K3)

At this third level of learning, you should be able to select the correct application of a concept or technique and apply it to a given context. This level is normally applicable to procedural knowledge. At K3, you don't need to evaluate a software application or create a testing model for a given software application. If the syllabus gives a model, the coverage requirements for that model, and the procedural steps to create test cases from a model in the Advanced syllabus, then you are dealing with a K3 learning objective. Watch for keywords such as *implement, execute, use, follow a procedure*, and *apply a procedure*.

For example, you should be able to do the following:

- Identify boundary values for valid and invalid equivalence partitions.
- Use the generic procedure for test case creation to select the test cases from a given state transition diagram (and a set of test cases) in order to cover all transitions.

This means that you should be able to apply the techniques described in the ISTQB Advanced Test Analyst syllabus to specific exam questions. Expect this level of learning to include lower levels of learning like K1 and K2.

Level 4: Analyze (K4)

At this fourth level of learning, you should be able to separate information related to a procedure or technique into its constituent parts for better understanding and distinguish between facts and inferences. A typical exam question at this level will require you to analyze a document, software, or project situation and propose appropriate actions to solve a problem or complete a task. Watch for keywords such as *analyze, differentiate, select, structure, focus, attribute, deconstruct, evaluate, judge, monitor, coordinate, create, synthesize, generate, hypothesize, plan, design, construct,* and *produce.*

For example, you should be able to do the following:

- Analyze product risks and propose preventive and corrective mitigation activities.
- Describe which portions of a defect report were actually observed and which were inferred from results.

This means that you should be able to analyze the techniques and concepts described in the ISTQB Advanced Test Analyst syllabus in order to answer specific exam questions. Expect this level of learning to include lower levels of learning like K1, K2, and perhaps even K3.

Where Did These Levels of Learning Objectives Come From?

If you are curious about how this taxonomy and these levels of learning objectives came to be in the Foundation and Advanced syllabi, then you'll want to refer to Bloom's taxonomy of learning objectives, defined in the 1950s. It's standard educational fare, though you probably haven't encountered it unless you've been involved in teaching training courses.

You might find it simpler to think about the levels this way:

- K1 requires the ability to remember basic facts, techniques, and standards, though you might not understand what they mean.
- K2 requires the ability to understand the facts, techniques, and standards and how they interrelate, though you might not be able to apply them to your projects.
- K3 requires the ability to apply facts, techniques, and standards to your projects, though you might not be able to adapt them or select the most appropriate ones for your project.

K4 requires the ability to analyze facts, techniques, and standards as they might apply to your projects and adapt them or select the most appropriate ones for your project.

As you can see, there is an upward progression of ability that adheres to each increasing level of learning. Much of the focus at the Advanced level is on application and analysis.

8.2   ISTQB Advanced Exams

Like the Foundation exams, the Advanced exams are multiple-choice exams. Multiple-choice questions consist of three main parts. The first part is the stem, which is the body of the question. The stem may include a figure or table as well as text. The second part consists of the distracters, the choices that are wrong. If you don't have a full understanding of the learning objectives that the question covers, you might find the distracters to be reasonable choices. The third part consists of the answer or answers, the choice or choices that are correct.

If you sailed through the Foundation exam, you might think that you'll manage to do the same with the Advanced exams. That's unlikely. Unlike the Foundation exam, the Advanced exams are heavily focused on questions derived from K3- and K4-level learning objectives. In other words, the ability to apply and to analyze ideas dominates the exams. K1- and K2-level learning objectives, which make up the bulk of the Foundation exam, are often covered implicitly within the higher-level questions.

In addition, unlike with the Foundation exam, the questions are weighted. K3 and K4 questions will be assigned two and three points, respectively, in most cases. K2 questions will be assigned only one point.

For example, the Foundation exam might typically include a question like this:

Which of the following is a major section of an IEEE 829–compliant test plan?

A. Test items

B. Probe effect

C. Purpose

D. Expected results

The answer is A, while B, C, and D are distracters. All that is required here is to recall the major sections of the IEEE 829 templates. Only A is found in the test plan, while C and D are in the test procedure specification and the test case specification, respectively. B is an ISTQB glossary term. As you can see, it's all simple recall.

Recall is useful, especially when you're first learning a subject. However, the ability to recall facts does not make you an expert, any more than my ability to recall song lyrics from the 1970s qualifies me to work as the lead singer for the band AC/DC.

On the Advanced Test Analyst exam, you might find a question like this:

Assume you are a test analyst working on a banking project to upgrade an existing automated teller machine system to allow customers to obtain cash advances from supported credit cards.

When the user first inserts a valid credit card type, the system considers the user to be in the *unauthenticated* state. Prior to requesting a cash advance, though, the user must enter the *authenticated* state. The user authenticates by entering the proper PIN.

When authenticating the user, the system should allow the user to enter their PIN up to three times before failing the authentication and rejecting the card. On the first and second try, the system should prompt the user to reenter the PIN.

Suppose you are concerned that, depending on the exact number of invalid PINs entered, the system might behave improperly. Which of the following test design techniques is specifically targeted at such failures?

A. Equivalence partitioning extended by boundary value analysis

B. Pairwise testing with orthogonal arrays

C. State-based testing using N-1 switch coverage

D. Classification tree testing using two-factor authentication

The answer is C. A, B, and D are distracters. A is wrong because these techniques can be used to generate valid and invalid PINs, but would not lead you to test each possible sequence of invalid PIN entries. B and D are both wrong for the same reason, as there is only one factor in play, the PIN, and you have nothing to combine with it. State-based testing with switch coverage is the exact technique to use when you are concerned with a sequence of events, in this case invalid PIN entry. As you can see, this kind of question requires analysis of a situation, along with a deep understanding of how and when to use each technique.

Scenario-Based and Pick-N Questions

Further complicating this situation is the fact that many exam questions will actually consider a scenario. In scenario-based questions, the exam will describe a set of circumstances. It will then present you with a sequence of two, three, or even more questions based on that scenario.

With a scenario-based question, it's very important that you study the scenario carefully before trying to answer the questions that relate to it. If you misunderstand the scenario—perhaps due to a rushed reading of it—you can anticipate missing most if not all of the questions related to it.

In addition to scenario questions, you'll also see another new type of question on the Advanced exams, Pick-N questions. In these questions, you will pick two or three answers out of a list of five or seven options, respectively. These questions are often a harder form of a Roman-type question, in that it is more difficult to use a process of elimination to select the right answer. And, if you only get some of the right answers—that is, one out of two or two out of three—you might not get partial credit.

Let me go back to this question of learning objectives for a moment. I said that the exam covers K1 and K2 learning objectives—those requiring recall and understanding, respectively—as part of a higher-level K3 or K4 question. There's an added complication with K1 learning objectives: They are not explicitly defined. The entire syllabus, including glossary terms used and standards referenced, is implicitly covered by K1 learning objectives. So, you'll want to read the Advanced Test Analyst syllabus carefully, a number of times.

Not only should you read the Advanced Test Analyst syllabus, but you'll need to go back and refresh yourself on the Foundation syllabus. Material that is examinable at the Foundation level is also examinable at the Advanced level, especially when material in the Advanced level builds on the Foundation level. It would be smart to take a sample Foundation exam and reread the Foundation syllabus as part of studying for the Advanced Test Analyst exam.

On the Structure of the Exams

So, enough about the questions on the exam; what can you expect from the exam itself? In the Advanced Test Analyst exam, you will get 60 questions. You'll have three hours (180 minutes) to complete it. (If your native language is not the same as the language of the exam, you'll be allowed an extra 45 minutes, for a total of 225 minutes.) Most of our customers find that the time limitation is not an issue, unlike with the Foundation exam, where a significant percentage of people need the entire hour.

Now, with the Foundation exam, you could estimate how many questions were going to be asked on each section by using the time allocated in the syllabus for that section. This trick will not work on the Advanced Test Analyst exams. In the Advanced Test Analyst exams, when we wrote the exam guidelines, we used a process of weighting the learning objectives for importance. So, for Chapter 1, here are the numbers of questions per learning objective:

- TA-1.3.1 (K2): 2
- TA-1.5.2 (K4): 1
- TA-1.8.1 (K2): 3

In addition to the six mandatory questions for Chapter 1, you will see three questions that cover at least three learning objectives from TA-1.2.1 (K2), TA-1.4.1 (K4), TA-1.5.1 (K2), TA-1.6.1 (K2), TA-1.7.1 (K3), and TA-1.9.1 (K2). There will be at least nine questions on Chapter 1. Remember that an exam question might cover multiple learning objectives, so it could be that a single question counts twice. For example, one question could cover both TA-1.2.1 and TA-1.3.1, so that one question would count toward coverage of each of the two learning objectives.

For Chapter 2, you will see two questions against TA-2.4.1 (K3). You will see at least one question that addresses optional learning objectives, TA-2.2.1 (K2) and TA-2.3.1 (K2). For Chapter 2, you will see a minimum of three questions.

For Chapter 3, here are the numbers of questions per learning objective:

- TA-3.2.2 (K3): 3
- TA-3.2.3 (K3): 3
- TA-3.2.4 (K3): 3
- TA-3.2.5 (K3): 3
- TA-3.2.6 (K3): 3
- TA-3.2.7 (K3): 3
- TA-3.2.8 (K3): 3
- TA-3.2.11 (K4): 3
- TA-3.4.1 (K2): 1
- TA-3.4.2 (K3): 1
- TA-3.4.3 (K4): 3

There are twenty-nine mandatory questions for Chapter 3 and a minimum of two questions on two of the five learning objectives, TA-3.2.1 (K2), TA-3.2.9 (K2), TA-3.2.10 (K3), TA-3.3.1 (K2), and TA-3.3.2 (K4). For Chapter 3, you will see a minimum of thirty-one questions. Notice that Chapter 3 accounts for about 50% of the exam.

For Chapter 4, you will see three questions against TA-4.2.4 (K4). You will see at least one question that addresses optional learning objectives, TA-4.2.1 (K2), TA-4.2.2 (K2), and TA-4.2.3 (K2). For Chapter 4, you will see a minimum of four questions.

For Chapter 5, here are the numbers of questions per learning objective:

- TA-5.2.1 (K4): 2
- TA-5.2.2 (K4): 2

There is an optional question against TA-5.1.1 (K2). You will see two questions that address the optional learning objective, TA-5.1.1 (K2). For Chapter 5, you will see a minimum of four questions and a maximum of five questions.

For Chapter 6, you will see three questions against TA-6.4.1 (K4). You will see at least one question that addresses optional learning objectives, TA-6.2.1 (K2), TA-6.3.1 (K2), and TA-6.5.1 (K2). For Chapter 6, you will see a minimum of four questions.

There are no questions specified for any of the Chapter 7 learning objectives. A minimum of one question must be included for one of the learning objectives, TA-7.2.1 (K2), TA-7.2.2 (K2), and TA-7.2.3 (K2).

Based on the suggested point allocation—one point for a K2 question, two points for a K3 question, and three points for a K4 questions—there are at least 108 total points available. You have to get 71 points (65%) to pass.

Okay, I realize that you might be panicking. Don't panic! Remember, the exam is meant to test your achievement of the learning objectives in the Advanced Test Analyst syllabus. This book contains solid features to help you do that. Ask yourself the following questions:

- Did you work through all the exercises in the book? If so, then you have a solid grasp of the most difficult learning objectives, the K3 and K4 objectives. If not, then go back and do so now.
- Did you work through all the sample exam questions in the book? If so, then you have tried a sample exam question for most of the learning objectives in the syllabus. If not, then go back and do so now.

- Did you read the ISTQB glossary term definitions where they occurred in the chapters? If so, then you are familiar with these terms. If not, then return to the ISTQB glossary now and review those terms.
- Did you read every chapter of this book and the entire ISTQB Advanced Test Analyst syllabus? If so, then you know the material in the ISTQB Advanced Test Analyst syllabus. If not, then review the ISTQB Advanced Test Analyst syllabus and reread those sections of this book that correspond to the parts of the syllabus you find most confusing.
- Are you comfortable with Chapter 3? Most of the points will be for questions about the material in this chapter, so if you're wondering where to focus, that's the place.

I can't guarantee that you will pass the exam. However, if you have taken advantage of the learning opportunities created by this book, by the ISTQB glossary, and by the ISTQB Advanced Test Analyst syllabus, you will be in good shape for the exam.

Good luck to you when you take the exam, and the best of success when you apply the ideas in the Advanced Test Analyst syllabus to your next testing project.

Bibliography

Advanced Test Analysis Syllabus Referenced Standards

International Standards Organization. ISO/IEC 25000:2005, Software Engineering—Software Product Quality Requirements and Evaluation.

International Standards Organization. ISO/IEC 9126-1:2001, Software Engineering—Software Product Quality.

US Federal Aviation Administration. DO-178B/ED-12B, Software Considerations in Airborne Systems and Equipment Certification.

Advanced Test Analysis Syllabus Referenced Works

Bath, Graham, and Judy McKay. *The Software Test Engineer's Handbook.* Rocky Nook, 2008.

Beizer, Boris. *Black-Box Testing: Techniques for Functional Testing of Software and Systems.* Wiley, 1995.

Black, Rex, Erik van Veenendaal, and Dorothy Graham. *Foundations of Software Testing.* Thomson Learning, 2011.

Black, Rex. *Managing the Testing Process: Practical Tools and Techniques for Managing Hardware and Software Testing.* Wiley, 2009.

Black, Rex. *Pragmatic Software Testing: Becoming an Effective and Efficient Test Professional.* Wiley, 2007.

Buwalda, Hans, Dennis Janssen, and Iris Pinkster. *Integrated Test Design and Automation: Using the TestFrame Method.* Addison-Wesley Professional, 2001.

Cohn, Mike. *User Stories Applied: For Agile Software Development.* Addison-Wesley Professional, 2004.

Copeland, Lee. *A Practitioner's Guide to Software Test Design*. Artech House, 2003.

Craig, Rick, and Stefan Jaskiel. *Systematic Software Testing*. Artech House, 2002.

Gerrard, Paul, and Neil Thompson. *Risk-Based E-business Testing*. Artech House, 2002.

Gilb, Tom, and Dorothy Graham. *Software Inspection*. Addison-Wesley Professional, 1993.

Grochmann, M. "Test Case Design Using Classification Trees." Conference Proceedings of STAR 1994.

Koomen, Tim, Leo van der Aalst, Bart Broekman, and Michiel Vroon. *TMap Next for Result-Driven Testing*. UTN Publishers, 2006

Myers, Glenford J. *The Art of Software Testing*. Wiley, 1979.

Splaine, Steven, and Stefan Jaskiel. *The Web Testing Handbook*. STQE Publishing, 2001.

van Veenendaal, Erik. *Practical Risk-Based Testing: The PRISMA Approach*. UTN Publishers, 2012.

Whittaker, James A. *How to Break Software: A Practical Guide to Testing*. Addison-Wesley, 2003.

Whittaker, James A. *Exploratory Software Testing: Tips, Tricks, Tours, and Techniques to Guide Test Design*. Addison-Wesley Professional, 2009.

Wiegers, Karl. *Software Requirements, Second Edition*. Microsoft Press, 2003.

Other Referenced Works

Beizer, Boris. *Software System Testing and Quality Assurance*. Van Nostrand Reinhold, 1984.

Beizer, Boris. *Software Testing Techniques*. Van Nostrand Reinhold, 1990.

Binder, Robert. *Testing Object-Oriented Systems: Models, Patterns, and Tools*. Addison-Wesley Professional, 1999.

Jones, Capers. *Software Assessments, Benchmarks, and Best Practices*. Addison-Wesley Professional, 2000.

Jones, Capers, and Olivier Bonsignour. *The Economics of Software Quality*. Addison-Wesley Professional, 2011.

RBCS
TIME TESTED.
TESTING IMPROVED.
www.RBCS-US.com

HELLOCARMS
The Next Generation of Home Equity Lending

System Requirements Document

This page deliberately blank.

I   Table of Contents

This page deliberately blank.

II   Versioning

Ver.	Date	Author	Description	Approval By/On
0.1	Nov 1, 2007	Rex Black	First Draft	
0.2	Dec 15, 2007	Rex Black	Second Draft	
0.5	Jan 1, 2008	Rex Black	Third Draft	

This page deliberately blank.

III   Glossary

Term[1]	Definition
Home Equity	The difference between a home's fair market value and the unpaid balance of the mortgage and any other debt secured by the home. A homeowner can increase their home equity by reducing the unpaid balance of the mortgage and any other debt secured by the home. Home equity can also increase if the property appreciates in value. A homeowner can borrow against home equity using *home equity loans*, *home equity lines of credit*, and *reverse mortgages* (see below).
Secured Loan	Any loan where the borrower uses an asset as collateral for the loan. The loan is secured by the collateral in that the borrower can make a legal claim on the collateral if the borrower fails to repay the loan.
Home Equity Loan	A lump sum of money, disbursed at the initiation of the loan and lent to the homeowner at interest. A home equity loan is a secured loan, secured by the equity in the borrower's home.
Home Equity Line of Credit	A variable amount of money with a pre-arranged maximum amount, available for withdrawal by the homeowner on an as-needed basis and lent to the homeowner at interest. A home equity line of credit allows the homeowner to take out, as needed, a secured loan, secured by the equity in the borrower's home.
Mortgage	A legal agreement by which a sum of money is lent for the purpose of buying property, and against which property the loan is secured.
Reverse Mortgage	A mortgage in which a homeowner borrows money in the form of regular payments which are charged against the equity of the home, typically with the goal of using the equity in the home as a form of retirement fund. A reverse mortgage results in the homeowner taking out a regularly increasing secured loan, secured by the equity in the borrower's home.

---

1. These definitions are adapted from www.dictionary.com.

This page deliberately blank.

000 Introduction

The Home Equity Loan, Line-of-Credit, and Reverse Mortgage System (HELLOCARMS), as to be deployed in the first release, allows Globobank Telephone Bankers in the Globobank Fairbanks call center to accept applications for home equity products (loans, lines of credit, and reverse mortgages) from customers. The second release will allow applications over the Internet, including from Globobank business partners as well as customers themselves.

At a high level, the system is configured as shown in Figure 1. The HELLO-CARMS application itself is a group of Java programs and assorted interfacing glue that run on the Web server. The Database server provides storage as the application is processed, while the Application server offloads gateway activities to the clients from the Web server.

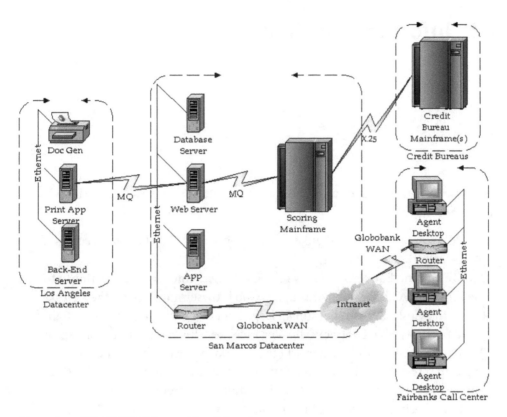

Figure 1   *HELLOCARMS System (First Release)*

001   Informal Use Case

The following informal use case applies for typical transactions in the HELLO-CARMS System:

1. A Globobank Telephone Banker in a Globobank Call Center receives a phone call from a Customer.
2. The Telephone Banker interviews the Customer, entering information into the HELLOCARMS System through a Web browser interface on their Desktop. If the Customer is requesting a large loan or borrowing against a high-value property, the Telephone Banker escalates the application to a Senior Telephone Banker who decides whether to proceed with the application.
3. Once the Telephone Banker has gathered the information from the Customer, the HELLOCARMS System determines the credit-worthiness of the Customer, using the Scoring Mainframe.
4. Based on all of the Customer information, the HELLOCARMS System displays various Home Equity Products (if any) that the Telephone Banker can offer to the customer.
5. If the Customer chooses one of these Products, the Telephone Banker will conditionally confirm the Product.
6. The interview ends. The Telephone Banker directs the HELLOCARMS System to transmit the loan information to the Loan Document Printing System (LoDoPS) in the Los Angeles Datacenter for origination.
7. The HELLOCARMS system receives an update from the LoDoPS System when the following events occur:
    a. LoDoPS system sends documents to customer;
    b. Globobank Loan Servicing Center receives signed documents from customer; and,
    c. Globobank Loan Servicing Center sends check or other materials as appropriate to the Customer's product selection.

Once the Globobank Loan Servicing Center has sent the funds or other materials to the Customer, HELLOCARMS processing on the application is complete, and the system will not track subsequent loan-related activities for this Customer.

Once HELLOCARMS processing on an application is complete, HELLO-CARMS shall archive the application and all information associated with it. This applies whether the application was declined by the bank, cancelled by the customer, or ultimately converted into an active loan/line of credit/reverse mortgage.

003 Scope

The scope of the HELLOCARMS project includes:

- Selecting a COTS solution from a field of five vendors.
- Working with the selected application vendor to modify the solution to meet Globobank's requirements.
- Providing a browser-based front-end for loan processing access from the Internet, existing Globobank call centers, outsourced (non-Globobank) call centers, retail banking centers, and brokers. However, the HELLOCARMS first release will only provide access from a Globobank call center (specifically Fairbanks).
- Developing an interface to Globobank's existing Scoring Mainframe for scoring a customer based on their loan application and HELLOCARMS features.
- Developing an interface to use Globobank's existing underwriting and origination system, Loan Document Printing System (LoDoPS), for document preparation. This interface allows the HELLOCARMS system, after assisting the customer with product selection and providing preliminary approval to the customer, to forward the pre-approved application (for a loan, line of credit, or reverse mortgage) to the LoDoPS and to subsequently track the application's movement through to the servicing system.
- Receiving customer-related data from the Globobank Rainmaker Borrower Qualification Winnow (GloboRainBQW) system to generate outbound offers to potential (but not current) Globobank customers via phone, e-mail, and paper-mail.

004   System Business Benefits

The business benefits associated with the HELLOCARMS include:

- Automating a currently manual process, and allowing loan inquiries and applications from the Internet and via call center personnel (both from the current call centers and potentially from outsourced call centers, retail banking centers, and loan brokers).
- Decreasing the time to process the front-end portion of a loan from approximately 30 minutes to 5 minutes. This will allow Globobank's Consumer Products Division to dramatically increase the volumes of loans processed to meet its business plan.
- Reducing the level of skill required for the Telephone Banker to process a loan application, since the HELLOCARMS will select the product, decide whether the applicant is qualified, suggest alternative loan products, and provide a script for the Telephone Banker to follow.
- Providing online application status and loan tracking through the origination and document preparation process. This will allow the Telephone Banker to rapidly and accurately respond to customer inquiries during the processing of their application.
- Providing the capability to process all products in a single environment.
- Providing a consistent way to make decisions about whether to offer loan products to customers, and if so, what loan products to offer customers, reducing processing and sales errors.
- Allowing Internet-based customers (in subsequent releases) to access Globobank products, select the preferred product, and receive a tentative loan approval within seconds.

The goal of the HELLOCARMS System's business sponsors is to provide these benefits for approximately 85% of the customer inquiries, with 15% or fewer inquiries escalate to a Senior Telephone Banker for specialized processing.

010 Functional System Requirements

The capability of the system to provide functions which meet stated and implied needs when the software is used under specified conditions.

ID	Description	Priority
010-010	*Suitability*	
010-010-010	Allow Telephone Bankers to take applications for home equity loans, lines of credit, and reverse mortgages.	1
010-010-020	Provide screens and scripts to support Call Center personnel in completing loan applications.	1
010-010-030	If the customer does not provide a "How Did You Hear About Us" identifier code, collect the lead information during application processing via a drop-down menu, with well-defined lead source categories.	2
010-010-040	Provide data validation, including the use of appropriate user interface (field) controls as well as back end data validation. Field validation details are described in a separate document.	1
010-010-050	Display existing debts to enable retirement of selected debts for debt consolidation. Pass selected debts to be retired to LoDoPS as stipulations.	1
010-010-060	Allow Telephone Bankers and other Globobank telemarketers and partners to access incomplete or interrupted applications.	2
010-010-070	Ask each applicant whether there is an existing relationship with Globobank; e.g., any checking or savings accounts. Send existing Globobank customer relationship information to the Globobank Loan Applications Data Store (GLADS).	2
010-010-080	Maintain application status from initiation through to rejection, decline, or acceptance (and, if accepted, to delivery of funds).	2

Priorities are:
1 Very high
2 High
3 Medium
4 Low
5 Very low

ID	Description	Priority
010-010-090	Allow user to abort an application. Provide an abort function on all screens.	3
010-010-100	Allow user to indicate on a separate screen which, if any, are existing debts that the customer will retire using the funds for which the customer is applying. Allow user the option to exclude specific debts and to include specific debts. For debts to be retired, send a stipulation to LoDoPS that specifies which debts that the customer must pay with loan proceeds.	3
010-010-110	Exclude a debt's monthly payment from the debt ratio if the customer requests the debt to be paid off.	3
010-010-120	Provide a means of requesting an existing application by customer identification number if a customer does not have their loan identifier.	4
010-010-130	Direct the Telephone Banker to transfer the call to a Senior Telephone Banker if an application has a loan amount greater than $500,000; such loans require additional management approval.	1
010-010-140	Direct the Telephone Banker to transfer the call to a Senior Telephone Banker if an application concerns a property with value greater than $1,000,000; such applications require additional management approval.	2
010-010-150	Provide inbound and outbound telemarketing support for all States, Provinces, and Countries in which Globobank operates.	2
010-010-160	Support brokers and other business partners by providing limited partner-specific screens, logos, interfaces, and branding.	2
010-010-170	Support the submission of applications via the Internet, which includes the capability of untrained users to properly enter applications.	3
010-010-180	Provide features and screens that support the operations of the Globobank's retail branches.	4
010-010-190	Support the marketing, sales, and processing of home equity applications.	1
010-010-200	Support the marketing, sales, and processing of home equity line of credit applications.	2
010-010-210	Support the marketing, sales, and processing of home equity reverse mortgage applications.	3
010-010-220	Support the marketing, sales, and processing of applications for combinations of financial products (e.g., home equity and credit cards).	4
010-010-230	Support the marketing, sales, and processing of applications for original mortgages.	5
010-010-240	Support the marketing, sales, and processing of pre-approved applications.	4
010-010-250	Support flexible pricing schemes including introductory pricing, short term pricing, and others.	5
010-020	*Accuracy*	
010-020-010	Determine the various loans, lines of credit, and/or reverse mortgages for which a customer qualifies, and present these options for the customer to evaluate, with calculated costs and terms. Make qualification decisions in accordance with Globobank credit policies.	1

ID	Description	Priority
010-020-020	Determine customer qualifications according to property risk, credit score, loan-to-property-value ratio, and debt-to-income ratio, based on information received from the Scoring Mainframe.	1
010-020-030	During the application process, estimate the monthly payments based on the application information provided by the customer, and include the estimated payment as a debt in the debt-to-income calculation for credit scoring.	2
010-020-040	Add a loan fee based on property type: • 1.5% for rental properties (duplex, apartment, and vacation) • 2.5% for commercial properties. • 3.5% for condominiums or cooperatives. • 4.5% for undeveloped property. Do not add a loan fee for the other supported property type, residential single family dwelling.	3
010-020-050	Capture all government retirement fund income(s) (e.g., Social Security in United States) as net amounts, but convert those incomes to gross income(s) in the interface to LoDoPS. [Note: This is because most government retirement income is not subject to taxes, but gross income is used in debt-to-income calculations.]	1
010-020-060	Capture the length of time (rounded to the nearest month) that the customer has received additional income (other than salary, bonuses, and retirement), if any.	3
010-030	*Interoperability*	
010-030-010	If the customer provides a "How Did You Hear About Us" identifier code during the application process, retrieve customer information from GloboRainBQW.	2
010-030-020	Accept joint applications (e.g., partners, spouses, relatives, etc.) and score all applicants using the Scoring Mainframe.	1
010-030-030	Direct Scoring Mainframe to remove duplicate credit information from joint applicant credit reports.	2
010-030-040	Allow user to indicate on a separate screen which, if any, are existing debts that the customer will retire using the funds for which the customer is applying. Allow user the option to exclude specific debts and to include specific debts. For debts to be retired, send a stipulation to LoDoPS that specifies which debts the customer must pay with loan proceeds.	1
010-030-060	If the Scoring Mainframe does not show a foreclosure or bankruptcy discharge date and the customer indicates that the foreclosure or bankruptcy is discharged, continue processing the application, and direct the Telephone Banker to ask the applicant to provide proof of discharge in paperwork sent to LoDoPS.	3
010-030-070	Allow user to indicate on a separate screen which, if any, are existing debts that the customer will retire using the funds for which the customer is applying. Allow user the option to exclude specific debts and to include specific debts. For debts to be retired, send a stipulation to LoDoPS that specifies which debts the customer must pay with loan proceeds.	3

ID	Description	Priority
010-030-080	Capture all government retirement fund income(s) (e.g., Social Security in United States) as net amounts, but convert those incomes to gross income(s) in the interface to LoDoPS. [Note: This is because most government retirement income is not subject to taxes, but gross income is used in debt-to-income calculations.]	1
010-030-090	Pass application information to the Scoring Mainframe.	1
010-030-100	Receive scoring and decision information back from the Scoring Mainframe.	1
010-030-110	If the Scoring Mainframe is down, queue application information requests.	2
010-030-120	Initiate the origination process by sending the approved loan to LoDoPS.	2
010-030-130	Pass all declined applications to LoDoPS.	2
010-030-140	Receive LoDoPS feedback on the status of applications.	2
010-030-145	Receive changes to loan information made in LoDoPS (e.g., loan amount, rate, etc.).	2
010-030-150	Support computer-telephony integration to provide customized marketing and sales support for inbound telemarketing campaigns and branded business partners.	4
010-040	*Security*	
010-040-010	Support agreed upon security requirements (encryption, firewalls, etc.)	2
010-040-020	Track "Created By" and "Last Changed By" audit trail information for each application.	1
010-040-030	Allow outsourced telemarketers to see the credit tier but disallow them from seeing the actual credit score of applicants.	2
010-040-040	Support the submission of applications via the Internet, providing security against unintentional and intentional security attacks.	2
010-040-050	Allow Internet users to browse potential loans without requiring such users to divulge personal information such as name, government identifying numbers, etc., until the latest feasible point in the application process.	4
010-040-060	Support fraud detection for processing of all financial applications.	1
010-050	*Compliance (functionality standards/laws/regs)*	
	[To be determined in a subsequent revision]	

020 Reliability System Requirements

The capability of the system to maintain a specified level of performance when used under specified conditions.

ID	Description	Priority
020-010	*Maturity*	
	[To be determined in a subsequent revision]	
020-020	*Fault-tolerance*	
	[To be determined in a subsequent revision]	
020-030	*Recoverability*	
	[To be determined in a subsequent revision]	
020-040	*Compliance (reliability standards/laws/regs)*	
	[To be determined in a subsequent revision]	

030 Usability System Requirements

The capability of the system to be understood learned, used, and attractive to the user and the call center agents when used under specified conditions.

ID	Description	Priority
030-010	*Understandability*	
030-010-010	Support the submission of applications via the Internet, including the capability for untrained users to properly enter applications.	2
	[More to be determined in a subsequent revision]	
030-020	*Learnability*	
	[To be determined in a subsequent revision]	
030-030	*Operability*	
030-030-010	Provide for complete customization of the user interface and all user-supplied documents for business partners, including private branding of the sales and marketing information and all closing documents.	3
	[More to be determined in a subsequent revision]	
030-040	*Attractiveness*	
	[To be determined in a subsequent revision]	
030-050	*Compliance (usability standards)*	
030-050-010	Comply with local handicap-access laws.	5

040 Efficiency System Requirements

The capability of the system to provide appropriate performance, relative to the amount of resources used under stated conditions.

ID	Description	Priority
040-010	*Time behavior*	
040-010-010	Provide the user with screen-to-screen response time of one second or less. This requirement should be measured from the time the screen request enters the application system until the screen response departs the application server; i.e., do not include network transmission delays.	2
040-010-020	Provide an approval or decline for applications within 5 minutes of application submittal.	2
040-010-030	Originate the loan, including the disbursal of funds, within one hour.	3
	[More to be determined in a subsequent revision]	
040-020	*Resource utilization*	
040-020-010	Handle up to 2,000 applications per hour.	2
040-020-020	Handle up to 4,000 applications per hour.	3
040-020-030	Support a peak of 4,000 simultaneous (concurrent) application submissions.	4
040-020-040	Support a total volume of 1.2 million approved applications for the initial year of operation.	2
040-020-050	Support a total volume of 7.2 million applications during the initial year of operation.	2
040-020-060	Support a total volume of 2.4 million conditionally-approved applications for the initial year of operation.	2
	[More to be determined in a subsequent revision]	
040-030	*Compliance (performance standards)*	
	[To be determined in a subsequent revision]	

050 Maintainability System Requirements

The capability of the system to be modified. Modifications may include corrections, improvement, or adaptations of the software changes in environments, and in requirements and functional specifications.

ID	Description	Priority
050-010	*Analyzability*	
	[To be determined in a subsequent revision]	
050-020	*Changeability*	
	[To be determined in a subsequent revision]	
040-030	*Compliance (performance standards)*	
	[To be determined in a subsequent revision]	

060 Portability System Requirements

The capability of the system to be transferred from one environment to another.

ID	Description	Priority
060-010	*Adaptability*	
	[To be determined in a subsequent revision]	
060-020	*Installability*	
	[To be determined in a subsequent revision]	
060-030	*Co-existence*	
060-030-010	Should not interact in any non-specified way with any other applications in the Globobank call centers or data centers.	1
	[More to be determined in a subsequent revision]	
060-040	*Replaceability*	
	Not applicable	
060-050	*Compliance*	
	[To be determined in a subsequent revision]	

This page deliberately blank.

A   Acknowledgement

This document is based on an actual project. RBCS would like to thank their client, who wishes to remain unnamed, for their permission to adapt and publish anonymous portions of various project documents.

This page deliberately blank.

Answers to Sample Questions

Chapter 1

1	B, E
2	A
3	B
4	D

Chapter 2

1	B
2	A

Chapter 3

1	D
2	C
3	B
4	A
5	C
6	D
7	C
8	A
9	A
10	D
11	B
12	A
13	B
14	C
15	B
16	D
17	B

18	A
19	C
20	A
21	C
22	B

Chapter 4

1	D
2	B
3	C

Chapter 5

1	D
2	B
3	C
4	A

Chapter 6

1	C
2	B

Chapter 7

1	A
2	B
3	A

Index

List Price: $ 54.95
536 pages | Soft Cover
ISBN: 978-1-937538-50-7
September 2014

Rex Black

Advanced Software Testing—Vol. 2, 2nd Edition

Guide to the ISTQB Advanced Certification as an Advanced Test Manager

This book teaches test managers what they need to know to achieve advanced skills in test estimation, test planning, test monitoring, and test control. Readers will learn how to define the overall testing goals and strategies for the systems being tested.

This hands-on, exercise-rich book provides experience with planning, scheduling, and tracking these tasks. You'll be able to describe and organize the necessary activities as well as learn to select, acquire, and assign adequate resources for testing tasks. You'll learn how to form, organize, and lead testing teams, and master the organizing of communication among the members of the testing teams, and between the testing teams and all the other stakeholders. Additionally, you'll learn how to justify decisions and provide adequate reporting information where applicable.

The book will help you prepare for the ISTQB Advanced Test Manager exam. Included are sample exam questions, at the appropriate level of difficulty, for most of the learning objectives covered by the ISTQB Advanced Level Syllabus. This second edition has been thoroughly updated to reflect the new ISTQB Advanced Test Manager 2012 Syllabus, and the latest ISTQB Glossary. This edition reflects Rex Black's unique insights into these changes, as he was one of the main participants in the ISTQB Advanced Level Working Group.

rockynook

Rocky Nook, Inc.
www.rockynook.com

Jamie L Mitchell / Rex Black

Advanced Software Testing—Vol. 3, 2nd Edition

Guide to the ISTQB Advanced Certification as an Advanced Technical Test Analyst

List Price: $ 54.95
480 pages | Soft Cover
ISBN: 978-1-937538-64-4
March 2015

This book is written for the technical test analyst who wants to achieve advanced skills in test analysis, design, and execution. With a hands-on, exercise-rich approach, this book teaches you how to define and carry out the tasks required to implement a test strategy. You will be able to analyze, design, implement, and execute tests using risk considerations to determine the appropriate effort and priority for tests.

This book will help you prepare for the ISTQB Advanced Technical Test Analyst exam. Included are sample exam questions for most of the learning objectives covered by the latest (2012) ISTQB Advanced Level syllabus.

Jamie Mitchell is a consultant who has been working in software testing, test automation, and development for over 20 years. He was a member of the Technical Advisory Group for ASTQB, and one of the primary authors for the ISTQB Advanced Technical Test Analyst 2012 syllabus. With over thirty years of software and systems engineering experience, author Rex Black is President of RBCS, a leader in software, hardware, and systems testing, and the most prolific author practicing in the field of software testing today. Previously, he served as President of both the International and American Software Testing Qualifications Boards (ISTQB and ASTQB).

rockynook

Rocky Nook, Inc.
www.rockynook.com

Printed in the USA
CPSIA information can be obtained
at www.ICGtesting.com
LVHW081357070724
784811LV00003B/70